Praise for Mark Atkeson's

Risky Business in Rising China

"Atkeson's evocative memoir brings to life an extraordinary passage of China's history. It gives the reader a fully sensory account of what living this journey was like."

— **James Kynge, Global China editor, *The Financial Times***

"Mark's observations while living and working in China are incredibly accurate and entertaining. His insights and experiences in China are unrivaled."

— **John Beliveau, CEO, Austin Currier; former general manager, United Technologies Corp.**

"If you want to understand today's China, and the forces changing it, you need to read Atkeson's book."

— **John Clasen, former director of China business development, Magellan Aviation Group**

"China's modernization has been every bit as fascinating, colorful and tragic as our own — and Atkeson offers an engrossing account."

— **Wang Xin, partner, VNE Investments Ltd.; former partner, Mobile Internet Asia Ltd.**

"Mark has captured every nuance of a fascinating and thrilling chapter in China. His story both captures the past recent decades and foretells the next ones."

— **Elle Carberry, cofounder, China Greentech**

"Atkeson brings the same intelligence, depth and wit to China storytelling that he brought to business building there. Valuable insights for anyone looking to up their game on doing business in China."

— **Matthew Estes, founder of China-based BabyCare Ltd.**

"Mark Atkeson has lived through the prime arc of China's hypergrowth. He has a unique perspective hard won through decades of ground-zero experience — not only surviving but prospering in its ultra-competitive business environment. It is a fascinating arc of personal growth, as well."

— **Kevin Czinger, founder, lead inventor and CEO of Divergent, and of Czinger Vehicles**

"Anyone wanting to experience China should read Mark's experiences to save themselves time, heartbreak, and money. He understood the language unfiltered through an interpreter, so had an uncensored interpretation of what was said and what was really meant. Even today when I hear the expression 'no problem,' I prepare myself for a problem!"

— **William Gormley former operations manager, Pratt & Whitney**

"Lots of Western businessmen, myself included, have China war stories, but few have a collection like Atkeson. What a treat to have one set of eyes on so many different adventures covering an amazing time in history for both the United States and China."

— **Doug Fieldhouse, former CEO of Vesta Corp.**

"Mark's story covers the excitement and pain of leading industrialization efforts in China. His tenure spans from before Tiananmen to the recent escalation in trade tensions with the United States. Mark managed to keep businesses moving forward with a great sense of humor through it all."

— **Broc TenHouten, former senior vice president, engineering, Coda Automotive, Inc.**

"With a sometimes hilarious accounting of his experiences, Atkeson takes a serious look at the future of China and its relationship with the West."

— **James Morrison, former Hines China Country head**

"Atkeson is a talented storyteller whose diverse and adventurous China business career winds along the path of China's progress and setbacks."

— **James McGregor, American author, journalist and businessman, and three-decade resident of China**

"Atkeson's book tells a personal story of China's transformation, powerfully and movingly."

— **William Plummer, former partner, Marathon Venture Partners**

"Mark Atkeson's China business memoir recounts his peripatetic career from the early days of the Open Door Policy to the Modern China of 2023 in an honest, humorous and detailed way. This book will be valuable for anyone seeking to understand the often messy 'inside story' of China's rise in the late 20th Century, and the role that foreign managers and investors played in the process."

— **David G. Brooks, former chairman, Coca-Cola Greater China and Korea**

"Mark has done a fantastic job of painting the picture of actual Chinese people's lives and characters. Chinese people are very much like Americans. If you think through Mark's conclusions and thoughts about the future, you can conclude that our two countries are absolutely better off working together to improve global conditions."

— **Phil Murtaugh, former CEO, Coda Automotive Inc.**

"When the history of the late 20th and early 21st centuries is written, the biggest story will be that of China's massive transformation and development. Mark's own story about the role he played in that drama provides tremendous insight about what China was like on the ground. Few people have the sweep of experience that Mark has had, and this book should be required reading for all interested in doing business with China."

— **Davin Mackenzie, former country manager for China and Mongolia, for International Finance Corp., and Greater China board director and advisor**

Risky Business in Rising China

冒险生意

Risky Business in Rising China

Deals, ordeals and lessons learned as an American entrepreneur
in a surging superpower grappling with growing pains

冒险生意

By Mark Atkeson

For my wife, Shannon, and our children: Lindsay, Trevor, Caroline and Julia.

From East to West, we shared these years.

Library of Congress Control Number: 2023918318

Print version: ISBN 979-8-9891025-0-1

Digital version: ISBN 979-8-9891025-1-8

To contact the author: markriskybusiness@gmail.com.

A note on the Chinese characters under the book's title:

冒险生意 (pronounced "Màoxiǎn shēngyì") can be translated as "Risky business" or "Risky venture," but the exact translation can vary with the context in which the phrase is used. It can mean, "Dare to take risks."

Printed in the United States of America

Contents

Author's Note

This book is a work of memoir. It is a true story based on my best recollections of various events. The names and identifying characteristics of certain people have been changed to protect their privacy. In some instances, I have rearranged or compressed events and time periods in service of the narrative. I also have recreated dialogue to match my memories of those exchanges.

Preface

A Morning Commute Through Timeless China

It's 7 a.m. on a weekday in April 2013, as I begin my commute to work across northern Beijing in a pleasant mood. Spring has that effect, wherever you live. This city I call home has clearly emerged from winter. The morning is dry and in the low 60s, the grass of the manicured lawns in my gated community is brown but should green up in a few weeks under the attention of gardeners. The morning sun has painted the sky a hazy pale yellow. The air, as usual, is tinged with the reek of coal smoke that cloaks the greater metropolitan area of the Chinese capital of 20 million residents.

I have long been used to this. China, after all, is an industrial giant modernizing at a dizzying pace — an economic superpower (as well as a military one) that only 30 years earlier had approximately 80 percent of its then 1 billion residents living below the poverty line. Now less than 1 percent of its 1.4 billion citizens fall beneath that level. The stunning transformation was the result of historic economic reforms begun in 1978 by the Communist Party of China, which has ruled the world's most populous nation since 1949. The go-go nature of China's economic growth was what beckoned me in the 1980s to learn

Chinese and then pursue a string of managerial and entrepreneurial opportunities in the fast-transforming economy that now was the world's second largest.

The pace of change was exhilarating as I rode the wave of China's modernization. I started by working in factories in the gritty industrial economy and later transitioned to ventures in the new economy of high-tech and finance. As one job ended, I'd find another — constantly reinventing myself to exploit opportunities by learning new skills and joining startup joint ventures in fields new to me. My expertise was serving as the bilingual expatriate general manager: a bridge between a joint venture's Western and Chinese partners.

On this particular morning, I am 49 and have lived about half my life in China. Over the course of two-plus decades — following stints working in Japan and Italy — I had held executive positions with a half-dozen pioneering joint ventures. These had been preceded by spending two years (1986-87) right after college as an on-site project manager in China, facilitating the technology transfer for a machine-tool product line from a U.S. company to a state-owned Chinese company. Since 1993 — when I'd left Europe behind and determined to surf the rising wave of China's economic tide — I'd held posts in industries ranging from aviation to automotive parts, venture capital, Internet, and electric vehicles.

These positions had taken me all over China, from teeming metropolises to remote deserts. China is where my wife, Shannon, and I raised our three biological children and one adopted Chinese child. All became (like their parents) bilingual. Now, on this day in spring 2013, I have just begun a new job as general manager for a joint venture between a U.S. company, GA Telesis, and the government-owned Air China. The company, GA Innovation China (GAIC), is selling surplus parts from disassembled aircraft such as decommissioned jetliners. I am overseeing the launch of GAIC's organization and operations. I am responsible for setting up offices and warehouse operations, recruiting, training and supervising 20 Chinese employees, managing the acquisition and disassembly of aircraft and directing sales of surplus parts in global markets.

As I steer my black Buick Lacrosse sedan along a quiet, smooth-paved street lined by landscaped lawns, trimmed hedges and pruned trees in my gated community, I reflect on the stark contrasts I always encounter on this seven-mile, 25-minute drive from a northeast suburban residential development (christened Yosemite by its developers) to our company's headquarters just south of Beijing Capital International Airport. Like a short film, the shifting scenes tell a story about China's breathless modernization from the 1980s to this moment:

• The $5 million, detached stucco villas in Yosemite resemble McMansions in Southern California, as do those in the similar high-end compounds named Beijing Riviera, Palm Springs, Merlin Champagne Town, and Chateau Regalia. Developers chose the architectural styles and designs to attract Western expatriates as well as Chinese nouveau riche — those upwardly mobile professionals and entrepreneurs prospering in the new economy, who desire homes that resemble America's, and crave easy access to golf courses, tennis and squash courts, swim pools, Starbucks, and Western-style shopping malls. Most of my neighbors are ambitious, educated Chinese, not expats like me, since foreigners have pretty much been replaced in managerial positions by the younger generation of Chinese professionals who have taken over, capably running joint ventures and other sizable companies. Shannon and I speak Chinese, not English, to our neighbors, as we do to our "ayi" (literally, "aunt" in Mandarin, but a term used for a combination nanny-maid) who cooks and cleans our house, and watches over our children, since Shannon is not a stay-home mom but an executive at International Finance Corp., a division of the World Bank.

• The Chinese security guards manually swing open the Yosemite front gates, and I proceed out to An Hua Road, which on this leg parallels the Wenyu River. To my right, I can see the modernistic, rectangular main building of the International School of Beijing, where my three youngest children — Trevor, 14, Caroline 11, and Julie, 6 — attend, alongside classmates most of whom are Chinese. Their parents have obtained U.S. passports so their children can attend this school with its dual Chinese and English language programs, and lofty academic standards tailored to award the International Baccalaureate diploma. (My oldest child, Lindsay, 17, opted to attend a boarding school in the United States, to play ice hockey and prepare for college in America.)

• I dart into traffic, jostling for space with shiny BMWs, Mercedes and Porsches driven by members of the rising class of affluent Chinese urban professionals: go-getters who've risen in the ranks of international companies, or are dogged grassroots entrepreneurs, or, perhaps, government officials adroit at the art of the secret deal. We are all residents of the suburban Shunyi District, which we leave daily to ply our professions in the city, where industrial grunge and the crush of hardscrabble masses show a less-glamorous side of China's breakneck growth.

I zip along the smooth, gray-asphalt of Tianbei Road — three lanes in each direction divided by a wide median of block tiles supporting a guardrail, as if in any major developed nation in the West. The billboards are in Chinese characters, and the smiling models Chinese, but the messages are universal. They tout the trappings of the good life: luxury houses for sale in Beijing Riviera or Palm Springs (the one in Beijing); international golf clubs such as the Jack Nicklaus Golf Club or the Beijing Orient Pearl Country Club; skin and hair products by Estée Lauder and L'Oréal; watches from Montblanc; men's fashion from Hugo Boss; women's fashion from Prada; Rémy Martin cognac. The ruling Chinese Communist Party asserts that China is not a capitalist country — despite the growing number of private capitalists and entrepreneurs doing business alongside public and collective enterprises — but the consumer appetite among prospering Chinese has their nation accounting for about 40 percent of luxury goods purchased worldwide.

• I whiz past another shopping mall being built, its structure shadowing the street. And then, a hulking reminder of the harshness of modernizing change: Towering beside the expressway are drab apartment complexes, 20 stories high. It was to these great, impersonal buildings that local government authorities relocated the farmers who, a decade before, had tended to corn and soy crops on the very land where high-end housing developments with Western names now stand, including the one my family calls home. It's a case of the present uprooting the past and building over it. *Progress.*

• The homogenized present — epitomized by Western-based chains — is well represented outside my windshield as the expressway reaches a bend alongside Tianbei Road. Here, the Euro Plaza Shopping Mall is situated: glistening with reflective window panels, bright red and blue signage and the obligatory McDonalds and KFC franchises. Further on is the Crowne Plaza Beijing International Airport hotel with its shiny brown and gray exterior of stone panels framing windows, and decorative patterns of vertical and horizontal black lines forming squares in an orderly grid. Topping the roof like a tiara is a neon sign spelling out Crowne Plaza in English script.

• The contemporary architecture is quickly juxtaposed with the lusterless past. Looming ahead are two massive rectangular blocks of concrete: the headquarters of Air China. These utilitarian, Stalinist-style edifices house this very important government-owned enterprise. Indeed, Air China is a symbol of the state. The only aesthetic consideration of these structures is that there is no aesthetic consideration. High-voltage powerlines cut right in front of the buildings, inelegantly framing them. Surrounding the Air China HQ are equally colorless two-story buildings housing industrial businesses such as autobody shops and warehouses.

• And now I'm passing slowly through a very different contemporary scene — one chaotic and teeming and occupying a seamless continuum with the past. The road is lined with flimsy shops and street-vendor booths. The working poor — the bulk of the population — is hard at commerce. Traffic snarls from the crush of ragged peddlers pushing carts, competing for space with passenger cars and plastic motor scooters, bicycles weaving in and out, trundling tricycles bearing bundles of agricultural goods or dumplings and cakes. Hustle, bustle. Haggling, honking. Congestion. And then I jam the brake pedal as a broken-down minivan crammed with migrant construction workers cuts into my lane with impunity. My blood pressure spikes.

• Finally, I have navigated through this shantytown district. I exit the main road and veer my Buick onto a two-lane road of cracked concrete that happens to be the very one I remember from my first trip to Beijing. My mind flashes back to what feels like another lifetime. *December 1982.* An exotic-sounding tour in China with my parents and siblings over the Christmas holiday, when I am but a college freshman far from any firm plan for my future. And here I am three decades later — still a bit frazzled behind the wheel from the maddening crush of the shantytown segment of my commute — motoring along on what all those years ago was the expressway to the airport, and now is a crumbling route leading to my workplace as a general manager of an aircraft surplus-parts supplier, in an industrial zone about a mile south of the modern Beijing Capital International Airport that replaced the original one where I'd disembarked as a 19-year-old, setting foot for the first time on Chinese soil.

As I draw nearer to the headquarters of GA Innovation China, I pass the rusty hangar buildings of the Aircraft Maintenance and Engineering Corp. — AMECO — a joint venture between Air China and Germany's Lufthansa

Technik that maintains, repairs and overhauls aircraft and their engines and components. Steam is belching out of pipes of this anachronistic colossus. At the end of the potholed two-lane road stands the 1950s Stalinist building of the old airport.

This sight is all too familiar to me, since AMECO was my first work assignment after I'd moved to China from Europe, 20 years earlier. My new employer, GA Innovation China, has set up its office in a dilapidated administration building adjacent to AMECO's campus and Terminal 2 of the airport. It is hardly plush digs. Bony stray cats steal up to our front door to nibble on scraps left by my office mates. The restrooms have leaky squat toilets from a previous era.

• As I park my Buick, relieved to have arrived without accident or injury, I realize I have come full circle in my time in China. GA Innovation's business is selling surplus parts salvaged from aircraft that Air China had purchased 20 years before, and now had retired and was divesting. In my office, I switch on my computer and wait for the company's virtual private network to help me skirt around the so-called "Great Firewall of China" so I can access Google and the *New York Times* and *Bloomberg* websites and connect to the outside world. Gazing out the window, I can barely see the outline of massive Terminal 3 in the sulfurous haze.

It is moments like these that tell you, in your bones, that you've done all you intended to do, or were able to do, on a specific life's journey, and it's time to step off this particular path and begin a fresh adventure on a new one.

NOW, AS I WRITE THIS preface, it is April 2023 — 10 years after that morning I just described. The position with GAIC turned out to be my last one as a resident of China. My wife and I decided it was time to return to the States. Our family moved to Marin County, California. But China has remained on my mind every day. And given the state of the world — a de facto Cold War having materialized between China and the United States — I remain keenly interested in developments in China beyond the headlines.

During my long residence in China, I kept personal notes, contemplating the idea that one day I'd write a little memoir for people in my life, primarily my children, to have as a keepsake, a piece of family history to preserve. But as I finally sat down not long ago to compose a draft of my experiences in China, I realized that they coincided with a historical transformation that surely is the most profound for the human race in my lifetime — even more significant than the collapse of the Soviet Union in 1991 and the cessation of the U.S.-U.S.S.R. Cold War that had persisted since the end of World War II.

I knew my business career in China had a type of uniqueness because of the breadth of work I'd done with a variety of new companies that had emerged in the previously closed Chinese economy. I'd witnessed a complete transformation of that economy from stagnant state-planned to dynamic market-driven. I'd directly experienced the rise of a vibrant private sector that is the key to China's long-term development. I'd worked alongside Chinese entrepreneurs striving to succeed despite barriers set up to protect the state sector. I'd watched local friends locked in state-allocated employment, earning hundreds of dollars per year, break out in the new economy to rise in economic status to middle income — owning cars and homes and asserting reasonable control of their futures.

From my Western perspective, China's modernization had brought me many opportunities to participate in, and contribute to, China's development. It also had given me great satisfaction observing the liberation of its people from the economic stagnation of the past. And I realized that sharing my experiences as an American businessman in China spanning four decades would not only describe the seismic shifts in that nation's economy and society but foretell where China is heading in the future. And since China now is the globe's chief superpower rivaling the United States, the implications for how China's economy grows, how it pursues its geopolitical aspirations, and how it handles climate change are critical for all humanity.

And so I decided to write this little book as more than just a piece of family history. I've written the chapters to inform (and, hopefully, entertain) a wider audience: anyone duly interested in understanding modernizing China. I've written what it's like to live and do business in China, how that great nation is grappling with its growing pains, and what the world may expect as China's ruling party navigates the needs and demands of its emergent capitalist class, its general populace, and its global trade partners and competitors.

Not many people, outside of Chinese citizens or expatriates, share a keener interest in that great nation's present and future than I. While I don't miss the daily grind of working there — and I never take for granted all the amenities of my present life in California — China is always in my heart. And I know its destiny, its welfare and prosperity, are inextricably entwined with that of its current great rival, my own country, the United States. One might say that the fate of the entire human race depends on these two superpowers working as partners to solve global problems such as climate change, nonproliferation of nuclear weapons, and development of clean-energy technologies. More importantly, trade between our two countries is mutually beneficial, and a driver of global wealth.

In the end — despite competition between our governments — we are not so different, and we share similar aspirations and desires as nations and individuals.

My hope is that the chapters ahead will provide you valuable insights into this ancient nation, China, as it continues modernizing and shaping all of our lives in the 21st century.

Introduction

An Ancient Civilization's Stunning Modernization Reaches a Crossroads

New arrivals to China have only today's snapshot perspective of bustling cities and vibrant urban life of what has ballooned into the world's second-largest economy, and they lack a sense of the unfolding drama of China's modernization over the past 40 years.

China exploded in an astounding transformation from the 1980s to today. The biggest event of the post-World War II generation is not the collapse in 1991 of the Soviet Union and the spread of capitalism and democracy in its former satellite states, but the modernization of China and the exit from poverty of 800 million of its 1 billion-plus people. Everything changed in the world's most populous nation — from people's living standards and aspirations, to how the country and economy are managed.

China has come charging onto the world scene. The nation's impact is felt all around the globe — from daily consumption of goods and services made in China (such as everyday items bought at Walmart or on Amazon. com, or the time you squander on the TikTok app on your phone), to inflation in commodities (such as oil and gas, copper, aluminum and lithium — in high demand by Chinese industry), to spreading pollution (China is the greatest contributor to greenhouse gases).

The rest of the world is struggling to reconcile China's seemingly miraculous emergence as an economic (as well as military) superpower. Nations are redefining their relationships with China. But China's dazzling transformation from a backward, agriculture-oriented nation to a modernizing industrial and high-tech giant might have been expected by those with a knowledge of history.

China is one of the oldest civilizations in the world — and for much of its existence has been a leader in technology and innovation. China's earliest writing system may date to 3,700 years ago, and China's first ruling dynasty, the Xia, emerged some 4,100 years ago. Through the millennia, China has influenced the rest of the world, including inventing paper making and movable-type printing, iron smelting and bronze, acupuncture and kung fu, gunpowder and rockets, the compass and the mechanical clock, alcohol and tea production, the kite and the toothbrush, row-crop farming and paper money.

But across the centuries, China also has endured lengthy periods of disunion and disorder, which compromised its security and stability and left it vulnerable to the predations of the world's powers. Since the late 19th century, China has struggled to modernize, to keep in step with the West and with its dynamic neighbor, Japan. Following the fall of the Qing Dynasty in 1911, China entered a long period of warlord rivalries leading to widespread poverty and deprivation for its masses, culminating in the nation's brutal consolidation in 1927 under the Kuomintang Party headed by revolutionary leader Chiang Kai-shek.

In the Chinese Revolution of 1949, the Chinese Communist Party under Mao Zedong overthrew Chiang with its promise to share the fruits of economic growth with the people. The Republic of China became the People's Republic of China, which it remains today. However, Communist Party mismanagement of the economy from the 1950s into the 1970s severely hampered China's modernization for another 30 years. Disasters included Mao's "Great Leap Forward" in the 1950s, in which collectivization of farms resulted in widespread starvation, and his implementation of the "Great Proletarian Cultural Revolution" in the 1960s and 1970s — with a stated aim of purging capitalist and traditional elements from Chinese society, instilling a reign of terror. The movement unleashed "Red Guard" units of fanatic youth around the country, who zealously absorbed and preached from *The Little Red Book* of Mao's quotations and attacked those they viewed as opposing Mao's vision of Communism.

By the time of Chairman Mao's death in 1976, the Chinese people were by and large exhausted by dogmatism and ready for change. They sought practical solutions to economic development and modernization without the baggage of political ideology. Mao's death and the downfall of his cronies freed the ruling Chinese Communist Party to adopt widespread economic reforms. The party struck an unspoken deal with the Chinese people: *We let you make money, you let us rule.* Deng Xiaoping, Mao's successor, focused on economic reforms and practical policies not rooted in ideology — setting the stage for early takeoff in the 1980s. Deng proclaimed, "No matter if it is a white cat or a black cat; as long as it can catch mice, it is a good cat."

From 1978 on, the Chinese Communist Party has pursued a strategy of transition toward a market economy. China's economic and political future loomed bright. China absorbed ideas and knowledge from around the world and implemented rapid development of its economy. Starting in the early 1980s, China's modernization began to build like a distant wave on the horizon barely perceptible in its approach. As economic reforms increased and China unleashed the entrepreneurial spirits of its people, its modernization began to swell in a rising tide of development. With the race of developed nations toward globalization, and the widespread outsourcing of labor and manufacturing to China in the 1990s, this wave started to surge. By the early 2000s China was a powerful economic force: a tsunami towering over the world economy and lifting other countries through trade. By the 2010s, this wave was cresting with Chinese cities fully modernized and urban people's daily lives completely transformed.

Consider these benchmarks of the transformation:

• Since China embarked on economic reforms in 1978, its gross domestic product grew at an average rate of almost 10 percent annually for more than 30 years.

• Over the past 40 years, China has lifted nearly 800 million of its citizens out of poverty, as defined by the United Nations.

• In 1978, no Chinese citizens owned property. Today, almost 90 percent of the population owns a home.

• In 1978, the bicycle was the primary means of transport, and there were no private cars. Today, there are more than 300 million private cars in China.

• Private firms, which did not exist in China prior to 1978, generate approximately 60 percent of China's GDP and 90 percent of new jobs.

• Chinese entrepreneurs have created unprecedented wealth, producing hundreds of billionaires today.

• China's middle class has grown to more than 400 million of its overall population of 1.4 billion.

• There has been huge migration to China's cities, with 65 percent of China's population urbanized.

• Chinese consumption is estimated to represent 40 percent of global luxury-goods sales.

• China is the global leader in renewable-energy installations, with the highest installed capacity of both wind and solar.

UNFORTUNATELY, A BACKLASH is slowing China's growth. The ruling Chinese Communist Party has begun exerting more control over the burgeoning private sector.

Here in the early 2020s, the wave of prosperity and growth is breaking on the back of more conservative government policies, producing diminishing returns from the political undertow. Consider these benchmarks of the current decline:

• China's GDP growth rate is slowing to between 2 and 5 percent.

• China's manufacturing-unit labor cost has climbed to nearly four times that of countries in Southeast Asia, such as Vietnam, Malaysia and Thailand.

• The Communist Party crackdown on the private sector has resulted in a significant loss of value. For example, two banner companies — Alibaba (e-commerce portals) and Tencent (videogame vendor) have lost two-thirds of their market value, and revenue growth has stalled.

• Chinese leadership insists that entrepreneurs need more "theoretical and political guidance" to understand their obligations to the party and the country.

• The Communist Party imposes its will on high-profile entrepreneurs. Examples include the disappearances and detentions of Jack Ma, cofounder of

Alibaba, and Bao Fan, former chairman and CEO of the China Renaissance investment bank.

• Ideology is creeping back into management of the economy, and the Communist Party is taking a more assertive role in the running of enterprises.

• China is suffering an unprecedented brain drain, in which the wealthiest and most capable choose to leave China. They are pursuing better educations for their children, and escaping the pollution and overcrowding in urban China.

• The crackdowns on the private sector exacerbate urban youth unemployment, which now stands at over 20 percent.

• The debt-fueled growth era seems to be ending now, while productive investment ended years ago.

• China's property-asset price bubble is at risk of deflating. Property values relative to income in Beijing and Shanghai are about three and four times higher than in major cities in the United States. The outlook for Chinese income growth does not justify such high property prices. This is a problem, because urban Chinese have 70 percent of their wealth tied up in real estate.

• China was the biggest emitter of carbon-dioxide emissions in 2021, accounting for nearly 31 percent of the global emissions.

• Across China, much of its groundwater is unfit for drinking, while half of its aquifers are too polluted to tap for industry or farming.

• Governmental corruption continues despite Communist Party crackdowns. The most prevalent forms of corruption in China are bribery, diversion of public funds, and favoritism.

• The state's welfare resources are heavily concentrated in urban areas, leaving hundreds of millions of rural Chinese without support.

• The vast labor pool that fueled China's low-cost industrial base is shrinking as its population ages rapidly. The country's population decline in 2022 followed years of slowing birth rates.

AFTER DECADES OF SPECTACULAR economic growth and social change, China has reached a key moment. The state sector holds China back from increasing the role of markets in determining the allocation of resources in the economy.

Some observers see China's influence ebbing as its government becomes pre-occupied with domestic problems that are a natural result of the breakneck economic growth triggered by the loosening of central-government constraints on private business. China is facing difficult challenges in rebalancing its economy to sustain growth. The current regime is opposed to reforms supporting privatization of state-owned businesses and empowerment of Chinese consumers, because these reforms would undermine the government's monopoly on political power. The Communist Party depends on ownership of key state assets, which are controlled by officials who are hostile to change. To preserve its hold on power, the Communist Party is focused on maintaining stability at the expense of faster economic growth.

At present, there is no groundswell for democracy from the wealthy. Richer urbanites have vested interests in expensive apartments and exclusive access to city services. They have no interest in broadening citizen participation in government, which would inevitably lead to wealth redistribution.

But just as the currents of history pushed China to its astonishing transformation from the 1980s to today, they may push China's governmental practices in a different direction tomorrow. After all, change can happen dramatically, but the forces that set it in motion are complex and build up gradually.

As for the present, the nations of the world are seeking to redefine their relationship with China. The chapters that follow chronicle this author's experiences and observations on China as an American expatriate working in joint ventures between foreign and Chinese-owned companies in a variety of industries critical to China's economic growth. As such, this author was a witness to China's stunning transformation as it modernized over three decades.

The chapters, therefore, can serve as an aid to understanding where China has come from, where it is today, and where it may go tomorrow.

Chapter One

Taking a Leap of Faith into an Alien World

The cruising Pan Am 747 gradually began its descent over nighttime wintry Beijing. Inside the aircraft, the dim glow of the cabin lights gave us a warm cozy feeling. Few travelers ventured to China that Christmas season of 1982, and the cabin was only a fifth full. My parents and us eight children were among the holiday-season passengers making the trip to this destination, which to us seemed exotic and mysterious.

We were somewhat seasoned travelers. Our family had visited Third World countries such as Egypt, India and several in Latin America, and lived two years in the Philippines. But China — this great ancient nation, the world's most populous and, in my short lifetime, a Communist superpower with a frosty relationship with the United States — had been closed to travel to Americans for three decades. That seemed like an eternity to an 18-year-old like me. But the slow, steady thaw in diplomacy initiated by President Nixon 10 years before had continued and reached the stage where, the previous year, Pan Am World Airways had begun flights to China — ending a 32-year freeze on aviation connections with the United States.[1]

We Atkesons had traveled from our home in Washington, D.C., up to John F. Kennedy International Airport in New York to board our Pan Am flight. As the jetliner lowered now over Beijing, we gravitated to window seats out of curiosity, as if we were touching down on the moon. We stared down from the winter night sky at the few dim twinkling lights below us and felt a strong sense of foreboding at our imminent landing in communist China. As the aircraft taxied toward the terminal building in the dark, we could see figures standing on the tarmac. Gradually, we could discern that these figures were soldiers in heavily padded winter coats and fur hats, armed with AK-47 rifles. The vapor of their breath hanging in the spotlights outside added to their menace.

As we shuffled toward the aircraft door and the terminal jetway, we were struck by rancid smells of disinfectant and foul coal smoke. The terminal was nearly empty except for a few cleaning staff lurking among the gates. When we reached the immigration desks, we found a row of coarse wooden tables painted a hospital blue. Chinese officers in olive-green uniforms received and studied our U.S. passports before banging a chop into them and handing them back to us. On entry into China, we met our tour guide, a young man with spectacles in a dark black overcoat.

His name was Mr. Zhang. He'd been assigned by the government to supervise our travel inside China. Our itinerary had been set by the Chinese travel company engaged to lead our family to famous sites and cultural events

---

[1] An executive order issued in 1950 by President Harry Truman, in a hardening of the U.S. stance toward the spread of Communism as the Cold War solidified and war broke out on the Korean Peninsula, listed prohibitions on direct dealings with Communist-ruled mainland China, including travel from the United States by ships and planes. In 1972, President Richard Nixon lifted the restriction. U.S. commercial flights, authorized by China, resumed when Pan Am began flights to China in January 1981.

in Beijing and other major cities. Mr. Zhang's English was passable, though not smooth. His speech was fairly formal, as he had no access to Western television or movies to see how average people spoke. Now he had custody, so to speak, of us 10 Americans — two middle-aged adults and seven young men or boys and one girl, the oldest 25 and the youngest 9 — for an itinerary spread over 10 days. He surely hoped we'd be a compliant lot.

Unlike most Americans who visited China now that travel had opened up, we hadn't come in the usual tourism months of summer. Going in winter had been my mother's demand, so we could avoid mosquitoes and the threat of viral encephalitis. That fate had tragically claimed the life of a former high school classmate of my brother Chris named John Zeidman. John had finished two years at Duke University but gone to China for a year of study and travel administered by the University of Massachusetts. He was studying at the Peking Normal University when he became ill from mosquito-borne viral encephalitis and was hospitalized in Beijing. He later was flown to Johns Hopkins Hospital, in Baltimore, where he died.

Touring in China had been my father's idea — and he was so eager for us to go, he'd obliged my mother's wishes, even though it meant sacrificing a normal Christmas holiday. My father had personal history in China, dating back to the era before Mao Zedong and his Communist People's Liberation Army had taken over the country and proclaimed it the People's Republic of China in 1949. My father's father, Clarence Lee Connor Atkeson, was a career Naval man assigned in 1938 to serve as lieutenant commander on the *USS Marblehead*: a cruiser with the U.S. Asiatic Fleet, based in the Philippines. Tim (my father) and Ted (my uncle) were pre-teens at the time; they attended boarding school in Baguio, the Philippines, for most of the year. In the summers of 1938 and '39, when the fleet steamed into Chinese waters and anchored at the port of Japanese-occupied Qingdao, Tim and his younger brother Ted would catch up with their parents (my grandparents) by boarding a Dutch steamer from Manila to Hong Kong and then Shanghai, China — the ports then being under Western control. From there, they trans-shipped on a Japanese troop ship (this being pre-World War II, before Japan and the United States were officially military adversaries) to Qingdao, where they stayed in hotel lodging. The thrill of their adventure aboard the ship was heightened by stumbling upon alien, fearsome Japanese soldiers in the hold, and by agonizing in terror when they temporarily lost their passports. Their memories of those summers in Qingdao were indelible, including watching brown-uniformed Japanese troops drilling daily with fierce discipline in the city they had occupied.[2]

My father's interest in the Far East continued into adulthood. After serving in the Marine Corps during World War II, he earned a law degree from Yale and studied at Oxford as a Rhodes Scholar, then worked variously in private practice and government posts, including general counsel of the Office of Technology Assessment, which advised Congress on public-policy issues related to technological change. Between 1967 and '69 (when I was ages 3 to 5), my father was general counsel in the Asian Development Bank in Manila, where we lived.

My father was an adventurous sort attuned to new opportunities, as well as the growing excitement in the United States in the 1970s about China opening up to cultural exchanges and business interests — capped by President Jimmy Carter normalizing diplomatic relations with China in 1979. This whetted his desire to explore what China looked like now — at least as much as was possible as foreign tourists, chaperoned by Mr. Zhang.

---

[2] My father's and uncle's experiences in those summers were shared by my Uncle Ted — Maj. Gen. E.B. Atkeson, USA (Ret.) — in the prologue of his book, *The Final Argument of Kings: Reflections on the Art of War*. The prologue is reprinted in Appendix A of this book.

The rest of us Atkesons were equally excited to see firsthand this country that had been off-limits. But we were apprehensive, as well.

AFTER RETRIEVING OUR LUGGAGE in the terminal's baggage-claim area, we went out into the frigid December air and boarded a bus that had no recognizable badge and looked like it had been hammered together in a junkyard. We then rumbled out onto a dark and cracked two-lane concrete road that took us into the city of Beijing.

The city we encountered was murky with almost no streetlights. A cheerless, ominous feeling pervaded. There was none of the illumination that one would expect from a city of 20 million people, such as glowing restaurant neon or radiant office buildings humming with activity. Another surprise was the lack of car headlights piercing the foggy night. We passed block after block of low-rise buildings, few of them taller than two or three stories. Among the few antiquated cars that we spotted on the road, we could see solitary dark silhouettes on bicycles. It was spooky.

On arrival at the Beijing Hotel in the heart of the city near Tiananmen Square, we dragged our luggage up to check-in, which was a long wooden counter with a single surly attendant. We grabbed our room keys and lugged our bags up the dusty stairs due to the elevators not being in service. From our hotel-room windows we had a panoramic view of a sea of darkness below us, punctuated by dim yellow lights here and there.

The next morning, my brother Andy and I emerged onto the frigid avenue in our running gear. Andy was a Yale senior, I, a freshman; we both ran on the track team. We had the idea of exploring a few miles out of the city center and then circling back into Tiananmen Square. A cacophony of jingling bells struck us from what appeared to be thousands of black bicycles mounted by dark figures in overcoats flowing down the misty avenue toward us. The streets seemed to be entirely flooded with bicycles rather than cars or buses.

As we swung back in the direction of Tiananmen Square, we suddenly had a funny feeling of being followed. *Indeed.* We noticed that pairs of young Chinese men in sweatsuits jogged not far behind us, and every few blocks they would be replaced by a new pair chasing doggedly after us. It was a shock to know we were actually being tailed. We figured that with so few foreigners on the streets, our Chinese pursuers were there either for our protection or to observe our movements.

We did realize that we stood out. Throughout our trip, whenever our tour group disembarked from the bus and strolled about, crowds often gathered, gawking. We didn't speak Chinese, so we had no idea what they were saying to each other, but we were cognizant that as non-Chinese and non-Asians, and wearing clothing that was colorful in contrast to the drab gray, blue or green so-called "Mao suits," we were a sight to see.[3] Yes, the Chinese viewed us as very strange aliens.

Our tour itinerary included the Imperial City and a section of the Great Wall in Beijing; the "Terracotta Army" sculptures in Xi'an — one of China's ancient capitals, 700 miles southwest of Beijing; the giant historic port city of Shanghai, on the East China Sea, with its famous waterfront promenade

---

[3] The "Chinese tunic suit" was originally known not as a Mao-style suit but as a Zhongshan suit, named for the early 20th century Chinese republican leader Sun Yat-sen (also known as Sun Zhongshan). As the first president of the Republic of China in 1912, following the overthrow of the Qing Dynasty, he'd introduced the style, basing it on the Japanese cadet uniform but intending it to serve as a form of national dress with political symbolism. The four pockets represented Confucianism's Four Virtues of propriety, justice, honesty, and shame. After the Communist victory in 1949, the suit style was modified to resemble the so-called Stalin tunic sported by Soviet strongman Joseph Stalin. Party leaders of the new People's Republic of China considered the suits a symbol of proletarian unity. Since Mao Zedong favored the style, the suit became known as the "Mao suit."

called the Bund; Suzhou, a city a bit inland of Shanghai, with its canals and classical gardens; Hangzhou, near Suzhou, with its ancient temples; and Guilin, in southern China, with the Li River meandering among limestone hills, surrounding waterway of lakes and rivers, and famous pagodas. In retrospect, though we were early arrivals in China's budding tourist industry, our stops were the same as those on standard tours today. The state of each attraction, though, was yet to be spruced up. For China was an impoverished nation in 1982.

Our impression of the Imperial City that winter was that most ancient sites were in a state of dilapidation and abandonment. However, this heightened the sense of mystery and authenticity of the palaces and temples. At each stop, Mr. Zhang gave us historical briefings of China that were laced with a strong Communist bias. Nowhere was this more pronounced than when we visited the Imperial City, which was basically cruddy from decades of neglect. The Old Summer Palace ("Yuanmingyuan Park") lay in ruins of toppled marbled pillars and stone bricks strewn among tall grass and weeds.

"China suffered one hundred years of Western imperialism, aggression and oppression, and therefore China is a very poor country," Mr. Zhang said, as if reciting the phrase by heart.[4] The reference was to the economic and military incursions of the United Kingdom, France, Germany, Russia and the United States in the 1800s and into the 1900s, which forced the weak Chinese government into granting humiliating trade concessions and access to ports, the permitting of embassies in China and free movement of missionaries. A major

---

[4] In 2021, China's National Cultural Heritage Administration — responsible for protecting cultural relics — ruled out restoring the pillars and other ruins of the Old Summer Palace. The agency's statement on the matter explained that the site's value lies in its "historical status of being destroyed by foreign aggressors," and that its ruins "serve as a warning to our descendants that they shall never forget the national humiliation."

issue of contention was the illegal opium trade that Western merchants plied in China, smuggling the narcotic into the country and profiting handsomely. (Ironically, this is similar to cartels trafficking fentanyl today in the United States.) China's Qing Dynasty rulers proved ineffective in quashing the illicit, ruinous opium trade; Chinese forces were defeated by superior firepower in two conflicts with Western powers, which became known as the Opium Wars. The second Opium War included an expedition in 1860 by a joint British-French force of 41 warships and 18,000 troops, who sailed north from the port of Canton (today, Guangzhou), ostensibly to punish China's emperor for not adhering to the terms of treaties. They fought their way to Beijing, sacked the Imperial Summer Palace and destroyed its adjacent Old Summer Palace, which was known as the "Garden of Eternal Brightness" for its intricate network of 200 ornate palaces and pavilions, courtyards and gardens.

Today, the deliberately neglected ruins are a Chinese shrine memorializing the Western aggression against China in what its government calls China's "century of humiliation" — from the start of the first Opium War in 1839 to the founding of the People's Republic of China in 1949. The day we Atkesons visited the Imperial City, we were the only visitors to these ancient sites, so we freely explored the empty palace buildings and clambered on top of the stone statuary.

We ascended the Great Wall at Badaling, where President Nixon had famously visited a decade before. At mealtimes, Mr. Zhang ushered us into musty, freezing banquet halls, where we dined while bundled in our winter coats, sitting before greasy tableware that we wiped off with paper napkins, spinning lazy Susans laden with steaming platters of various entrees, such as chunks of chicken bearing bone, which we chuckled was "chainsaw chicken." From Beijing, we proceeded on to the old imperial city of Xi'an.

The morning following our arrival in Xi'an, I woke up with a lingering pain in my abdomen. During breakfast, I guessed that the pain was probably caused by eating contaminated food. However, as we drove to the famous site of the buried terracotta warriors, the pain gradually intensified. Filing through the large pit among the unearthed terracotta warriors, I suffered a spontaneous desire to vomit to try to relieve the stabbing cramps in my abdomen.

Outside the excavation building, I found a latrine: a rough old brick building with breezy open doors and windows. Inside, I faced a long trench and immediately puked in reflex to the revolting smell and squalor. After emptying my innards, I joined my family in yet another cold, gray banquet hall set aside for foreign guests. Instead of subsiding, the pain worsened. My mother made a special request to Mr. Zhang to escort me to the local hospital in Xi'an.

Our grim-faced guide and I rode our tour bus through the city streets to the hospital. Inside, we bypassed a large, rundown waiting room of cracked plaster and peeling paint, packed with members of the general public waiting in line. Everyone in there was dressed against the winter cold in threadbare Mao suits. Mr. Zhang ushered me into a waiting room in a relatively more sanitary section for party cadres. This room was not spotless but was sanitary by local standards — meaning those akin to 19th century America. There was only one other patient in this room: an older, rotund man wearing a Mao suit, including the cap. He likely was some local official getting a checkup. He periodically bent over to hawk phlegm into a little round spittoon.

I was brought into an examination room. The doctor was wearing a white cap that resembled a baker's hat and a smock spattered with blood and chemical stains. With hand gestures, he requested I lie on a table so he could probe my abdomen. After a few moments of poking me, he spoke to Mr. Zhang, who translated that the doctor had diagnosed my malady as appendicitis. The doctor decided to inject me with a large dose of penicillin to see if that would remedy the problem. A Chinese nurse entered the room and plunged a metallic syringe into my naked bottom.

Mr. Zhang and I returned to the hotel and rendezvoused with my other family members. The message from our guide was that I should immediately go to bed and rest to see if the pain would disappear. That was wishful thinking. It later became obvious to me that he was very worried he would be held responsible for my illness. He concealed his anxiety beneath a stoic expression, hoping for a miraculous recovery so this problem would simply go away.

Being forced into bedrest at least relieved me from having to attend the highlight of that evening — a screechy Peking opera in a crowded theater littered with bits of snacks chucked by the local audience wrapped in heavy overcoats. My siblings later told me I was lucky to have missed it. When my family returned to the hotel late that evening, my condition had significantly worsened, and my parents determined to immediately take me back to the hospital for an appendectomy.

At the hospital, nurses lifted me onto a gurney while the doctors met with my parents and Mr. Zhang in a separate room. I later learned that the doctors were uneasy about the risks to me in the operation, and had informed my parents that I might die. The doctors did not want to be blamed in a worst-case outcome.

Nurses wheeled me outside from the section for party cadres, through dark alleys lightly dusted with snow to the building that housed the operating room. Inside the operating room, I observed that the various machines and instruments looked like they were 1950s vintage. The operating surgeon in his apron and white cap requested that the heater in the room be turned off, to lessen the noise so the team members could hear each other.

The operating team administered a local anesthetic and placed a small curtain below my chin to obscure my view of my lower body. As the room temperature gradually dropped toward freezing, I became aware of a slicing sensation in my abdomen. Finally, just as they cut out my diseased appendix, I felt an intense stab of pain, triggering uncontrollable heaving. The team stepped back as I writhed and tossed on the operating table. When my spent body eventually lay still, the doctor presented to me my deflated, bloody appendix: a shriveled red balloon the size of an index finger, lying on a piece of white gauze.

Our small group then returned to the segregated section at the hospital, wheeling me back through the snowy lane with a sheet over my head. The sight of me under a sheet shocked my parents until they realized that I was not dead. Nurses parked me in a separate bedroom while the doctors celebrated their success with my parents over tangerines, sunflower seeds, and Chinese tea. My mother volunteered to spend the night in my room in the bed adjacent to me. As the numbing anesthetic wore off over several hours, I became increasingly miserable from the throbbing pain from the large, raw wound in my side, bandaged with gauze. I tossed and turned, groaning and moaning, with little sympathy from my mother, a bit callous to whimpering after raising eight children.

The following morning, we decided that the family would continue their tour of China with Mr. Zhang, with stops in Hangzhou and Suzhou, while I stayed behind in the hospital to recover. My father remained with me in Xi'an and made daily visits to the hospital. During these visits, he brought along whiskey and cigars and regaled me with stories of his youthful experiences in China in the 1930s. Our new Chinese minder, similar to Mr. Zhang, was appalled at my father's stories of Western decadence in pre-communist China. I'm sure the whiskey and cigars bothered him, too. I can only suppose that my father — worldly as he was, and possessed of a wry sense of humor — was drinking and smoking and storytelling to deliberately cause consternation in our Chinese chaperone.

MY FATHER, TIMOTHY BREED Atkeson, certainly had an international and historical perspective of the world, particularly when it came to Asia. His childhood experiences in China observing the Japanese army — combined with witnessing the terrible struggle to defeat imperial Japan in World War II — had permanently impressed him with the dynamic power inherent in the Japanese culture. He marveled at Japan's miraculous postwar economic revival — especially as Japanese automobiles and consumer electronics gained ever-larger shares of the world market.

Japan's stunning growth influenced him to encourage his children to learn Asian languages. He primed us at an early age to view Japan and Asia as a future place of growth and opportunity. But my brother Andy and I were his only children to heed this encouragement.

Andy chose the study of the Japanese language and traveled to Japan for work, so, naturally, I opted for a different path by studying Chinese. Andy did work briefly in Japan, but didn't pursue a career in Asia. I attended Chinese-language courses while pursuing an electrical-engineering degree at Yale.

It is true that China had seemed a very unpromising nation to me during our family's trip in 1982. After our return, I'd contemplated what I'd seen and experienced on that brief circuit from Beijing to Xi'an, Shanghai and Guilin. My impression was that China was backward, colorless and chaotic, its people desperately poor. India, in contrast, was very poor, too, yet its people wore colorful ethnic clothing and were not stoic like the Chinese. I'd sensed a quiet resignation in the Chinese. Beijing was a drab city coated in dust deposited by winds from the northern plains. In other cities, I'd seen how residents lived in brick houses clustered around a common courtyard, with shared tap water and a communal outdoor latrine. They lacked variety in their lives.[5] They had bad haircuts to go along with their Mao suits, a legacy of the anti-bourgeois sentiment of the Mao era. Females cropped their hair short and wore it straight; males had clipped bangs across the brow and basic block cuts in back. No sideburns, parts or gels. They also constantly spat on the ground, indoors and outdoors. I grew to expect expectoration, the hawking sound simply part of China's soundscape.[6]

Nevertheless, my father continued to be high on China's future. He would cite news stories about China's markets opening up, about such-and-such U.S. company building a factory there. China, he believed, was a new frontier for business opportunity. Independent of his enthusiasm, I followed China in the news myself. The communist country was continuing to open its economy to capitalism — to market forces and foreign investment — albeit while maintaining trade protections. While China permitted foreign companies to construct factories on Chinese soil, employing Chinese labor, it restricted the companies' ability to sell its goods and services in China. It also required the companies to share their technology with Chinese companies. This was not laissez-faire capitalism. Yet it was a big step toward industrialization, toward free enterprise.

---

[5] As a positive note, though, in a society where almost everyone was equally destitute, many people feel a sense of solidarity with others who are in the same circumstances. I ascertained that among the Chinese, life was relatively free of envy among friends and neighbors.

[6] There are several explanations why many Chinese habitually spit on the ground in public. One is that in traditional Chinese medicine, spitting is seen as ridding the body of an excess of one kind of fluid to balance the system. Another is that Chinese from rural backgrounds were used to spitting on the ground and covering the spittle with dirt; they retained the habit after relocating to cities during China's fast-paced modernization. Yet another is that heavy air pollution in cities accompanied China's rapid industrialization, causing chronic nasal congestion. The attitude is: "Better out than in." It's worth mentioning that the Western habit of blowing noses into handkerchiefs or tissues then pocketing them is seen as disgusting by non-Westerners.

I felt a twinge of excitement about preparing myself for a possible post-college career in China. Youthful wanderlust certainly contributed to my motivation, as did the chance to pursue something eccentric. Surely, the mysterious attraction of China — what in a different era might have been characterized as the allure of the Orient — played a part. And then there was the low-risk factor. I could afford to gamble a couple years of my life after college, seeing if I could catch a good opportunity in China. That's the advantage of being young, with zero responsibilities or commitments to anyone or anything other than oneself.

And so, the summer after my freshman year, I enrolled to study Chinese in an intensive language course at Middlebury College, in Vermont. This required a sacrifice of sorts. I was showing promise as a long-distance runner on the Yale track team, and had capped my spring season with a win against Harvard that qualified me to join a combined Yale and Harvard track team that would travel to England to compete against a Cambridge and Oxford team. I agonized deeply over the timing conflict, but in the end chose Chinese language study over joining the trip.

At Middlebury, I encountered an oddball class of China Program students made up of kung fu enthusiasts and oilmen, who were in stark contrast to and greatly outnumbered by the Cold Warriors studying Russian, and the pragmatic businesspeople studying Japanese. Chinese language study was not highly sought at that time in 1983. Learning Chinese occupied all my time, with grueling memorization of conversation dialogs and characters.

As college graduation loomed in spring 1986, my engineering classmates were scheduling job interviews with major U.S. corporations, pursuing solid career opportunities with the likes of AT&T and Bell Labs. I did explore positions with Corporate America, but with a mind to be stationed in China. This made me a target of ridicule by my peers, who were incredulous about this incongruent career path of their classmate. I shrugged off their barbs. I was embracing this leap of faith — gambling my future on China — even though I still had visions from the 1982 trip, of a billion people in threadbare clothing, riding bicycles to get around.

My fellow students weren't the only ones put off by my plan. I advanced to a second-round interview with the investment bank Salomon Brothers, but the interviewer abruptly terminated our conversation when I expressed my interest to go to China. That country was not on Salomon Brothers' radar. The firm had no business operations there. When it came to Asia, Japan was the economic superpower that financial prognosticators viewed as potentially usurping the United States as the prime mover on the globe. The Land of the Rising Sun was the big player in Asia, not its enormous — and enormously backward — Communist neighbor across the Sea of Japan.

I quickly discovered that finding job opportunities in China was extremely difficult. I enlisted the help of the U.S.-China Business Council, a nonprofit group promoting trade between the nations. This led me to an obscure headhunter named Christine Casati, who ran a one-woman operation finding job candidates for companies doing business in China. Christine found two completely different prospects for me. One was to join a team from Portman Property Group developing a large commercial and residential property in downtown Shanghai, in a joint venture with a Chinese company. This didn't appeal to me when I considered that the construction schedule was uncertain, and I'd likely be sitting in an office in America, spending work hours on the phone with someone in Shanghai. I wanted to be physically stationed in China.

The other opportunity Christine turned up was a project-management position with a machine-tool company, Cincinnati Milacron. That's the one I chose. My tasks would be coordinating the transfer of technology for an automatic grinding machine to a Chinese company, and supporting the sale of machine tools in China.

If the job didn't work out? My fallback was resuming a traditional career track as a young man with an electrical-engineering degree.

My father, the non-traditionalist — the man always keeping an eye out for opportunities — was very supportive of my decision. "Mark," he said with a laugh, "is going to become a captain of industry."

Well, one step at a time. First, I'd have to learn the machine-tool business. I would be diving into that at the company's plant in Cincinnati. There also was the matter of my Chinese language skills being shaky. I'd have to bring them up to speed on the job, while working in China. *Sink or swim.*

The main worksite would be in Wuxi, west of Shanghai in eastern China. But the job also would take me to many remote sites, such as Yumen City, a small oil-drilling town in the far west of China. My boss ribbed me that I would often be out of touch and might go for a week or more without being able to communicate back to headquarters in America.

After three months in Cincinnati, learning about machine tools and the details of the technology-transfer project, I boarded a Japan Airlines flight and headed to China. As the smartly dressed flight attendants of Japan Airlines politely bid me farewell at the aircraft door in Beijing, I grew uneasy at the old familiar smell of disinfectant and coal smoke.

What was I getting myself into?

Chapter Two

Trading Knowhow for Uncertain Sales

The smell was sickeningly familiar. After disembarking from the Japan Airlines flight in Beijing on a warm afternoon in late summer 1986, my nostrils filled with the acrid aroma of coal smoke and ammonia of disinfectant — just like when I'd landed with my parents and siblings in 1982.

I met our company driver, a Chinese man sporting sunglasses, driving a bright-red Mercedes sedan that our company leased to impress customers. When we sped into the city on a new motorway, it was my first indication that China was rapidly modernizing. The freshly paved highway was a huge improvement over the narrow two-lane road of cracked concrete I remembered from my family's trip.

I also noticed the abundance of cars and trucks in Beijing. What had been streets filled with bicycles in 1982 now were crawling with yellow minivan taxis, used Japanese Toyotas, tiny Fiat hatchbacks, and Chinese-made Hóngqís ("Red Flag Limousines") whose rectangular design was based on a 1955 Chrysler. Numerous Chinese-made Jiefang (meaning "Liberation") trucks built from old International Harvester designs from the 1930s spewed sooty exhaust as they lumbered along the streets. I also noted small stores and restaurants with neon signs, and tall buildings under construction. An economic transformation was taking place before my eyes.

The driver dropped me off at the Lido Beijing, which Holiday Inn had opened two years earlier as one of the first international hotels in China since the Communist takeover in 1949. Hotels were to be my home in China, as I would be constantly traveling throughout the country. I was not quite 23, young and free, and the prospect of living out of a suitcase didn't stress me. But I had other trepidations. If I'd been anxious about traveling to mysterious China as an 19-year-old for that vacation tour in 1982, I was even more so about going there on a work assignment in 1986 — equipped as I was with a fledgling understanding of the machine-tool industry I'd joined, and untested skills in communicating in Chinese as I handled my twin duties of facilitating consultations of my American employer's engineers with their counterparts in China buying our high-tech equipment — so they could gain the technical knowhow — and drumming up sales of our equipment to additional Chinese customers.

My employer, Cincinnati Milacron, had its office in Beijing in a cramped room in the Jinglun Hotel, about three miles from Tiananmen Square in the city's center. It had four wooden desks piled high with papers and scraps left over from the day's boxed lunches. I had three office mates — English-speaking Hong Kong Chinese who dressed Western style, and carried Hong Kong passports and identification cards. Anthony Wong and his wife, Athena, presided over the company business. They were in their early thirties. Anthony wore a decently tailored business suit from Hong Kong; Athena, a nice dress or pants and a blouse. They squabbled constantly in Cantonese, a dialect so different from Mandarin that I had no clue what they were saying. Just as well. Their bickering presented a delicate challenge to peaceful office harmony, particularly in such a small space. The other office mate was Qi Li, a swinging bachelor in his late twenties whose dress and demeanor was that of a nightclub gigolo who'd stumbled out of Hong Kong's 1970s disco scene. Qi Li sported blow-dried hair, a dress shirt unbuttoned to his breastbone, a gold chain and aviator glasses. He constantly chased local women. He was the whole "Saturday Night Fever" package, Chinese style.

Qi Li teased me about my alien status in China with a mischievous Chinese adage, roughly translated as: "Americans are very hairy — therefore, they do not look that intelligent." He would often serenade me with a comical rendering of, "Play that funky music, white boy!"

The primitive office electronic communications, typical of Beijing in the 1980s, challenged us. We needed to arrange the logistics of visits to clients and prospects. We had to shout madly into our fixed-line phones, which crackled with static whether the call was local or long-distance, to try to be understood by the person on the other end. A common greeting on the phone is, "Wei wei!" — meaning, "Hey, hey!" — and we'd holler that, and the person on the other end would holler it back.[7] When we were lucky to connect to more sophisticated customers, our communications were by fax machine. Athena would translate the information I needed into Chinese characters.

Some of our customers had no phones, much less fax machines, so we resorted to terse cable messages. This meant going down to the telegraph office near us. Miraculously — despite the uncertainty of whether these messages had successfully been delivered to the correct addressee — someone would usually appear to greet me at my sales visits.

When I was traveling for business in China, I'd periodically send telex messages to the home office in Cincinnati when I was in a city large enough to

---

[7] If you overhear Chinese speakers using cell phones today, you'll be sure to hear, "Wei, wei!"

have a telex office. Telex required the keying of a message in punched holes on a pre-prepared ribbon of paper tape, followed by threading the tape into a reader to transmit the message. Messages were necessarily short because of the limited length of tape. I felt like a submarine briefly surfacing in the ocean, spitting out a message, then submerging again for a lengthy period, out of sight and unreachable in backwards China.[8]

In those years, neither the Lido hotel in Beijing nor hotels in smaller cities had spa and gym facilities, so I improvised a hotel-room workout. I traveled with a portable, screw-in pullup bar and positioned it in a bathroom doorframe. Sometimes, the frame would crack from the pressure. I also did incline pushups with my feet elevated on the edge of the bed and my hands set on the dusty floor. I got used to peering at hotel carpets scarred with cigarette burns. The Chinese in their slowly modernizing nation of 1986 were as nonchalant about spreading ashes and butts from their cigarettes as they were about spitting in public.

AS I MOVED AROUND Beijing outside the hotel and my workplace, I observed that life for residents in the great capital proceeded at only a slightly faster tempo than what I recalled from 1982. Still lacking many cars or retail stores in comparison to the metropolises of the developed world, Beijing largely moved at the pace of commuters on bicycles and pedestrians dining and shopping at sidewalk stalls. I acquired a single-speed Flying

---

[8] In those days, I carried a Sony shortwave radio, which enabled me to access news from outside of China. Many Chinese citizens were able to hear *BBC* and *Voice of America* programming — banned from Chinese radio stations — via shortwave. I remember waking in China on Oct. 20, 1987, to the news on my shortwave radio of the "Black Monday" stock-market crash plunging the Dow Jones Industrial Average by over 22 percent.

Pigeon black bicycle — the ubiquitous Chinese-made model — to explore the city's back alleys and to take marathon rides to the Old Summer Palace on the city's outskirts.

Two very pleasant realities about Beijing were the virtual non-existence of beggars (a rare exception being extremely destitute souls I might encounter in train stations), and the serene recreation of senior citizens in the parks. In mornings or evenings, common sights in the parks were groups of 20 or so retirees gracefully following an instructor in a series of flowing Tai Chi movements, and couples waltzing to "Blue Danube" playing on a boombox. Old men carried pet birds or crickets in cages. There'd also be street performers. Artists dipped broom-sized brushes in buckets of water and painted poetic phrases on the pavement, the calligraphy lasting for a few minutes until fading in the sun. A musician might show up with an erhu — a two-stringed fiddle with a long stick-like neck and a small, cylindrical sound box at one end — and stroke a hauntingly stirring tune of soaring high notes on the Chinese pentatonic scale, evoking the atmosphere of mountains and valleys and intricate gardens. To Western ears, erhu's strains conjured the ancient mystery and beauty of China. Neither the painters nor musicians were performing for tips from passersby. They were simply engaging in pastimes they loved.

This gentle aspect of the Chinese culture was in stark contrast to the spectacle of street vendors haggling in the markets, and the petulance of surly sales staff in the state-sponsored department store, which (to my amusement) was named the Friendship Store.

My interactions with the Friendship Store clerks honed my skills in one of the subtle aspects of communicating in Chinese when in China. That is, the ability to interpret nuanced or hidden meanings in statements or responses. A few examples:

Me: "Do you have any thermos bottles for sale?"

Staff: *"Méiyǒu."* [There are none.]

Actual meaning: "I cannot be bothered to find any because I have no incentive to do so."

Me: "Do you mind if I look in the shelves behind you for any thermos bottles?"

Staff: *"Bùxíng."* [Not possible.]

Actual meaning: "I don't want to get into trouble with my boss, so I don't dare to help you."

Me: "When will you get some more thermos bottles?"

Staff: *"Bù zhīdào."* [I do not know.]

Actual meaning: "It's been a long day; I want to go home so I don't want to help you."

Me: "Is there someone else who can help me?"

Staff: *"Bù tài qīngchǔ."* [I'm not sure.]

Actual meaning: "I don't know what you want, however, my boss may know; I don't know where he is."

The street vendors, however, were more than eager to engage me to make a sale. I recognized these hustlers as shoots of free enterprise emerging in China. These purveyors of black-market goods and money-changing services were popping up all over the place. One site was "Silk Alley," next to the Friendship Store. Here, hardy hawkers set up folding tables heaped with T-shirts, jeans, and fake watches and other cheap knockoffs, such as poor replicas of Sony Walkman portable cassette players with earphones, and cassettes with Western pop music. These freelance vendors did brisk business. While the Chinese Communist Party complained about the import of decadent ideas from abroad — labeling the likes of long hair, jeans, sunglasses, and cassette tapes with pop music as evidence of "the disease of individualism" —

the central government did not move to uproot the street merchants peddling items that fed this putative social malady.

I was grateful for that. At that time, foreigners such as I were allowed to spend "FEC's" (foreign exchange certificates), which looked different from the Yuan bills of Chinese renminbi currency. As a U.S. passport holder, I couldn't spend local money at hotels, although I could on the street. The exchange rate for U.S. dollars at Chinese banks or stores was not as good as what I could bargain for with a street vendor. So I did money changing that way. I also bought some T-shirts and a fake Rolex illegally made in southern China. The street vendors were avid traders, eagerly haggling and even chasing after me to do business.

My biggest criticism of the black-market offerings — and of Chinese-made merchandise in general — was that its quality was utterly shoddy and never should have seen a store shelf or even an outdoor tabletop. Electronics didn't work. Cups were cracked. A thermos had broken glass inside. T-shirts were of inferior fabric and poorly cut, their designs or logos crude or amateurish. The "Rolexes" didn't keep time.

Still, the ubiquitous appearances of the street vendors, and the masses of customers they attracted, was proof to me that a great change was taking place.

THIS IS A GOOD POINT at which to provide some historical context.

At this juncture in the mid-1980s, the Chinese government's post-Mao embrace of accelerating modernization by rejecting the Communist dogmatism of the past was gaining steam. The new approach involved relaxing many restrictions to a free-market economy, so as to encourage entrepreneurialism. And this included opening up trade and business partnerships with the West.

China's leaders wanted their nation to leapfrog the West to jump ahead in production and trade. To do so, they sought foreign capital and modern technology. Thus: an open-door policy — though the door wasn't fully ajar. China was luring foreign companies into joint ventures, as well as so-called "transfers of knowhow," by which the Chinese would be provided with technical information on manufacturing equipment by a foreign company, in return for opening their markets to the foreign company to sell its equipment. My employer, Cincinnati Milacron, was one such U.S. company that had been attracted by China's gigantic potential market for sales of machine tools. My bosses were eager to curry favor with the Chinese government by providing technical guidance for equipment we were selling.

The Chinese government's new party line — under the reform-minded stewardship of paramount leader Deng Xiaoping — was: "Practice is the sole criterion for testing truth."[9] It meant that any policy must be tested in practice, in the real world. The implication was that if the outcome proved positive, that was proof that the policy was sound.

China's economic and social policymakers began experimenting with a multitude of ideas for spurring development — all aimed at propelling the nation forward out of poverty. Results were all that mattered. For example, the dreadful central-government requirement (forced on the populace during the 27 years of Chairman Mao's rule) that farmers must work in communes on publicly owned land, and meet specific harvest quotas, went by the wayside. The new policy — allowing families to return to their ancestral plots and to be empowered to sell excess crops for personal profit — had passed the only test

---

[9] The phrase comes from an article by Chinese intellectual Hu Fuming, published in 1978 in a Chinese philosophy journal, *Theoretical Trends*. Fuming supported "anti-dogmatism" and generating new solutions for the economic and social problems the nation faced. Deng Xiaoping, who became China's de facto leader that year, and ended up serving as chairman of the Central Advisory Committee 1982-87, advocated this approach.

that mattered: the plots were more productive.

My brief glimpse of China on my family's tour in December 1982 had revealed to me an impoverished, colorless nation, not one buzzing with entrepreneurial potential. But by the time I'd returned in 1986, the "Contract Responsibility System" (also known as the "Household Responsibility System") was firmly established for farmers (as well as for urban, industrial "work units"), and the communal farming system had been officially dissolved for four years. The new system was a hybrid of communism and capitalism. While the state still owned land and much of the means of production, the production itself was now the responsibility of households. The households still had to contribute to state-set quotas, but could decide for themselves, for example, which crops to plant on the contracted land. They also could sell their produce in a multi-tier price system. The lowest price was used to sell to the state until the quota was satisfied; a higher price was for above-quota sales to the state; a market price was for crops sold at fairs.[10]

In other words, families now had a measure of control of their economic destiny. They could sell surplus goods on the open market and collect profits accordingly. They had gained an economic incentive to succeed. It's also worth noting that this flip-flop by the Communist Party had come about organically. Desperate, starving villagers had simply moved en masse back onto their ancestral lands and resumed the traditional ways of farming. The local Communist Party authorities had been powerless to prevent them. The draconian policies of Mao's reign — including his second Five Year Plan (known as "The Great Leap Forward") from 1958-62, that had implemented the policy of people's communes and directly led to mass starvation — had worn out much of the Chinese population. So had doctrinaire social movements

---

[10] Weber, Isabella. *How China escaped shock therapy: the market reform debate.* Abingdon, Oxon. Routledge, 2021. Page 163.

such as the Cultural Revolution of the 1960s and '70s that aimed to quash dissension to Chairman Mao's edicts.

Mao had wanted to transform China from an economically backward agrarian-oriented society to one increasingly urbanized and industrialized. Yet his anti-capitalism beliefs — his opposition to the profit motive — had itself prevented progress. It took his death in 1976, and the will of the general population, to force the central government into taking a fresh approach to priming the economy. This approach included adopting the philosophy that "Practice is the sole criterion for testing truth": opening the possibility of free-market capitalism, at least to a degree. Farmers moved away from cultivating monocultural crops (such as just rice, wheat or cabbage — to meet state-mandated quotas) to profitable produce consumers wanted to buy on the market.

Change, however, was slow. In 1986, as in my short visit in 1982, cabbage was still a main food staple, and I didn't see vegetables that Americans commonly associate with Chinese cuisine, such as broccoli or snow peas. Chinese families in Beijing would fill up their outdoor balconies with stacks of cabbage, which was easily preserved in the cold, dry winters. They'd break off pieces of cabbage, peel them and boil them to serve with rice garnished with hot peppers. Heads of cabbage were everywhere when I returned in 1986. (That would end up changing as the years passed, as rural farmers discovered which crops could earn them the best profits on the open market, such as broccoli, green beans and bok choy.)

The Contract Responsibility System also applied to so-called "work units" — communal enterprises — in the cities. The state created work units to produce the goods or services it deemed were needed by society, and assigned people to the units when they finished school. The state provided the capital for the work units to procure machines and other equipment. But under the new system, the government shifted from specifying which products to produce, and setting production quotas, to taxing work units on their output and allowing the work units to seek financing from banks. Now the work units could control their own destinies, just as the farmers could. The work units could sell what they produced, and accumulate earnings.

Mao's so-called "Iron Rice Bowl" policy was thusly retired. Whereas those in work units had been guaranteed they would always be housed and fed and provided with healthcare, now their work units had to produce goods or services of market value. They became profit oriented.

That's the new mindset I encountered as I strove to land sales of machine tools with Chinese companies. The work units enjoyed the autonomy to purchase equipment themselves, although they did need to apply to the Ministry of Machine Building for an allocation of U.S. dollars to pay for the equipment. Nevertheless, China's economy was opening up. The potential seemed infinite in this nation that constituted approximately 20 percent of the world's population. I was sensing a change in the Chinese population's mindset about the new economic opportunities — the confidence that economists term "animal spirits."

And since one of my chief duties for my employer was selling machine-tool equipment to Chinese buyers, I believed I was in the right place at the right time.

MACHINE TOOLS ARE USED to make a wide variety of industrial widgets, such as molds and dies for the plastics industry and engine blocks for the car industry. They come in all shapes and sizes — from the common garage drill press to gigantic machines such as the one I saw in a Shanghai factory, where McDonnell Douglas was assembling MD-80 jetliners for China's domestic airline, in a co-production agreement with the state-owned Shanghai

Aviation Industrial Corp. The Shanghai factory used one of our enormous machines for milling aircraft wing spars 100 feet long; an operator rode in a control box that glided on railroad tracks next to the machine bed. Machine tools are used for metal cutting, milling, drilling, punching, stamping, turning, grinding — and any other process to shape and form metal into useful products. China wanted these machines very badly, to accelerate industrialization.

In addition to my duties as the project manager for Cincinnati Milacron — which meant supervising the transfer of machine-tool technology to our Chinese partner — I was responsible for pursuing Chinese customers for our machine tools. My sales calls mostly led me to grimy factories far from the heart of China's export-driven economic boom. The pioneering new economic zones in the south, near Hong Kong, best symbolized China's early dramatic rise in the 1980s. The go-go south's light industry was pumping out enormous quantities of cheap household goods, garments and shoes, consumer electronics and plastic toys to satisfy world demand. When I took a trip to Hong Kong toward the end of 1986, I was shocked by the bright lights and big-city vibrancy.[11]

But the environments in which I traveled in the machine-tool business were hardly glamorous or exhilarating. My work took me to remote, satanic, smoke-belching factories in China's metal-bashing, rust-belt northeast, and backwater frontier towns such as Yumen in China's barren west. In the 1950s,

---

[11] This highly developed, densely populated global financial center and commercial port of high rises and factories — on a peninsula and island on China's coast with the South China Sea — was still a decade away from being returned to China by terms of a 99-year lease agreed to with the United Kingdom, which had taken it over as a colony after the 19th century Opium Wars. However, in advance of China's 1997 regaining of Hong Kong and turning it into a special administrative region, China's leaders had recognized Hong Kong as a needed middleman for capital to finance new Chinese industry, and as an interface with the outside world for trade. The Chinese government created special economic zones, such as Shenzhen, in the south, near Hong Kong, to try to incubate a market economy but not let it "pollute" the rest of China. Hong Kong-based investors could put factories in Shenzhen, and the factories could export goods directly back to Hong Kong.

Mao Zedong had ordered much of Chinese heavy industry to be moved inland to locations far from the risk of capture by invading foreigners. At one factory I visited near Harbin, barefoot kids fed red-hot machine parts into a diabolical, furiously pounding forge hammer in a sweltering shop. Cincinnati Milacron's polished precision machines with their blinking lights stood as shiny monuments to the modern world surrounded by the shabbiness of dim and decaying factories.

The company that employed me was nearly a century old itself and had grown up with America's robust modernization in the late 19th and 20th centuries. Cincinnati Milacron had been founded in 1889 by German immigrants as the Cincinnati Milling Machine Co., which in turn had been formed from one founder's previous partnership, the Cincinnati Screw and Tap Co. Then Milacron had grown into America's largest machine-tool builder, expanding its product line to include planers and grinding machines, before reincorporating as Cincinnati Milacron.

The company's factory in Cincinnati looked like it was vintage World War II era, with large, dark brick halls, and sunlight streaming down in dusty rays from dirty skylights. My on-the-job apprenticeship for my first three months as an employee had consisted of shadowing machinists as they carefully bolted together large assemblies with precision movements driven by jackscrews, electric servo motors and computer controls. As we bantered together in the factory, these craftsmen grew aware of my Yale pedigree, my study of Chinese language, and my time spent in the Marine Corps Officer Candidate School back in the summer of 1984. They speculated that I was a CIA plant tasked to spy on Red China. We had fun during those months with relaxed weekend barbecues, and my middle-class, blue-collar friends' chitchat would occasionally focus on the question: "Why do U.S. workers have to change in response to China's rise?"

Their concerns were fueled by the ascendence of Japanese carmakers and electronics manufacturers, and Japan's soaring economic clout and fierce competition with U.S. companies for our domestic market. This was the era when Americans were increasingly subscribing to the viewpoint to "Buy American" and, "Don't buy a Japanese car." My blue-collar friends at Cincinnati Milacron performed highly skilled labor, putting together machinery that demanded clockwork precision. But they felt pressure from Japan's rise, and fears that the Japanese would take over industries and threaten their livelihood by replacing U.S. workers they deemed inefficient. Cincinnati Milacron's primary customers for machine tools were mold and die-makers, carmakers, and aircraft manufacturers. My friends lumped the Chinese in with the Japanese.

Our company wanted to sell our latest machine tools, costing hundreds of thousands of dollars each, to Chinese industrial customers, who were hungry for new and productive equipment to meet their rapidly industrializing nation's growing demand. An export license was approved by the U.S. commerce department, which had determined that our equipment could not be used for military purposes. On the Chinese side, its government permitted us to court Chinese customers for our machines — with, however, a quid pro quo. In exchange for allowing us the opportunity to capture a share of China's scarce allocations of foreign exchange, Cincinnati Milacron would have to transfer our knowhow for one of our machine products (a grinding machine) to a customer in China: the Wuxi Machine Tools Co., whose factory was upriver from Shanghai.

My main duty was serving as project manager for the technology-transfer project. This meant working directly between U.S. and Chinese teams to coordinate the technology transfer and localization of the grinding machine. My other duty was working (as I mentioned) to close equipment sales of Milacron machines in the Chinese market. Following my three months of training at the factory in Cincinnati, I'd embarked on my first business trip to China, knowing I would be spending most of the next two years in China with only infrequent returns to the States.

This first business trip involved visiting Wuxi Machine Tools' headquarters. I traveled south to Shanghai to transfer by train to Wuxi for meetings with the Chinese engineering team. Passing through Shanghai, I stayed at the old brick Jinjiang Hotel, which must have been strikingly glamorous in the 1930s with its Art Deco interior, but now was a bit timeworn. While dining at the hotel restaurant, I had to compete with cockroaches scurrying about, vying for my food on the greasy tablecloth. I visited the new, gleaming Sheraton hotel one evening and found myself the object of attention of a multitude of Chinese pedestrians outside, staring in through the lobby windows.

I enjoyed strolling on Shanghai's leafy streets outside the stately mansions of the Foreign Quarter. The 1930s bank and hotel buildings of the Bund, the waterfront district along the Huangpu River, had housed banks and trading houses, foreign consulates and social clubs for the expatriate European and American communities that had made it a major financial hub in east Asia. My father had a childhood memory of riding in a Packard Limousine along the Bund in the late 1930s. The Communist victory in 1949 in the Chinese Civil War had pushed the foreigners, and the national banks of the Republic of China, out. But the majestic buildings of the Bund, with their Beaux Arts columns and balustrades, still dominated Shanghai's skyline. I would climb up the worn wooden staircase of the Peace Hotel to the rooftop restaurant and slurp down xiǎo lóng bāozi steamed dumplings while gazing out at the tugs and barges chugging along the Huangpu. On boat tours down the Huangpu, I observed the hustle and bustle of riverboat life aboard puttering junks enlivened with old women cooking, children playing, and farmers tending animals on these gliding vessels. I occasionally caught glimpses of rusty Chinese naval ships and submarines moored at the mouth of the Yangtze River. It was clear to me China wasn't spending effort upgrading its military.

But I was there to work, not sightsee. And there certainly was work to be done, as the American-Chinese partnership I'd signed onto lurched clumsily forward.

The train ride from Shanghai to Wuxi took me through the damp green countryside of the coastal Jiangsu province. Paddy fields stretched out in every direction, with groups of farmhouses dotting the landscape here and there. The farmers seemed to be benefiting from the new household responsibility system, by which they could sell crop surpluses for private gain. This was evident from significant farmhouse construction activity, renovations and additions — all financed by the earnings on direct sales of cash crops. The rural farmers outside the cities were the first to benefit from China's early economic liberalization.

On disembarking from the train at the Wuxi railway station, I met a representative of the machine-tool factory. We drove in a battered Toyota Crown Royal Saloon sedan through the crowded streets and markets of Wuxi. A high, white-washed wall, spattered with mud and topped with broken glass shards, enclosed the gray factory buildings. Bars obscured the windows of the offices. After entering the main lobby, we ambled down a dark hallway to a door with a sign above that I deciphered as, "Negotiation Room." As the door swung open, I felt deep unease over how the Chinese delegation might receive me. Were they expecting a gray-haired, senior American engineer? Would they be offended by my youth and inexperience? Would I be able to communicate with them using my limited language ability?

On entering the room, I observed a half-dozen Chinese men and women huddled around a table in the center of the room. They stood, and with stiff smiles and limp handshakes greeted me one by one. I exchanged my business card with theirs and learned that my hosts included the factory general manager, the chief engineer and lower-level engineers. The era of the Mao suit was waning. These professionals were dressed as best as they could in Western fashion. The women wore simple black pantsuits to go with their basic short-cropped hair. The men wore ill-fitting business suits with sagging jackets draped on their skinny frames, and baggy trousers cinched far above their waists with extra-long belts. I attributed the ill-fitting clothes to the fact these people were emaciated, most having grown up under great deprivation during the Cultural Revolution. The belts appeared to be about five holes too long, and I credited that to a purchasing mentality formed in poverty. They must have decided that buying a long belt at the same price as a short one meant getting more material.

Several large blueprints — slightly worn and soiled with oil stains — lay unrolled on the table in front of them. Cigarette smoke drifted up from butts resting in tin ashtrays perched on the edges of the blueprints. The general manager was a short, balding, energetic man. It was his duty to deliver the official opening speech in Chinese. It was brief and businesslike, rather than flowery and ceremonial:

"Welcome Mr. Mark! We are happy to partner with your highly esteemed machine-tool company. We look forward to your company's experts visiting us. The objective of our cooperation is mutual friendship and benefit!"

With that, he turned to the chief engineer: a tall, bony, nervous man who chain smoked. He was the one facing the most pressure to make the technology transfer work. The formalities completed, he began interrogating me in Chinese.

"We have sent many inquiries summarizing our list of questions," he said, pushing a lengthy telex with numbered requests at me. "When can we get answers from your team?" His exasperation was evident in his tone.

While I dodged demands with clarifying questions and assurances that I would expeditiously follow up with our U.S. team, I felt the stress of a tricky situation in which China and U.S. teams had a broad disconnect. My role was the connector, but I had yet to plug in each end. The Chinese sensed that squeezing me would not produce any substantive answers to their questions that day. The general manager rescued me with a proposal that we adjourn and reconvene for an evening banquet at their cafeteria after a brief respite at my hotel. It dawned on me that the Chinese looked forward to these work-unit banquets as a rare, sumptuous meal far superior to their meager diet at home. So, at least, my visit was providing them that.

On my arrival at the cafeteria that evening, I was gratified to see that my counterparts' demeanors had transformed to broad smiles and good cheer in anticipation of the abundant food. Dish after dish of tasty Wuxi delicacies arrived.

Me: "This is an amazing spread of interesting dishes!"
Team: " *Duìbùqǐ.* " [Please excuse us.]
Actual meaning: "It is customary to impart that the banquet food is inadequate and insufficient, and expect you, the guest, to unanimously praise the spread of stinky tofu, rooster testicles, silkworms and partially developed duck eggs.

Me: "Thank you for preparing this banquet for me."
Team: *"Bùyào kēi qǐ. "* [No need to be polite.]
Actual meaning: "We're done with the small talk; please start eating!"

Me: "Mmm, tasty food!"
Team: *"Hǎo. "* [Good.]
Actual meaning: "Bat soup and tuna eyeballs are good for you, eat more!"

When we could barely cram any more mouthfuls, the cook dramatically presented the signature dish of Wuxi: white fish of Lake Tai. Each diner discreetly spit bones, cartilage, and other inedible tidbits onto small piles next to his or her plate. Drinking centered on shot glasses of fiery Moutai or Baijiu: Chinese white-lightning liquor. According to Chinese custom, each member of the delegation individually toasted me with a lively challenge to down my glass in one swallow.

OVER THE NEXT FEW months, I was able to defuse Chinese rancor with the perceived slow pace of progress. I extracted written responses from the Milacron engineers and scheduled dates for visits by our technicians to China, and the Chinese team to America. My counterparts in Wuxi deeply desired an opportunity to travel to the United States and lobbied me for endorsements of them to join the traveling group. The Chinese requested an itinerary that would transit Washington, D.C., for tours of our capital. (They had not yet discovered the allure of Las Vegas. Despite the decades under Communism and the party's criminalizing of gambling, betting remained firmly ingrained in Chinese culture.)

The delegation of eight staffers from Wuxi Machine Tools Co. were the jolly general manager, the nervous chief engineer, three additional male and two female engineers, and a translator. They set off for America with an insatiable curiosity about our way of life — and a naïveté about the hazards of our free society. I greeted them on their arrival at the Cincinnati airport and then, as their chauffeur, led them to the Chevrolet van I'd rented. I drove them to their motel, where I had booked rooms for all of us. They were thrilled to discover that their rooms had telephones, and they excitedly posed for photos pretending to be deep in officious conversation with the handset to their ears.

Curious about the local neighborhood and stores, they ventured out in the evenings to window-shop in the suburban strip malls. One evening, they headed out by themselves to a nearby grocery store. A thief exploited their innocent display of their wad of cash at the grocery store and shockingly relieved them of their money in a snatch and dash. They were embarrassed by the episode, and — given their cultural aversion to involving police — did not report the crime. They certainly were thinking about money, though. They cleverly asked me if I could help them invest their company per-diem cash advances in the U.S. stock market.

America enchanted them. I did my best to culturally acclimate them. The motel staff frowned on their spitting in the pool and forbade their smoking indoors. I translated the concerns, explaining that, "Americans don't like it" when it came to spitting in the pool or elsewhere in public, and that it was forbidden to stub out cigarette butts on the carpets of their hotel rooms.

My guests gleefully tried driving for the first time in our van in the motel parking lot. Outside of the sometimes-adversarial business environment, we solidified our friendships via these amusing exposures to life in America.

While the slowly thawing relationship between the governments of the United States and China was not contentious, it did have an underlying tension regarding Chinese goals to gather U.S. technology. One day, two straitlaced American men in suits showed up at our factory's executive offices and presented business cards bearing no insignia or information other than their names and phone numbers.

"We're with the FBI," one explained. "We're here just to understand if the Chinese nationals visiting you have been doing anything suspicious."

They asked me if I had seen the Chinese snooping inappropriately or fishing discarded material out of our trash cans. The agents' visit struck me as comical. They had not been pre-informed of the identity of our Chinese guests, and they lacked basic information about our joint project. I assumed that the sheer volume of Chinese visitors to the United States at that time was overwhelming the FBI's efforts to track them all.

The agents were not imperious, just inquisitive. From their tone, I ascertained they didn't think Chinese nationals posed much of a threat, unlike, say, if our guests had been from the Soviet Union.

OVER TWO YEARS, WE completed our project milestones for the transfer of knowhow and launched a fully localized Wuxi version of the grinding machine. Not that matters always ran smoothly between our team at Cincinnati Milacron and my associates at Wuxi Machine Tools Co.

Me: "When will you send the money for payment for our knowhow?"
Team: *"Děng yīxià."* [Wait a moment.]
Actual meaning: "We can't tell you right now, or how long you have to wait."

Me: "It is important that we receive payment before we ship the technical documents."
Team: *"Méiyǒu guānxì."* [It doesn't matter.]
Actual meaning: "The reason why you can't get what you want is because you don't know the right person."

Me: "Can you help find a way to get us paid?"
Team: *"Méiyǒu bànfǎ."* [No way.]
Actual meaning: "I know the correct person to talk to, but it would take too much trouble to convince them."

We sold a modest number of Cincinnati-built machines in China. The Chinese government's capital allocations for investment in our products were slow and unreliable. China was still very poor, and its takeoff as an economic giant was not yet perceptible, based on what I'd observed of industrial activity in the nation's north and west. Dramatic changes in the export-driven south — where the "animal spirits" were truly unleashed — might have altered my view, but I'd had no direct contact with it in my working world.

Etched permanently in my memory is the following scene:

The train coach is clicking along the rails in the northwestern desert as a dry and dusty scene passes by my open window — conjuring again a fleeting feeling I am in the Old West, though this is late 20th century China, not late 19th century America. Gusts of coal smoke are belching from the antiquated steam locomotive and blowing through the window, choking us passengers.

My body has gotten used to the swinging and rocking of the coach. I've been on this train for 40 hours and still have 10 more to go before arrival in Beijing. I've read all the books I have brought, and exhausted frivolous conversation with my sleeper cabin's Chinese travelers.

With tired eyes, I watch a fly dance among the half-eaten snacks on our little table, then buzz off toward the soiled sleeping clothes in the racks above our bunks. Suddenly, a screeching sound from the speaker in our compartment jars us upright. Martial music blares dramatically for a few moments, followed by the recording of an announcer with a nasal voice delivering a droning recitation of Communist Party propaganda. These exasperatingly long bulletins have interrupted our daily routine many times over the past few days.

Me: "Do you mind if I adjust the volume on the speaker in here?"
Travelers: "*Kěyǐ.*" [It's acceptable]
Actual meaning: "You can try if you like, but the conductor in charge is not around, and you probably won't be able to adjust it yourself.

Me: "I think lunch is being served in the dining car."

Travelers: "*Chīfàn, xiūxí.*" [Let's eat, rest.]

Actual meaning: "Chatting with you this morning was *so* exhausting, we will go eat, rest and come back later."

As soon as my three traveling companions have shuffled out of the compartment to eat lunch in the dining car, I pull out my Swiss Army knife and disassemble the speaker volume-control panel. I quickly cut the wires to the control and reassemble the panel into the wall. After the other travelers return to the compartment, they scratch their heads as they fumble with the volume for the now-muted speaker.

This train trip has been my escape from Yumen City, a small oil-drilling town in the far west of China. Yumen — in ancient times an outpost on the Silk Road — is one stop farther out at the edge of Chinese civilization beyond the city of Jiayuguan: the most western point on the Great Wall of China. A week before, I'd joined a technician from our employer, Cincinnati Milacron, to travel by train from Beijing to Yumen — one of two oil-producing sites in China — to install a new grinding machine at an oil equipment-repair facility there, run by the buyer of the grinding machine. The machine was needed for honing the long cylinder from a "nodding donkey" oil pump so that it would better fit its cylinder casing after suffering wear-and-tear issues from hard use.

As our steam engine had chugged across the desert that October of 1987, I'd assured my American co-worker — I'll call him "Joe Sixpack," because he was a regular guy, a tattooed blue-collar man in his late thirties who didn't speak a word of Chinese — that we would be met by representatives of the Chinese customer at the train station.

"Don't worry," I'd told him several times on our train trek. "It's a long train ride but everything's going to be fine."

We'd disembarked at the desolate depot. There was no town in sight. To my chagrin, there also was no sign of a representative of the Chinese customer. We'd stepped down from the train and found a small shack with chickens pecking about outside in the dusty yard. With no telephone and no means of communication, we'd stoically sat on our bags in the dust and watched the train disappear into the distance, dark exhaust billowing from its smokestack.

Eventually, a dusty, battered black Russian Lada coupe had rolled up and the driver, dispatched by our client, had transported us to a rundown, dirty guesthouse in the town of Yumen. It was no-frills frontier lodging. The toilet paper consisted of a stack of cardboard wedges ripped from a packing box. The guesthouse had no power or hot water except for brief periods in the evenings, when the staff alerted us to jump in the shower:

Staff: *"Kuài kuài! Chèn rè xǐzǎo!"* [Hurry up! Take a shower while it's hot!] Actual meaning: "It's normal to wait all day for only 10 minutes of hot water!"

Joe and I had spent every day on site in the equipment-repair facility installing the machine. A foundation was needed to be built and leveled for the installation. The grinding machine had to be lubricated to be operated. Getting it ready for operation was complicated by the fact it had been jostled along its 7,000-mile journey from Cincinnati. It had been shipped by train to a Pacific port in America, then spent two months on a container ship, then bumped around some more on trains, and then on trucks traveling bad Chinese roads. At the site in Yumen, it had been hoisted into position via Chinese rigging that was less than conventional. By the time it was in place, this giant piece of precision equipment had been bent or smashed here and there, and Joe had taken pains to render it functional.

He'd checked that the foundation was sound, then set to calibrating the machine. He'd set up the electronic-control system. It looked to be a two-week operation. In the evenings after dinner, I'd walk from one end of the treeless town, which was bordered by huge ponds of oozing crude oil, to the other end, which was flanked by a cemetery for those who had died in the oil fields.

As the days crawled by and the machine installation progressed, it had become evident that our hosts had no plans for our return to Beijing. My repeated inquiries in the mornings and afternoons had been met with typically elusive replies that they were working on arrangements for our return trip.

Me: "Are there any train tickets available to send me back to Beijing?"
Them: " *Méiyǒu.* " [There are none.]
Actual meaning: "There are some, but we are waiting for you to finish your job first."

Me: "Where is the person who is responsible to arrange my train ticket to Beijing?"
Them: *"Bùzài."* [Not present.]
Actual meaning: "The person you want to speak to is here, however, is not prepared to see you."

Me: "Is there a problem getting a ticket to Beijing?"
Them: *"Méiyǒu wèntí."* [No problem.]
Actual meaning: "Please have confidence that you will eventually arrive at your desired destination."

Joe and I had realized we were hostages until we'd completed the installation. However, I'd needed to return to Beijing to handle another sales-related task. I'd persisted in my demands that my return trip be booked, and finally been awarded with a 50-hour train ticket home.

The sensation of my body rocking with the endless train movement persisted long after I'd stepped off the train in Beijing.

IT WAS EXPERIENCES LIKE that one that eventually convinced me it was time to move on. Two years of toiling in China's awkwardly modernizing economy were enough for me. My sights, in fact, were readjusted. They were set eastward: toward Japan.

By 1988, Japanese cars and electronics were flooding into the United States. The so-called "Japan, Inc." was marching into markets across the world, and Japan beckoned with opportunity. Western media portrayed Japan as an economic juggernaut that looked bound for global domination. I yearned to ride that wave.

The lure of bustling Japan overshadowed the languor of backwater China. Japan beckoned me with bigger surf.

So, in spring 1988, I said, *"Zàijiàn"* to the Land of the Red Dragon, and *Konnichiwa* to the Land of the Rising Sun.

Chapter Three

Beholding Bubbly Japan

Martial music blared from the speakers, and 100 of us stood beside our desks and display terminals and faced the general manager — balding, middle-aged, bespectacled Matsumoto-san — at the front of the cavernous room. Everyone wore identical tan uniform vests with "SONY" emblazoned in red letters across our chests. A robotic voice from the speaker instructed us to begin our morning calisthenics.

All of us — tall, short, heavy, thin, mostly men but a few women — moved in unison with the bright ding-dong music that sounded like an arcade videogame jingle. We followed the singsong counting for the repetitions ("Ichi, ni, san, shi . . ."): stretching, bending, twisting, and jumping in front of our desks. For my Japanese coworkers, this was customary; they'd been conditioned by years of morning workouts in school. When the 15-minute routine ended, the general manager addressed our ranks with his daily briefing.

One by one, Matsumoto-san instructed each section to complete its tasks. *Prepare the report for last month's sales. List the top customers. Prepare the sales plan for next month.* Each section leader acknowledged the directions

43

with a bow. The general manager then picked out one of our colleagues to step to the front of the room to blather a short spontaneous speech about himself or herself, for public-speaking practice. This morning's misfortunate was Ms. Horikiri. The rest of us shifted on our feet out of boredom as Ms. Horikiri, nervous in her skirt and vest, shared her experience of riding the train to work that morning.

Finally, we all crumpled into our chairs to begin the daily hustle of selling silicon chips.

It was summer 1988. I was an employee of Sony Corp., working in the Shinagawa district of Tokyo. Prior to moving to Japan, I'd spent two months in a crash course of Japanese comprehension. I'd been hired as a semiconductor sales manager — a small cog in the marketing and sales group for Sony semiconductor components. Sony had chosen years before to sell its high-end integrated circuits and video microchips — which went into Sony-branded stereos and televisions — to other manufacturers of consumer electronics. I worked in the greater China section to develop markets and sell these tiny chips to companies in Taiwan, Hong Kong, and mainland China. I was a non-Japanese face in a sea of mostly Japanese employees in our large, open-plan office. The Japanese favored this type of workspace to facilitate communication and coordination among marketing and sales sections — each section working hard to outperform the others.

At the end of the 1980s, the Japanese dominated world markets for memory chips. Chip shortages in the United States, Europe and other parts of Asia fed foreigners' fears that Japan would control this strategic market and fuel Japanese arrogance. It was a bit like the alarm about Japanese military empire building from the first half of the 20th century. But this new international anxiety was of a rising Japanese economic empire steadily dominating key industries, expanding into ever more markets, investing earnings in foreign property, buying up foreign competitors and wielding ever-greater clout — ultimately asserting financial hegemony over the United States and the rest of the world. The vision was of Japan conquering the world through exports of superior products and ruthless trade deals, rather than via warplanes and ground invasions.

As a foot soldier, if you will, in Sony's campaign of selling chips to Asian manufacturers of stereos and TVs, I saw how Japan aggressively seized the initiative in negotiations with U.S. companies. CEOs of U.S. computer and device companies were begging Sony for allocations of memory chips to keep their factories in Singapore running. Sony sought leverage by insisting that these allocations be granted on the condition that the U.S. companies buy more of Sony's higher-value, application-specific integrated circuits.

The timbre of the times was reflected in a collection of highly provocative essays — half of them written by Sony co-founder and chairman Akio Morita, the other half by Japan's minister of transport, Shintaro Ishihara — titled, *The Japan That Can Say No: Why Japan Will Be First Among Equals.* Though intended only for publication in Japan, the essays were translated into English: shocking U.S. business executives and government leaders. Ishihara's essays claimed that the Japanese character was innately superior to the American; Japanese products were of higher quality because their workers were better; the United States now depended on the superior Japanese technology, and therefore Japan could refuse to sell components for U.S. missiles — and even share secrets with the Soviet Union as a bargaining weapon. Morita was less belligerent, yet highly critical of the United States. He assailed U.S. companies for focusing more on mergers and acquisitions and creating short-term profits by moving manufacturing overseas, than on focusing on creating manufacturing power and better products to capture markets abroad. He also lambasted U.S. executives for earning outrageous compensation that harmed their companies.

I felt that the essays reflected the truth about the state of U.S. industry, and Japan's threat to establish economic domination. They instilled me with unease about America's future.

As a Sony employee, I was keenly aware of the supreme confidence, even chauvinism, of Japanese companies, fostered by "Japan, Inc.'s" steady takeover of U.S. consumer markets for automobiles and electronics. When it came to the fast-growing computer industry, the Japanese had their sights initially set on taking over the market for computer memory. The strategy then called for swallowing up the microprocessor business, then desktop computers, and — finally — high-end computers. U.S. business leaders, as well as American workers, feared that they would be victims of an industrial domino effect in which Japan grabbed all the high-value opportunities in the high-tech digital world.

The chain reaction wasn't confined to computers, electronics, and automobiles. Japanese corporate profits were being sunk into foreign investments. Already there had been high-profile Japanese acquisitions of marquee American properties. Sony had purchased CBS Records in 1988 and Columbia Pictures in 1989. Syndicated radio commentator Paul Harvey warned of "an economic Pearl Harbor."

To many people, there seemed no limit to Japan's economic rise, and I had an in-the-trenches view as a Sony employee between 1988 and '89. I was witnessing this modern, developed country with a proud and ancient history morphing unremittingly into an economic superpower — overtly shedding traces of its submissive post-World War II posture as a defeated empire. Japanese discipline impressed me. Tokyo, the capital, exhibited extraordinary orderliness and cleanliness in contrast to China's chaos and grimy poverty. Japan seemed set on toppling the United States to become the largest economy in the world.

From that standpoint, it was obvious to me I had chosen wisely to shift my business career from the People's Republic to the Land of the Rising Sun.

SONY MARCHED RESOLUTELY FORWARD, staffed by self-important salarymen from Keio University and Tokyo University sporting the tan company vests that had been designed by the legendary Japanese fashion mogul Issey Miyake, hired by Morita-san. The regimented office culture required groupthink and consensus decisions — really everyone just agreeing with the boss. Management snubbed creativity and individual responsibility. Soliciting ideas from the group was unheard of. Dull workdays extended late into the evenings, whereupon everyone halfheartedly joined the general manager for obligatory drunken revelries and karaoke at local dives. *Nomi ni iku!* ("Let's go out for a drink!")

Every day, I walked the mile from my tiny, unheated cell (36 square feet, the size of two tatami mats) in the Sony bachelor dormitory, to the office for another daily routine. After work, it was off to the neon-lit Roppongi nightclub district for karaoke partying and heavy drinking of Japanese Suntory whiskey. I was officially part of the crew, but felt more like a spectator at Sony, due to the restricted society and xenophobia. I'd grown used to being called *henna gaijin* ("strange foreigner") by my workmates whenever I made a flub in understanding Japanese culture.

Why had Sony hired me? Simple: It needed non-Japanese sales agents selling its products as it expanded into foreign markets. The brass at Japanese corporations were keenly aware that buyers abroad would be intimidated by Japanese salespeople selling superior Japanese products, and thus be resistant to purchases. Therefore, they wanted a more international "face" representing them. Sony initially wanted to hire me to help develop the U.S. market for chips. I'd requested to be assigned to the Greater China market, due to my background working there and my Chinese-language ability.

I adapted as best I could to my status as a *henna gaijin*. But there were days when culture shock would overwhelm me, and I would bolt outside the office for fresh air and a reset. Fortunately, there were places for me to escape the oppressive atmosphere of Japan, Inc. The aesthetic of Zen temples and the serenity of Shinto shrines soothed my soul. Trips to open-air hot baths (*rotenburo*) reinvigorated my flesh. Hole-in-the-wall eateries lured me with tasty grilled seafood and other delicacies. Hikes in lush bamboo forests offered a respite from the urban concrete jungle.

Some of my colleagues presented me a welcome break from the uniformity of Japanese corporate life. I enjoyed being around self-assured Nomura-san. In her late twenties and unmarried, she was considered "unsold Christmas cake" by the rest of the office clan. The phrase referred to the airy sponge cakes (which the Japanese pronounced, 'CRISS-mahs-a-KAY-kee'), often made with strawberries. This Western dessert is highly perishable; thus, calling someone "unsold Christmas cake" is cruel, but how women unmarried past age 25 are viewed in Japan. It implies they had passed their use-by date. Nomura-san probably frightened men away with her assertive personality and blunt way of speaking. While she was an expert speaker of Chinese, she was still expected to serve tea to the Sony men. It was the same for the vivacious Yuko Sakamaki, who dressed like a groovy go-go girl of the 1960s in colorful miniskirts and boots. Outside of work, she sang lead vocals as a Japanese Chrissie Hynde for a Pretenders cover band.

I did encounter the gentler side of the Japanese character. Affable Nagai-san, a slim, unassuming man in his late thirties, invited me for a weekend stay with his extended family at a farmhouse outside Tokyo. While huddled over the heated table (*kotatsu*) sunk into the floor in Nagai-san's frigid wood-

and-paper (*shoji*) farmhouse, I listened to his father recount his experiences during World War II in the Imperial Japanese Army, climaxed by being taken prisoner by U.S. forces on Okinawa in 1945. The old man tearfully thanked me for the humane treatment he had received from the U.S. Army four-and-a-half decades earlier.

America's military power was still present in Japan. My coworker Kobayashi-san, who had graduated from the Japan Self-Defense Forces, took me on weekend excursions on his Yamaha motorcycle. One day, we rode to the Yokosuka Naval Base, where we stared up at the USS Midway aircraft carrier towering over us at the pier.

One coworker who was utterly unimpressed by America was bombastic Yamamoto-san, my section leader. He represented a different facet of the Japanese nature. He was not my favorite coworker.

Yamamoto-san was short and potbellied with a mustache, wore a comb-over haircut to hide a growing bald spot, and had a darker skin complexion than most Japanese (for which he was self-conscious). He tested my patience. Yamamoto-san sometimes lectured me with his forecasts that Japanese economic growth would rocket Japan past America, resulting in a dire outcome in which the U.S.A. would have only oranges and its women to offer to the Japanese.

Yamamoto-san was a perfect example to me of how many Japanese had become brainwashed about how strong their nation had become. Japanese media heavily promoted this message. There were even *manga* — Japanese comic strips or graphic novels — about super salarymen who would lead Japanese corporations to dominate the world. I believed Yamamoto-san was overestimating Japan's future performance. He lacked credibility in my eyes. He'd drunk the Kool-Aid.

But I kept these thoughts to myself.

YAMAMOTO-SAN ORGANIZED a business trip with me in April 1989 to Hong Kong and China, focused on introducing new Sony products to our customers. In preparation, we considered what samples of semiconductors we could safely carry into China.

In those days, the United States and its allies enforced bans on technology exports to Soviet Bloc countries. Toshiba Corp. had enraged the U.S. government by selling sophisticated machine tools to the Soviet Union despite the ban. The Soviets had used this equipment to machine quieter propellers for their submarines to evade the U.S. fleet. U.S. military analysts estimated damages from the diminished ability to track submarines to exceed $1 billion. As a result, Japan was very sensitive not to allow another renegade sale of technology, and Sony was careful to limit what semiconductors we would carry into the People's Republic of China. Yamamoto and I chose 64k memory chips, and Sony Walkman-on-a-chip — a microchip consisting of a digital processor and memory functions for a Walkman, and which could be inserted onto a circuit board and then housed in a casing to be sold as a portable player similar to a Walkman.

During our Japan Airlines flight from Tokyo to Hong Kong, Yamamoto-san became irritated by the Japanese flight attendants persisting in addressing him in English. Apparently, his darker complexion, mustache and wavy thinning hair had led the attendants to mistake him for a foreigner (perhaps Turkish). He resigned himself to downing several cocktails to smother this indignity.

After our plane navigated its heart-pounding final approach to Kai Tak Airport — veering over the drab apartment towers of Kowloon, across

Victoria Harbour from Hong Kong Island — then making a bumpy landing on the tarmac, we made our way into the mob of travelers outside the terminal. Our local sales agents for Hong Kong met us and escorted us downtown to their office. These young Chinese men expressed surprise to me that I was employed by Sony. They whispered that a *gweilo* ("white devil" in Cantonese slang, but a word generally used in Hong Kong simply to refer to a foreigner) like me should not be working for the Japanese.

We all boarded a ferry for a night at the casinos in Macau for gambling and partying before our trip into China.[12] The casinos presented a scene from 1970s Las Vegas of cigarette smoke-filled gambling halls with tattered interiors, and tuxedo-attired dealers and skimpily clad call girls competing to relieve visitors of their cash. After walking off the fog of the morning hangover, we boarded a ferry to take us back to Kowloon to start our trip into China.

Selling Sony semiconductors in China took us to Japanese owned and operated consumer-electronics factories, and to an assortment of local manufacturing businesses and traders across the country. Japanese companies such as Sharp and Hitachi were longtime consumers of Sony chips, and the factory representatives greeted Yamamoto-san warmly. Our Chinese customers consisted mostly of consumer-electronic device and desktop PC assemblers. During a stopover in Nanjing, our team happened to visit a street-side dealer selling electronic components. When we asked him if he had any interest in our 64k memory chip, he chuckled and showed us a 128k Sony memory chip in his glass case.

---

[12] In 1989, the former Portuguese colony of Macau, about 42 miles southwest of Hong Kong in the western Pearl River delta near the South China Sea, was a Chinese territory under Portuguese administration. An agreement specified Macau would be transferred to full Chinese control in 1999, but Macau's political and economic systems — including its legal casinos — would be guaranteed by China for the following 50 years. Today, as a special administrative district of China, it has a gambling industry seven times larger than that of Las Vegas. Mainland Chinese comprise most of its tourists.

"How did you get that?" exclaimed Yamamoto-san.

The street dealer grinned mischievously.

We later learned from our Chinese sales agents that it was common knowledge that memory chips were being smuggled into China. They said "everybody knows" that Hong Kong agents ran a brisk business carrying suitcases filled with semiconductor contraband into China to sell at marked-up prices.

So much for U.S. bans on technology sales to communist China!

In Guangdong, Yamamoto-san and I visited a small manufacturer of consumer electronics. Its workers were soldering Sony's Walkman-on-a-chip onto circuit boards, together with power electronics and other components. They then inserted the circuit boards into pink or lime green, plastic-injection-molded cases that featured control buttons and a headphone jack, and sold the cases as Chinese-made Walkmans. Sony was happy to provide the chip hardware guts and take the lion's share of profit on these local-label Walkman knock-offs.

While we were traveling in China that April, I observed thousands of protesters gathered in Beijing's Tiananmen Square. They were mostly college students. I wasn't too surprised. I knew that 20th century China had a tradition of students protesting, going back to the so-called May Fourth Movement begun during the First World War, when young Chinese intellectuals, motivated by national pride, had agitated for governmental reform, the strengthening of Chinese society and the modernization of Chinese culture in the face of Japanese encroachment.[13]

---

[13] Japan had aligned itself with the Allies in World War I (in contrast with what it would do in World War II, joining the Axis powers). On May 4, 1919, 3,000 students in Beijing held a mass protest against the decision at the Versailles Peace Conference to transfer

In following decades, students would demonstrate at symbolic times to protest the humiliation of China or some sort of grievance. Often, these demonstrations would be in response to a death or funeral of some leader whom students thought was a reformer on their side. I understood that the reason students had massed in Tiananmen Square here in April 1989 was the death of Hu Yaobang — a leader the students loved. Hu had served as general secretary of the Chinese Communist Party, and under the direction of Chairman Deng Xiaoping had pushed forth economic and political reforms, until being forced to resign by party elders.

My awareness of political and economic reforms demanded by the protesters — combined with my direct experience of the stirring "animal spirits" in China's go-go south — renewed my optimism that my investment in learning Chinese and committing time to the Chinese economy would pay off as China someday accelerated its development.

I could sense democracy taking hold, as a natural byproduct of the rising tide of free enterprise.

I couldn't have been further from the truth! But neither I, nor the rest of the world, would find that out until the events that took place in Tiananmen Square that June. And by that time, I'd already left Asia.

---

the former German concessions in China's Shandong Province to Japan, instead of to China. The Republic of China's government had acquiesced to the terms of the major powers who'd defeated Germany. In response, the enraged students razed the house of the minister of communications and attacked China's minister to Japan. Demonstrations spread around the country, and strikes and boycotts against Japanese goods lasted two months. More than 1,000 students were arrested, and several were killed or wounded. The Chinese government acquiesced to the students' demands and refused to sign the peace treaty with Germany.

THAT SPRING OF 1989, I decided to return to the United States for a graduate business degree. A number of reasons motivated me.

One was a feeling that I was just an insignificant salesperson in the Sony corporate world. Another was being a bit fed up with Japanese ethnocentrism. I enjoyed the Japanese lifestyle and respected the culture, and didn't begrudge the Japanese their success in business, but I felt like a permanent outsider. Beyond all that, I wanted to do something more purposeful in my career. I wanted to boost my knowledge of finance and operations. I knew that a master's of business administration would give me that foundation.

In addition, I wanted to reconnect with my generational peers in America. I'd essentially disappeared into Asia for three years. I was nearly 26. I felt it was time to go home.

My applications were accepted at both Harvard's and Stanford's business schools. However, in the process of researching MBA programs, I'd discovered the Leaders for Manufacturing Program at the Massachusetts Institute of Technology. It intrigued me. LFM was offering both an MBA and a master's in engineering in an intensive two-year program.

The LFM Program had been created by a consortium of MIT and 12 U.S. industrial companies to fund a program to turn out operations managers to make U.S. manufacturing more competitive. That mission spoke to my heart! The intent was to shore up the U.S. industrial base. The sponsoring companies were so keen on this idea, they were offering enrollees paid tuition, with a stipend on top for living expenses.

I was elated to be accepted into the program. I left for Boston in May 1989 with a vision of fixing America.

Chapter Four

Pursuing Alternatives to China

The headlines in the *New York Times* on June 4, 1989, blared: "Troops attack and crush Beijing protest; thousands fight back, scores are killed." The article summarized: "Tens of thousands of Chinese troops retook the center of the capital early this morning from pro-democracy protesters, killing scores of students and workers and wounding hundreds more as they fired submachine guns at crowds of people who tried to resist."

Acting out of fear of threats to their regime, the Chinese central government felt compelled to use force against peaceful demonstrators. Those thousands of students I'd seen gathered in Tiananmen Square two months before, on a business trip for Sony before I'd left China, had been joined by a great many more students, as well as workers and others. Their ranks had swollen to as many as 1 million protesters and triggered demonstrations in many other Chinese cities. Their demands included political reforms, an end to corruption by Communist Party members, and protection of social security.

From having lived in China for two years, I understood their discontent. The long, difficult transition from the planned economy of the Mao era to the market economy post-Mao meant that supply and demand could get completely out of sync. At this point, inflation had reached a level that ordinary people believed was painfully high. When they went shopping, their money wouldn't buy as much as it had. They began to greatly resent corruption among party officials — how these politically connected insiders enjoyed the fruits of favoritism and graft. A party member might have a car, whereas the average citizen rode a bike.

As the protests swelled, the central government finally sent in troops and tanks to clear Tiananmen Square and begin a harsh crackdown on dissent. And overnight, China went from most promising emerging market, to most hated pariah country.

What did this mean for the China-U.S. relationship? Was my investment in learning Chinese and spending time working in China wasted? Did this mean that my ever working in China again — as quickly modernizing as it was, as fast as its economy had been growing — was now only a remote possibility?

At a minimum, I knew, China was consigned indefinitely to the penalty box of outcast nations.

Despite the blow to my China career aspirations, I got on with the basic blocking and tackling of studying accounting and corporate finance in the intensive Leaders for Manufacturing Program at the Massachusetts Institute of Technology, to earn my master's of business administration and a master's in engineering.

In the MBA program, I took courses in operations management and learned about critical paths and bottlenecks. I enjoyed diving into a study of the Toyota Production System, based on simple factory-floor, visual-management methods and Kanban inventory controls — a strategy that avoids the complexity of enterprise-level software systems.

But soon my career sights had shifted entirely from Asia to a different continent: Europe.

AT THE START OF the 1990s, the world began paying attention to European economic and political integration. The goal of European federation, in the minds of its architects, was the establishment of a multinational, politically cohesive zone with a single currency, in which capital, goods, services and labor could circulate freely. Observers outside Europe came up with the "Fortress Europe" label to describe an impregnable, self-reliant and closed European economy.

Lester Thurow, the dean of MIT's business school, was a well-known economist who was pushing a concept of zero-sum competition among the United States, Fortress Europe and Japan. Thurow concluded that Fortress Europe would prevail over the U.S.A. and Japan. During one of his lectures at MIT, I raised my hand and asked what his prediction for China was. Dean Thurow responded that China would not amount to much in relation to the contest among America, Fortress Europe and Japan.[14]

Thurow published his predictions in his book *Head to Head*, which came out in early 1992. It didn't take long for his forecasts to be proved myopic. That year, the Italian lira and the British pound were forced out of the European exchange-rate mechanism, posing a crisis for European integration.

---

[14] Ironically, Lester Thurow ended up working in China by founding the MIT-China Management Education Program in 1996. He stated at the program's founding that U.S. business schools needed to understand Chinese-based economies. Chinese faculty came to the MIT Sloan School of Management as faculty fellows, for training and to develop courses; MIT faculty, including Thurow, visited China campuses to lecture and teach short courses. Students attended learning laboratories to address business issues at host Chinese companies, and then visited the companies to work alongside Chinese students who had attended the MIT labs.

This clearly demonstrated that Fortress Europe was not as resilient or unified as some — including the MIT business dean — had imagined, even if the European Union would officially come into being the following year, 1993.

Thurow also had failed to predict the struggles that the Japanese economy would suffer, starting with the collapse of their asset price bubble in late 1991. To economists and historians, it was a familiar pattern. While the manufacturing and marketing prowess of the automobile and electronics companies dubbed "Japan, Inc." had boosted Japan's gross national product, yielded trade surpluses and created unprecedented wealth for its citizens, easy credit and speculative investments during this boom period of the 1980s also had resulted in overvalued equity markets and overpriced real estate. In America, the Roaring Twenties had silenced into whimpers and wails after the artificially inflated stock market crashed in October 1929, with the Dow Jones Industrial Average falling 25 percent in four days.[15] Japan's moment of reckoning struck in August 1990, when the Nikkei stock index plunged to half its peak. Other asset prices, including for real estate, followed the stock-market drop, and Japan's economy stagnated for more than a decade, a period economists call "the Lost Decade."

Professor Thurow also had failed to perceive the rise of globalization, in which developed economies, only a few years after the Tiananmen Square Massacre, outsourced their production to low-cost China, fueling the continued rise of Chinese capitalism and rapid growth of the Chinese economy.

Events in the real world can defy what academics hypothesize.

Outstripping all the value I earned in my graduate studies, meeting

---

[15] The Dow Jones Industrial Average had lost almost half its value by mid-November 1929, and by summer 1932 had shed 89 percent of its peak value in the 1920s. It didn't regain its pre-crash top until 1954.

a fellow MBA candidate named Shannon was by far the best thing I gained from business school. We shared common interests in the outdoors and travel adventures, we thought alike, and we each had spent time abroad. Shannon, an Alaska native, had grown up in Massachusetts and studied economics and French at Brown University, in Rhode Island. She'd briefly worked in New York at Fuji Bank, with Japanese colleagues. While she had yet to visit East Asia, she could sense that China was rapidly rising on the world stage.

Shannon also had worked in several European countries — including at a bank in Portugal, a bank in France, and at the U.S. Embassy in Belgium — and spoke fluent French. She was a shoo-in for leading Corporate America's effort to build a foothold inside Fortress Europe. As we prepared to re-enter the working world after finishing our MBA program, Shannon won job offers to re-locate to popular destinations across Europe, including Paris and Prague.

Setting aside my interests in Asia, I followed her to Europe in 1992 for a new expatriate adventure.

"GOOD NEWS! WE HAVE been awarded the grant!"

Those exciting words spoken over the phone to me in January 1993 were from Gabriel Bugeda Castelltort of the University of Catalunya, in Barcelona, Spain. It meant a consortium I had assembled had won funding of Euro 900,000 (equal to $1.1 million) from the European Union for a project consisting of academic institutions and private enterprise jointly developing software solutions to optimize 3D Printing processes.

Shannon and I had settled in summer 1992 in Bologna Italy, situated between Milan and Florence. She worked in Bologna at a local subsidiary of Otis Elevator, which in turn was a subsidiary of United Technologies Corp.: a multinational conglomerate headquartered in Farmington, Connecticut.

I commuted to another subsidiary of UTC, based near Milan in the grimy industrial city of Monza. My job was piecing together a consortium of UTC subsidiaries located in multiple European countries, as well as universities in three European nations, to jointly develop rapid prototyping services using a network of 3D Printing technologies. It involved developing computer-aided designs of new products captured in 3D files — which would be shared via a network, and fabricated on centralized 3D Printing equipment.

3D Printing, also called additive manufacturing, involves constructing three-dimensional objects from computer-aided design (CAD) models, under computer control. It was being adopted as a futuristic technology to supplement and even replace the traditional subtractive manufacturing found in factories, where workers use machinery to slice, cut out or hollow out pieces of metal, plastic, textiles, ceramics or other materials. 3D Printing allows for making more complex shapes while using less material than traditional machines. It's also more efficient: adding the materials together in layers. It can be employed in endless industries and fields, including making automotive parts, airplane parts, dental products, prosthetics, footwear, jewelry, movie props, scale models for architecture, replication of ancient artifacts, reconstruction of fossils, and reconstruction of evidence in forensic pathology, to solve murders.

Now it was January 1993. I had worked hard to cajole three European institutions of higher education — the University of Catalunya, in Spain; Turin Polytechnic, in Italy; Stuttgart University, in Germany —and a German start-up company, Electro Optical Systems GmbH, to cooperate with my employer's subsidiaries in the joint-research project. We were operating at the forefront of 3D Printing technology and simulation software. We believed (and rightly so) that 3D Printing Technologies would revolutionize the future of manufacturing.

I had written most of the grant application and shepherded the participants through the process of meetings with EU officials. I was very excited! Here was a chance to participate in a high-tech business project far different from selling machine tools or computer microchips, as I had done in China and Japan.

Overall, I was very happy in life. As for our new home, Shannon and I had quickly fallen in love with Italy. As newlyweds, we savored our new lifestyle, though we didn't have much leisure money. Bologna sits in the rich gastronomic paradise of the region of Emilia Romagna. Bologna is a vibrant city with an 11th-century university, soaring stone towers, and arched porticos lining the streets and squares of its medieval core. Shannon leveraged her knowledge of French and Latin and quickly developed fluency in Italian, while I struggled with complicated Italian conjugations not found in Chinese.

Shannon and I savored the cuisine, culture, language, and art of Italy, despite the austerity of our lives in Bologna. Our modest apartment offered a closet-sized kitchen and a shower powered by a rickety, rumbling hot-water heater. We frequently zoomed off at hazardous speeds on the Autostrade to escapes in Tuscany, Cinque Terre, and the northern mountains of the Tyrol. We encountered petty thievery on trains, undisciplined traffic in labyrinthine villages, warm welcomes in *agriturismo* farmhouses (that were bed and breakfasts or dining stops), breathtaking views in the Dolomites and picturesque sunsets over the Mediterranean. The Italians' ability to shrug off the chaos of their daily lives and laugh at themselves made our experience even more charming.

A different cultural aspect I soon discovered that persisted throughout Europe rendered my work experience less charming.

FROM THE START, THERE were significant challenges from the

participants from the different countries — Spain, Italy and Germany — working together in the consortium I'd assembled. The barriers ranged from differences in language and culture to a parochial unwillingness to share information.

We were building resin parts using stereolithography and printed parts in nylon and other materials using selective laser sintering. We created simulations of part fabrication using finite-element analysis. We marveled at the beauty of curling airfoil prototypes for air-conditioning units, and complicated hydraulic-pump prototypes for aerospace use.

One of the challenges I faced was getting agreement on design standards, file formats and the location of the printing equipment. Our progress was impaired by the diverse business models, languages, and cultures of the participants. Everyone had a territorial view of how the operation should be configured.

Managing this project turned out to be an early lesson for me in how only an outsider, such as myself, could surmount these challenges to get disparate Europeans to work together. My training was in engineering and business administration. Now I had to add diplomacy to my toolbox.

In any event, I succeeded in negotiating a master services agreement with the young German startup participating in our European Union-funded project: Electro Optical Systems (EOS GmbH). And I managed to connect most of United Technologies' European divisions to EOS GmbH for 3D printing of prototype parts.

This experience taught me how much disunion remained in the European Union. I wondered what dean Thurow back at MIT would have made of this syndrome. For me, it was clear: The weakness of Fortress Europe was the fragmented nature of its member states. Whereas my employer's rapid prototyping operation in the United States consisted of multiple divisions around the country working efficiently together in a common language and culture to share files and 3D Printing services, our activity in Europe was hampered by multiple and profound differences among the participants.

Meanwhile, it was hard for Shannon and me to miss the steady drumbeat of positive media reports about China's comeback.

CHINA WAS EXITING THE penalty box. China was beckoning — the gold rush was on!

In the aftermath of the Tiananmen Square Massacre, the Chinese Communist Party had tightened its grip on power and doubled down on its commitment to the Chinese people: *We let you make money, you let us rule.* Paramount leader Deng Xiaoping wanted to re-focus the country away from political reform and toward economic development. He launched his southern tour in 1992, visiting various cities in China's most prosperous regions, while advocating for further economic reforms. In response to Deng's initiatives, by the mid-1990s China was again pursuing market liberalization on a scale even greater than that seen in the reforms of the 1980s. Western media reported the return of foreign multinationals to China.

After two years in Italy, Shannon and I were beginning to feel redundant as foreigners working in seemingly stagnant Europe. Europe was beautiful, and our time there had been delightful, but could we really make an impact in our careers there?

When we finally decided it was time to go to China at the end of 1993, our Italian friends unanimously questioned why we would want to leave. And to China, of all places!

La vita in Italia non era bella? Was not life in Italy good?

Yes, it was. But it was lacking in economic opportunities. Our friends could not envision a future of opportunities in China.

Shannon and I could.

Chapter Five

Lurching Toward a Bumpy Takeoff

"Air China has the worst engine in-flight shutdown rate in the world! This is killing our reputation! They are not doing the required maintenance to keep their planes flying," growled white-haired Bill Kerr, vice president of aftermarket services for Pratt & Whitney Aircraft Engines.

"Get a SWAT team of our mechanics together and go fix the problem!"

It was January 1994. Two months before, I'd joined Pratt & Whitney, the famous aircraft-engine manufacturer, which was a subsidiary of United Technologies Corp., my employer in my previous position in Italy. My new job was in Beijing as project manager for negotiating a joint venture that would include the Chinese government-owned Air China airline, and Germany's state-owned airline, Lufthansa, as our partners.

Pratt & Whitney was seeking to enter as a shareholder into the Aircraft Maintenance and Engineering Corp. — itself a joint venture between Air China and Lufthansa. We wanted to establish Pratt's managerial control of AMECO's engine-overhaul and repair facility for aircraft at the Beijing Airport. This facility — which had a very poor track record for maintenance— would be key to keeping Air China's planes safely airborne. And since Air China's fleet largely used Pratt & Whitney engines, the facility's performance would be vital to preserving Pratt's stellar reputation.

As project manager, I had to use my business-school training to develop — in tandem with consultations with AMECO's management — a feasibility study for investing in major upgrades to the engine shop at Beijing Airport. The feasibility study would be the basis for our negotiation of a joint-venture partnership with Air China and Lufthansa. But that wasn't my only task as project manager.

Regardless of the outcome of our joint-venture discussions — we at Pratt needed to solve the maintenance problems contributing to Air China's engine inflight-shutdown rate. And it was urgent.

In short order, I found myself helping oversee the "SWAT team" (as Bill Kerr termed it) of Pratt mechanics dispatched from our factories in the United States to the AMECO maintenance facility at Beijing Airport, to provide direct support to the Chinese mechanics. My employer was providing this vital assistance free of charge to Air China. I'm sure the leadership at Air China was secretly pleased with this generous offer. After all, the airline's engines had a bad rate of shutting down in flight, and this posed a danger not only to Pratt's reputation but to Air China's. And that's not even mentioning the danger to passengers and pilots — as well as to whatever people or property on the ground that might be imperiled should a plane crash. There was no upside. It was bad for everyone.

I sprang into action. A colleague, Steve Myers, and I drafted four licensed mechanics from Pratt. They arrived from the United States, and we all hurried off to the AMECO facilities at the airport. We planned to work nightshifts, maintaining, and updating the aircraft — duties that Air China had neglected over the previous months. We needed to install safety updates to the engine hardware without delay.

Night after night, our American mechanics worked alongside the Chinese mechanics from AMECO. One night, we towed a Boeing 747 into a cavernous hangar at Beijing Airport for work on all four of its gaping engines. The Chinese mechanics arrived at AMECO, stumbling unsteadily from their van after boozing it up over dinner. We paired each Pratt mechanic with a Chinese counterpart to work on the engines simultaneously. All through the freezing night, they perched on ladders and mobile stairs underneath the jumbo jetliner's wings, cranking wrenches and performing delicate adjustments to the engines and their complicated external plumbing.

The discovery of a major crack in the gearbox of one of the engines temporarily distracted everyone from their work. Obviously, this was an important find. Bill Kerr's stern orders were justified.

The mechanics finished their repairs at dawn. The 747 rolled out of the hangar and taxied to a distant tarmac for engine-thrust tests. I joined the Air China pilot, co-pilot and several AMECO engineers in the cockpit. I stood behind them as they pushed the throttles to full takeoff thrust with the aircraft brakes locked on. The enormous plane — shoved forward by the thundering engines while gripped by the brakes — lurched back and forth while kicking up a torrent of dust behind us.

The pilots concluded that engine thrust was satisfactory. They cleared the 747 for return to service. I deboarded, feeling relieved, and prepared to return to the AMECO office after a long, long night . . .

Passengers boarded the flight on schedule, filling the seats. As the jumbo jetliner sat, engines whirring, at the terminal gate, the pilots performed pre-flight checks. They were puzzled by bizarre readings of oil pressure and quantity but shrugged them off, figuring they were likely the results of faulty gauges. The 747 charged down the runway and lifted into the sky.

What none of us knew was that lubricating oil was bleeding from the maze of tubing on one of the engines inside its nacelle covering. The first notion we at AMECO had that there was trouble was the sight of Air China leaders pedaling madly on bicycles toward the airport's main administrative building. We quickly learned that the pilots had shut down one engine in flight, due to lack of lubricating oil, and turned the aircraft back to Beijing.

The passengers deboarded, the 747 was towed back to the AMECO hangar, and I set the mechanics to work on the silver bird again. Deeper examination of the stricken engine revealed that a Chinese mechanic had not tightened one of the bolts on the section of the engine he'd worked on. Due to the use of safety wiring of bolts, the Pratt mechanic assigned to this Chinese mechanic hadn't been able to double-check if the bolts had been properly torqued. Once attached, the safety wire needs to stay in place. A second mechanic must trust that the first mechanic has properly torqued the bolt prior to safety wiring.

Using safety wire is a standard method of wiring two or more hardware units together, so if one of the units loosens because of a plane's vibration, the safety wire will tighten and hold it in place. It's like wearing suspenders in addition to a belt to keep a pair of pants from slipping. However, bolts, nuts and screws need to be properly tightened to begin with, because even safety wire cannot always ensure that the hardware remains in place.

In the case of the loose engine bolt on the 747, the safety wire hadn't helped.

AMECO was, simply, a fiasco in maintaining and overhauling engines in 1994. Many engines entered the shop for service only to spend over a year in overhaul, followed by an almost 50 percent failing to pass test-cell certification for return to service. In contrast, the best engine shops in the world completed overhauls in two to three months, with 95 percent of engines passing in the test cells.

We at Pratt grew firmly convinced that we needed to step in and take a direct role in managing the Air China engine fleet and supervise the hands-on maintenance work. This was the aim of our proposed joint venture with AMECO.

PRATT & WHITNEY'S RELATIONSHIP with Air China — the flag carrier of Chinese commercial aviation — dated to the thaw, two decades before, in U.S.-China relations, symbolized by President Nixon's surprise, historic visit to China in 1972 aboard Air Force One — which, incidentally, was a Boeing 707 powered by Pratt & Whitney engines.

In short order — thanks to an export license granted by the Nixon Administration to the Boeing Co. to sell 707s to China — the Chinese had ordered 10 of these 200-seat, long-range commercial airliners. Boeing 707s had made air travel more popular than train or ship travel throughout the 1960s, and in 1972 still were a mainstay of commercial aviation, though more modern airliners, such as 727s, 737s and 747s had come into service.

Air China continued buying Western aircraft for its fleet. Most of Air China's aircraft were powered by Pratt engines. Back then, in the 1970s, the Chinese were accustomed to unreliable Soviet engines. They assumed U.S. engines might be as problematic, so they ordered one spare Pratt engine for every engine on wing. In the following years, the Chinese came to learn about the superior reliability of Western-made engines. Over 20 years later, our Pratt mechanics discovered many of the unused spare Pratt engines for 707s from the early 1970s still in their original packing crates, covered in dust in the AMECO shop. They had never been needed as replacements.[16]

Yet, the Chinese still blamed Pratt for Air China's horrible engine in-flight shutdown rate in 1994. This complicated my efforts to negotiate with Air China and Germany's Lufthansa — the partners in AMECO — to bring Pratt in as a shareholder, and to grant Pratt control of managing the engine-overhaul and repair facility at the Beijing Airport.

AMECO was a Chinese-German joint venture born in the period following the 1989 Tiananmen Square Massacre, in which China had been relegated to the status of pariah nation among democracies in the developed world. Of course, that blacklisting had heavily impacted China's ability to recruit foreign investors. China's government was desperately seeking to lure them back. Premier Li Peng had offered German Chancellor Helmut Kohl and Germany's state-owned airline, Lufthansa, a sweet deal to invest in a joint venture with Air China to create AMECO, an entity charged with maintaining Air China's planes and engines.

The challenges (to use a polite term) for my Pratt negotiating team of working out the bugs in a joint venture with a Chinese company were quite interesting, there in 1994. China was industrializing and modernizing at breakneck speed. But the growing pains were pronounced when it came to adapting to the technology of the developed world.

Air China's management lacked a strong commitment to building a disciplined maintenance organization. Maintenance was an expense that

---

[16] Incidentally, around that time, a savvy American trader spotted an opportunity and acquired all the remaining Pratt & Whitney spare engines for 707s for next to nothing, then flipped them to carriers in Africa at profitable prices.

could only detract from top management performance (meaning: profits). Air China's executives did not fully appreciate the safety implications of failing to properly maintain their fleet. They wanted favors from Pratt — such as the ability to freely borrow spare engines to compensate for their airline's poor management of maintenance. (And, again, they certainly didn't object to the free labor and expertise Pratt was providing with its mechanics it assigned to AMECO's facility at Beijing Airport!) For its part, Lufthansa's management was more interested in winning maintenance business from China for the German company's Frankfurt and Hamburg operations.

Pratt's goals were to expand its role in Chinese aviation by servicing Pratt engines, and — ultimately — to sell more engines in China. My colleague, John Beliveau, and I created detailed analyses of process improvements for engine overhauls, and produced a comprehensive feasibility study to assess the investment return on upgrading the AMECO engine shop. We met frequently with our counterparts from Air China and Lufthansa.

Negotiations were thorny. Lufthansa acted as a gatekeeper on maintenance investment opportunities sought by other potential partners, such as Pratt. The German team was difficult to work with. The Air China representatives, meanwhile, deftly played us foreigners off against each other, and Lufthansa relished its role as a spoiler in our talks. This became the negotiation from hell.

John Beliveau and I worked hard to win the rights for our company to run the AMECO engine shop. We spent many days studying the flow of engine parts and modules in that shop. We tweaked our financial models and plotted a path to profitability for engine overhauls. When the logic of our investment analysis failed to convince the teams from Air China and Lufthansa, we tried schmoozing them with a boondoggle to New York City. John and I boarded our corporate Sikorsky helicopter in Connecticut and buzzed down to John F. Kennedy Airport in New York to pick up our AMECO VIP guests directly from the tarmac next to their Air China plane just arrived from Beijing. We then zoomed around Manhattan and whizzed around the Statue of Liberty. Landing at the 34th Street helipad next to the East River, we whisked our guests by limousine to Tavern on the Green, followed by the Rockettes show at Radio City Music Hall.

Failing to impress them, we called in the ultimate "door opener": Alexander Haig, retired four-star Army general, former secretary of state under President Reagan, former Supreme Allied Commander Europe (in charge of NATO), and now a strategic adviser to United Technologies Corp. We flew Gen. Haig to Beijing. I met him one-on-one at the VIP lounge of the old Beijing Airport and escorted him by limousine to meet our friends at AMECO.

Gen. Haig performed well in a take-charge manner at a ribbon-cutting ceremony at AMECO. However, we probably wasted his influence-peddling value on the relatively minor Chinese officials of AMECO and Air China.

Despite our Pratt mechanics' scrupulous efforts, our partners in Air China and the central government continued blaming Pratt for poor reliability of its engines, despite the substandard maintenance performed by AMECO engineers.

The numerous in-flight shutdowns continued threatening Pratt's market position. I grew disillusioned. Finally, I decided two years of negotiating this joint venture were probably enough for me.

I DO RETAIN SOME fond memories from my two years working on the AMECO joint venture. During that pre-9/11 period of lax security, I would sometimes drive our company's Beijing Jeep out onto the active taxiways at Beijing Airport. I recall glancing in the rearview mirror and panicking at the sight of an enormous 747 bearing down on me.

There were some amusing events — including a much-anticipated ping-pong match between our young star U.S. mechanic and an elderly female employee from AMECO. The reputation of the Chinese to be experts at table tennis proved warranted. She beat our man soundly, 21-0, to our embarrassment.

Despite our adverse negotiating conditions, we did find time for raucous banquets with AMECO staff. We laughed at the shock of our U.S. mechanics on being served deep-fried scorpions presented with stingers arching menacingly.

When we weren't at the airport negotiating the terms of our participation in the joint venture, we huddled downtown to develop strategy in an office suite at one of the first high-rise buildings in Beijing: the original 22-story CITIC Tower, affectionately referred to as the "Chocolate Building," due to its cladding in brown tiles. Shannon had taken a job working on the development of a joint venture between Pratt and Aviation Industry Corp. of China, for the local manufacture of parts for Pratt engines.

Shannon worked in an office near where our teams were meeting. She heroically continued working right up to the birth of our first child, Lindsay, in 1995, and returned to the office shortly after Lindsay was born. I can remember our project meetings sometimes being interrupted by the steady humming of Shannon's breast pump in the room next door.

One unforgettable episode was hardly amusing. Shannon and I employed an elderly Chinese woman, Dr. Yu (a retired anesthesiologist) to care for Lindsay at our apartment while we commuted to the CITIC Tower for work. In violation of official Chinese labor laws, we employed our nanny informally without registering her status with the authorities. Registering her would have required paying a commission to the government, in addition to our nanny's compensation. With the tight budget of a young family, we skipped that extra fee.

One day, Shannon and I learned that a police dragnet had surrounded our apartment building to ensnare all non-registered staff. I raced home from the office and discovered that Dr. Yu and Baby Lindsay were missing from our apartment. Lacking any means to contact our caretaker (this era preceded the standard usage of cell phones), I imagined that they either had been arrested and were in police custody, or had escaped into the streets.

Neither scenario thrilled me.

While pondering my next move, the door to our apartment cracked open, and Dr. Yu peeked in with Lindsay in her arms. On hearing the approaching police, she'd cleverly sought refuge in a neighbor's apartment.

We managed to avoid the reach of the authorities for the rest of our time in Beijing.

WHILE MY JOINT-VENTURE project floundered with reluctant partners Air China and Lufthansa, Shannon's project developed into a signed deal approved by the relevant Chinese government ministries. Pratt would join with the Chengdu Engine Co. to build a new factory to manufacture engine parts, starting in early 1996.

Faced with bleak prospects in Beijing, I volunteered to join this joint venture — Chengdu Aerotech Manufacturing Co. — in remote Chengdu in Sichuan Province, 950 miles southwest of Beijing, as operations manager.

A famous Chinese proverb is: *"Shāngāo huángdì yuǎn."* Translated, it means, "The mountains are high, and the emperor is far away." It implies the inclination of local officials in places such as Chengdu, far from Beijing, to ignore the wishes of central-government authorities, and instead follow their own agenda.

It was time for Shannon and me to go down to the countryside (*"Xià xiāng"*), beyond the mountains that are high, and where the emperor is far away.[17]

---

[17] The practice of sending people to the countryside, known as *Xià xiāng* ("go down to the countryside"), took place in 1955-56. This policy was revived in the early 1960s. The policy of *Xià xiāng* had several motives or objectives. According to party rhetoric, its function was to relocate intellectuals, officials or skilled workers to provide leadership and direction in the countryside. This, it was claimed, would accelerate China's economic development. Mao Zedong promoted this relocation as an opportunity: "In the vast rural areas, there is plenty of room for [participants] to realize their talents to the full."

Chapter Six

Going Down to the Countryside

"We need you. You are the only guy out there who can do this."

Those were the pleading words from Bob Robinson, vice president of international partnerships at Pratt & Whitney, by long-distance call from the company's headquarters in Connecticut.

It was May 1996. Four months prior, I'd joined Pratt's new joint venture with the Chinese government-owned Chengdu Engine Co. as operations manager. Shannon had worked on developing this joint venture to create the Chengdu Aerotech Manufacturing Co. while we lived in Beijing, and she was now commuting every few months, as a passenger on aging Russian Tupolev 154 jetliners operated by Sichuan Airlines, between Chengdu (where we now lived) and Xi'an to work with a Pratt team negotiating another engine-parts joint venture with a state-owned company in Xi'an. We and our infant daughter, Lindsay, had relocated to a house in the Orchard Villas compound in Chengdu — the provincial capital of Sichuan Province, nearly 1,000 miles from Beijing, and thus somewhat removed from the kind of central-government oversight that can constrict a business's operations. Instead, local officials in Sichuan

Province would have a hand (or hands) in monitoring our construction of a factory — with all that might entail in securing governmental approval and cooperation.

Chengdu Aerotech would be Pratt's first joint venture in the Chinese aviation industry. The company would manufacture spare airplane-engine parts. Pratt was engaging in this "greenfield" investment — a startup company that would be a Pratt subsidiary — with a $22 million outlay. That was a significant sum in 1996. Pratt was the majority shareholder with 52 percent, to 48 percent for Chengdu Engine Co.

The joint-venture investment included building a factory, fitting it with equipment and raw materials, and staffing it with 150 Chinese workers. The business plan called for securing U.S. Federal Aviation Administration certifications so that we could export our aircraft-engine parts to the U.S. aftermarket. That meant the factory had to be run according to FAA-approved processes and procedures. No shoddy work standards could be tolerated. I appreciated what a challenge this could be after my previous two years working in aircraft maintenance in Beijing!

And now Bob Robinson, Pratt's VP of international partnerships, was asking me to move up from operations manager to the top on-site job: general manager. The original GM had resigned after only a few months, due to "pressing personal matters." In the eyes of my superiors at Pratt, I was the go-to man already on site in distant Sichuan Province.

The GM had responsibility for all functions of the enterprise — from factory construction and equipment investments, to manufacturing and quality control, to human resources, finance and accounting. My response to Bob Robinson:

"OK, I'll do it. But I need to choose my own people."

A BIT OF BACKGROUND on the startup company I'd committed myself to running:

China's central government must approve all aircraft and engine orders by Chinese airline operators. There in 1996, China wanted industrial participation in Pratt's aviation manufacturing in exchange for buying Pratt engines, such as those used by Air China. Pratt had set up the Chengdu Aerotech joint venture with China's state-owned Chengdu Engine Co. to fulfill offset obligations incurred by Pratt to the Chinese government — arising from Pratt's sales of commercial jet engines to Air China and other Chinese airlines. Pratt was required to localize some of its production in China. Therefore, Pratt proposed a factory producing a variety of spare engine parts for planes in the United States.

The reason I'd insisted on choosing "my own people" to help me run the joint venture was that I wanted allies who would support me in leading the challenging manufacturing startup from factory construction to the launch of first product sales. I needed a loyal, results-oriented team with me. I didn't want to deal with workplace politicians.

With Bob Robinson's blessing, I put together a strong team. To fill the post of operations manager, I drafted an old Pratt shop veteran, Bill Gormley, who late in life was looking for an exotic challenge liberated from meddling upper management in our U.S. factory. Bill would serve me well in troubleshooting new production lines and training the shop staff. I excused some of his old-school ways and his passion for whiskey and smoking, because he had a take-charge attitude and never hesitated to get jobs done. In such a remote location where we mostly relied on ourselves, I highly valued his action-oriented approach.

For finance manager, I recruited a competent certified public accountant from Hong Kong, Alvin Liu, out of Price Waterhouse's accounting and audit engagements in China. Alvin would deftly navigate the pitfalls of tax, accounting and other financial matters raised by our Chinese joint-venture partner or by local authorities. Alvin had an unwavering commitment to financial integrity, which is what I wanted, but sometimes he interpreted untidy local tax and accounting issues in an overly rigid manner. This occasionally required me to mediate between Alvin and our JV counterparts at Chengdu Engine Co.

My team's first task was planning the production processes for each engine part we would make. Fully committed to the new manufacturing management methods from Japan that I'd studied at M.I.T., we insisted on laying out our production lines in accordance with the Toyota Production System. In contrast to the typical Chinese factory, we steered away from segregating equipment into departments based on processes such as milling, grinding or turning. Instead, we organized cellular production lines dedicated to each product, with equipment arranged in the sequence of process steps for making the product. For example, we built "burner cans," which are used in the combustion section of older Pratt engines. Our cellular production began with punching semicircular blanks from special alloy metal sheets imported from the United States. These were then rolled into cylinders, and the can was assembled from multiple cylinders stacked and welded on top of each other. This burner-can assembly, which would need to endure super-high engine combustion temperatures, was coated with a special heat-resistant layer using plasma spray, and then baked in a heat-treatment chamber. The burner-can top was capped with a cast-metal fuel-injector nozzle. The final burner-can assembly was then inspected, tagged "airworthy," and packed for export to the United States.

On the factory floor, we used simple visual-management aids and inventory containers to track production and keep workers oriented. One could easily track the progress of part production from start to finish. This represented a new way of thinking for our Chinese partners — and for some of my older U.S. colleagues: including the operations manager, Bill.

I leaned on my superiors at Pratt to provide help wherever possible. I visited Bob Robinson's brother, Mike, who ran a Pratt factory in North Berwick, Maine. Mike presided over a plant that covered more than 1 million square feet as the largest manufacturing facility under one roof in Maine. Pratt's North Berwick facility produced modules, components, and parts for commercial and military jet engines. Mike stared at me from his chair behind his large desk in his executive office as I stood before him, pitching him on the idea of allocating to our plant in the Chinese joint venture some declining parts from older engine models, so we could replicate and produce them in Chengdu. He reluctantly agreed to offload some of his parts for engine models that were nearing obsolescence.

I continued scrambling. Needing to borrow staff from our U.S. plants to help train our Chinese recruits, I selected young Pratt employees eager for adventure in China. I found bargain used machines at Pratt that we refurbished for use on the factory floor in Chengdu — saving millions in equipment costs. But one objective I didn't achieve was convincing my superiors at Pratt to release the joint venture to compete for outside business from other foreign aerospace manufacturers sourcing parts from us.

I wanted Chengdu Aerotech Manufacturing Co. to be a stand-alone company with its own branding. Selling Pratt parts via Pratt's channels under the Pratt brand limited our sales, due to their price markups. Chengdu Aerotech would have been much more profitable if Pratt had cut us loose, to produce and sell third-party parts rather than parts from older Pratt engine models. However, Pratt's corporate decision makers wanted to limit the mandate of our JV to fulfilling Pratt's offset obligations in China, and to playing a role in supporting new Pratt engine sales in China. The JV was serving a larger corporate agenda: supporting Pratt's new-engine sales in China.

While Chengdu Aerotech needed to make money on every product line we launched, we were never intended to become a major profit center for the parent company.

OUR TEAM SET THE scene for our JV groundbreaking ceremony, which took place on an overcast day in January 1996. Looming in the center of the five-acre grassy field was a stage draped in the bright red colors of China's national flag and decorated with gold calligraphy proclaiming the founding of Chengdu Aerotech Manufacturing Co. Colorful banners shaped like dragons fluttered in the breeze overhead. Among the invited dignitaries gathered on stage were the Sichuan provincial governor, the Chengdu mayor, the Aviation Industry Corp. of China vice head, the Chengdu Engine Co. president, and Bob Robinson himself.

The master of ceremonies, borrowed from among the anchormen at Chengdu Television, announced the launch of the JV over loudspeakers. An audience of local bureaucrats and reporters and our plant employees stood in a throng gazing up at the stage. At the end of several lengthy speeches, a music troupe roused attendees from their stupor with the vigorous pounding of drums and clashing of cymbals. The VIPs descended from the stage — each receiving a shiny new shovel from slender, pretty models clad in tight-fitting silk *qipao* gowns, hired for the ceremony. The VIPs gathered in a circle, and in unison drove their shovels into a dirt pile prepared for the event.

This turnout of high-ranking officials from central and local governments impressed me — and made me feel the weight of responsibility for the JV's success that extended beyond the confines of the company's grounds and the factory that would imminently be under construction. The ceremony concluded, and we were in business!

The JV site quickly transformed into a large, vacant, muddy lot torn up by earth-moving machines. Mechanized brigades of dump trucks and bulldozers, and formations of helmeted workers on foot, armed with pickaxes and shovels, stormed in to clear and level the field to prepare the foundation for the factory building.

Hundreds of construction workers hurried about: straining behind wheelbarrows filled with cement, erecting bamboo poles for scaffolds, welding steel rebar and steel beams into place. Their safety gear was hardly up to U.S. union standards. Their headgear ranged from yellow plastic hardhats to knitted wicker helmets. They wore mostly threadbare, faded-blue utility shirts and trousers, and canvas sneakers or flipflops. What would be a hulking, rectangular, 50,000-square-foot factory would now be gradually rising from a sprawling cement foundation.

The work carried on, nonstop, for more than a year, both during daylight and at night under spotlights. I took my management team, including our deputy general manager and operations manager, to periodically tour the site to inspect construction progress and haggle with the general contractor over price and schedule changes. He had been hardened by the brutal struggle of endless construction work in Chengdu, and looked prematurely aged and scarred with graying hair and permanent beard stubble. Whenever he called for cost escalations and schedule delays, we relied on our Chinese counterparts at Chengdu Engine Co. to put the squeeze on him.

My management team implemented a revolutionary approach in recruiting our manufacturing team from among Chinese candidates. Our JV had a completely free hand in choosing staff both from our Chinese JV partner and from the local labor pool in Chengdu. Based on concepts from the Toyota Production System, my managers looked for new recruits having a high capacity for teamwork, collaboration, and creative thinking. Our interview process focused on having the candidates roleplay while solving real-world problems. This was at odds with the traditional Chinese approach of choosing candidates who scored highly on skills-based testing. The Chinese utilized a top-down style of management, with shop managers dictating what workers should do. We knew that our cellular manufacturing environment would require more worker self-reliance, resourcefulness, and collaboration.

Initially, many candidates registered surprise during their interviews that we wanted them to explain how they would lead their worker teams to solve production line problems. It was eye-opening for them to learn that we encouraged listening to line workers' feedback, and that we empowered line managers to shut down production when quality problems arose. Like anywhere in the world, a few capable candidates rose to the challenge and demonstrated the leadership capacities we were seeking.

Our initial group of 40 engineers — consisting of production cell teams with cell leaders paired with an American engineer — laid out the production processes on paper, and itemized a long list of machines to be purchased. I adopted multiple bidding rounds with several local equipment agents, and succeeded in having them bid aggressively against each other. Even our Chinese partner — whose procurement processes were heavily corrupted by kickbacks and bribes — expressed admiration for the bargain prices we paid for our machines.

In April 1997 — 15 months after breaking ground — we moved excitedly into the factory. As machines kicked into life and began stamping, punching, welding, turning and milling metal sheets and forged blocks, we could see our products take shape. In addition to building burner cans, we were manufacturing two types of engine disks on three separate production lines. We choreographed cell workstations to match the cadence of parts moving along the line. Process engineers and quality managers worked to finely tune parameters to produce conforming parts. Five months later, our machines and production processes were in place for us to begin mass producing parts.

"Graduation Day" came when we held an official grand-opening ceremony, in September 1997 — complete with dignitaries from the United States and China cutting a ribbon and toasting with Moutai, an ancient Chinese distilled liquor, the start of production, on a decorated stage built for the occasion in the center of the factory.

Not long after our grand opening, U.S. Sen. Chuck Hagel — a freshman Republican lawmaker from Nebraska, as well as a decorated Vietnam veteran who would become secretary of defense under President Obama — led a congressional delegation of several congressmen to visit our joint-venture factory to learn more about U.S. investment in China's hinterland. Sen. Hagel expressed amazement that we had transplanted a slice of U.S. aerospace manufacturing into remote Sichuan Province. He understood our objective to support Pratt commercial engine sales in China, and there was no tension at that time over whether American jobs had been sacrificed for this goal.

OUTSIDE THE FACTORY, LIFE in Chengdu wilted under the pall of humid, overcast skies and thick, malodorous pollution. Coal soot from factories accumulated everywhere, blackening tree leaves and depositing in floating slicks on the surface of the swim pool in the center of Orchard Villas. A steel factory across the street from our house coughed purple and red smoke in satanic emissions from its furnaces. Our nasal discharges and saliva showed signs of sooty particulate.

Shannon and I uneasily worried over our baby Lindsay's exposure to the pollution. Our nanny, Dr. Yu, who had escaped the police dragnet back in Beijing, lived with us and cared for Lindsay. She protectively did as much as possible to limit Lindsay's exposure to the outdoors. However, we did make excursions with Lindsay and Dr. Yu outside the city whenever possible. There were a few other foreigners living in houses nearby, including some representatives from the giant, ill-fated Enron Corp. (which would declare bankruptcy in 2001 after revelations that accounting fraud had sustained its financials), searching for natural gas in Sichuan Province — and a fun-loving Aussie general manager, Stephen Davies, running a hot-water heater manufacturing plant in Chengdu. We enjoyed raucous drinking parties alternating between our house and his. The rest of the neighborhood consisted of local Chinese residents.

Dr. Yu led us on local outdoor shopping trips to purchase our groceries. Supermarkets did not exist yet in Chengdu. Open-air wet markets reeked of swine feces and buzzed with flies around the chicken, pig and sheep carcasses hanging by iron hooks among the stalls. Exotic smells wafted up from tables laden with spices and peppers. These markets overflowed with a wide variety of green and colorful Sichuan vegetables we could not recognize and had never seen in Beijing.

A minivan owned by Chengdu Aerotech would convey me, and any temporarily assigned American Pratt engineers, from Orchard Villas to our factory each morning and afternoon. One time, on our early-morning commute, we shuddered at the sight of a prone human corpse: the victim of a hit-and-run by an errant vehicle from the night before. Clearly, the local police had not yet arrived to investigate the incident. One day, a lunatic vagrant assaulted our minivan outside the JV gate, beating on the outside of the vehicle. Our driver giggled nervously and sped up beyond the man's reach. Another time, a Chengdu government VIP vehicle collided head-on with one of our JV employees on his bicycle outside our factory gate. Given the immunity of high-level officials, we were left to escort our employee to the hospital for treatment of the severe bruises and lacerations on his face, without compensation from the offending official.

After turning into bed, Shannon and I were occasionally jolted awake by exploding firecrackers shattering the night to disperse the spirits of the recent dead in the neighborhood. Grieving relatives chose inconvenient hours to shoot off these pyrotechnics. Rats freely shared our kitchen, despite poison pellets spread everywhere outside by Orchard Villas groundskeepers. Dr. Yu worried that Lindsay might be visited by rats in her room at night. We had Lindsay sleep with us most nights.

One morning, local uniformed police adorned the house next-door to us with crimson seals designating a crime scene, after the local inhabitants fled overseas, making off with millions of dollars looted from their bank.

Urban Chengdu was a city of contrasts. New construction and affluent development — consisting of villa compounds, high-rise apartments and new Western-style retail malls catering to the newly wealthy — went side by side with horribly overcrowded slums where people lived in the worst conditions. These were mostly crowded shantytowns beyond the boundaries of new development populated with migrants from the countryside of Sichuan.

The president of our Chinese JV partner, Chengdu Engine Co., fit in well in this "Wild East" setting. Chain-smoking Lin Zuoming, standing tall at over 6 feet, with oily, slick-backed black hair and a bulky black overcoat, looked like a young thirtysomething mafioso staking out his turf. Fifteen years earlier, he'd have been garbed in a Mao suit like most Chinese, with no chance to apply his special enterprising talents to claw and connive his way up the ladder to prosperity. Lin was the charismatic head of a state-owned manufacturer of MIG fighter aircraft engines. He'd likely attended an aviation college. He spoke no English, and we conversed in Chinese. He once brazenly proposed a deal to me to sell the JV his battered black Lexus, which he'd flipped into a rice paddy, injuring himself on impact.

"Why not have the JV general manager ride in a classy car despite a few dents here and there?" he proposed.

I politely declined his offer, saying it was too great an honor for me to accept. Not long after that, Lin, clearly in some pain from his auto-crash injury, gamely propped himself in an armchair and received visitors from Pratt's top management. At least his injury was real.

Lin would rise many years later to take over the reins of ministry-level Aviation Industry Corporation of China, in Beijing. Little did we realize how far his political skills and personal relationships would carry him out of Sichuan and to the center of power in Beijing! I admired him for that.

Shi Lei was my quiet and composed Chinese counterpart. Shi Lei was in his early thirties, with a prematurely receding hairline. He maintained constant self-control and remained unflappable despite the challenges we faced in our startup period. While he played the official role of deputy general manager, in practice he leveraged his local connections and relationships to local party officials, as well as to local wheeler-dealers and hustlers, to propel our operation forward. Most actions and initiatives — such as promoting JV staff to higher management and purchasing big ticket items — had to be floated by him. He was very helpful as a local problem solver and consigliere.

One day, while seated in Shi Lei's office in a huddle of JV managers, we were interrupted by a distraught worker who burst into the room with awful news. There had been a serious accident on the factory floor. When I rushed through the factory, I encountered several men bearing the wounded victim rapidly to an exit. The injured man was semi-conscious and moaning in severe pain. His bloodied foot had been crushed, with all his toes severed and white bones protruding from torn flesh. After bundling him into a van outside, Shi Lei set off for the hospital with a bag of cash to capture the attention of doctors and procure the best treatment possible. Navigating Chengdu hospitals required stepping over the blood and guts on the floors to aggressively seek urgent care.

I stayed behind to carry out an investigation of the accident. This involved taking photographs and physical measurements of the scene, and identifying and collecting forensic evidence. I questioned several workers in Chinese who had witnessed the events from their workstations nearby. The unfortunate worker and his group, seeking to expedite installation of a machine, had slung the heavy machine high overhead from raised forks on a forklift, and had swung the arrangement — causing the forklift to tip over and plunging the machine onto his foot, crushing it.

After documenting the accident evidence, I rushed to the hospital to console our mangled employee. Upon arrival, I was confronted by his hysterical, pregnant wife. The amputation of half her husband's foot was too much for her to bear. It took a long time to calm her down with assurances that the JV would generously compensate her injured husband. I then went home and braced myself to make a late-night mandatory call back to Pratt headquarters in Connecticut, to report the accident to our CEO, Karl Krapek.

Karl wanted to know if I had followed all of our Environmental, Health and Safety procedures, and if so, how had this accident happened? I explained that the JV workers had not notified us of their intention to install the machine and were not authorized to use a forklift in the manner they did. (Pratt protocol required me to travel to the United States not long after the accident and present the details of the accident, and any corrective actions, in front of Karl, who presided over a review board of the executives who reported directly to him.)

Getting things done in Chengdu sometimes required unconventional methods. I engaged a tall, emaciated character, whom I privately referred to as "The Undertaker." Shi Lei had sent him to me. Dressed in a black Western business suit and tie, with slicked-back black hair and a pencil-thin mustache, The Undertaker worked miracles performing special assignments for us. One time, we engaged him to figure out how to move an enormous marine diesel engine weighing many tons into our generator building. The Undertaker strategized effectively. He copied the Egyptians by employing a horde of workers to push the monster on rolling steel pipes into position. Overnight, he erected a towering neon sign on our factory roof radiating our "Chengdu Aerotech" name across the city.

We gave him smaller jobs, too. One time, The Undertaker arranged for exotic burlesque entertainment for board members of our JV.

The Undertaker personified the rebellious view that in Chengdu "the hills were high, and the emperor was far away."

I realized I wasn't in Beijing anymore.

MY TIME IN CHENGDU was productive. Over three years we built a factory, and launched production of three jet-engine parts certified by the FAA and successfully exported to the United States. We earned a modest profit and anticipated additional production launches in the future. We fulfilled the joint-venture mandate to produce offset value for Pratt in China.

Shannon and I enjoyed our trips outside raucous Chengdu. Sichuan

Province offered an abundance of delights. We spent many weekends hiking in the misty mountains and bamboo forests, and even spotted a few pandas. Qingcheng Mountain, near Chengdu, the 1,300-year-old Leshan Giant Buddha (a 233-foot-tall statue carved out of a red sandstone cliff) and 9,843-foot-tall Emei Mountain were all world-class nature sites. Everywhere, the local people were friendly. One could take refuge in Taoist temples and serene tea gardens. Best of all, the tasty, hot-and-spicy cuisine of Sichuan, such as *Gān biān sì jì dòu*: fresh green beans slowly roasted until blistered and beautifully charred, then tossed with ground pork, ginger, garlic and chili peppers, Sichuan peppercorns, soy sauce and wine easily beat northern Chinese fare.

After three years in Chengdu, I concluded that it was time for my family to move on. By 1998, Chengdu Aerotech was steadily exporting products to the U.S. aftermarket. Pratt sold our parts to U.S. overhaul shops that were maintaining aircraft for airlines worldwide.

The Atkeson family was now a foursome. Our son, Trevor, had been born in April 1998. Daughter, Lindsay, was now 4. Shannon and I were seeking to return to Beijing for pre-school options and a less polluted living environment. I visited Hong Kong and poked around the headhunters there for new opportunities in China. One of these recruiters ended up connecting me with a U.S. private-equity fund — Asian Strategic Investments Corp. — and Tim Clissold, ASIMCO's president.

He arrived one day at Chengdu Aerotech to chat with me about a new opportunity in the automotive-parts industry. My response: "You've got to be kidding. Automotive suffers from over-capacity, low margins, and nobody gets paid in China."

Years later, in 2004, Tim would write an entertaining book titled, *Mr. China* about extraordinary and bizarre tales of value destruction as ASIMCO mishandled its early investments in automotive components-makers in China. ASIMCO had been founded in 1994 by Jack Perkowski, a veteran Wall Street investment banker, who intended to capitalize on the emerging China market. Tim's book chronicled how ASIMCO ended up losing most of its $400 million invested in China (though it later recovered this loss).

ASIMCO's business model was based on accessing and transferring capital, technology, and managerial techniques from the United States and Europe to upgrade existing automotive-parts makers in the ASIMCO portfolio. The early investors ended up losing many millions of dollars due to lack of controls and to significant financial leakage among the portfolio businesses. However, the debacle of ASIMCO investments was not fully apparent in 1998 when Tim met with me.

While the automotive-parts industry sounded dull to me, I gravitated toward what I wanted to hear about investment management. I wished to move on from manufacturing and elevate myself into fund management. Little did I realize that ASIMCO intended to keep me in manufacturing by inserting me into one of its most problematic and distressed portfolio businesses in Beijing — a diesel-fuel injector/pump company — to lead a turnaround.

In the process, I would discover levels of corruption in China I had never imagined.

Chapter Seven

Combating Corruption

It was Fall 1999. I sat in a drab meeting room and greeted Wang Gang when he entered. This self-assured man in his thirties was the manager of our export business at Beijing Fuel Pump & Fuel Injector Co. — BYC for short. Gang was tall and skinny and sported a short, spiky buzz haircut that made him look hip and Western, despite the light-blue utility jacket bearing our company's faded logo that he also wore. As I shifted uneasily and cleared my throat, I informed him, in Chinese, that we had an important issue to discuss.

Important, indeed. It was the sort of issue any general manager, such as myself, dreaded and needed to decisively resolve if he wanted to accomplish what he was hired to do: make the company profitable. The day before, three women employed on BYC's fuel-injector production line had surreptitiously sought out me and my trusted colleague, James Li, manager of our nozzle shop, to tip us off about Wang Gang's secret operation of stealing nozzles from our shop, packaging them as parts from our overseas competitors, and selling them on the black market in Southeast Asia for huge profits. The women, in their late forties, were very fearful about sharing this information, but were determined, nonetheless. As I questioned them, I gathered that Wang Gang had seen them as a threat, since they could observe what Gang's gang was up to. They explained that he'd snarled a veiled threat against their families if the three ever reported his corrupt activities. The intimidation had rattled the women enough that they'd decided they couldn't remain silent. After all, they reasoned, Gang might carry out his threat, merely based on suspicion. The women determined that they would only be safe if Gang were removed from the company and his operation quashed by us in management.

I understood the broader cultural context of why the women had approached me. The busybody factor — people watching the actions of others and ratting out perpetrators of illegal activities — was ingrained in Chinese culture from decades of autocratic Communist rule. During Mao's Cultural Revolution, staunch Communist Party members populated neighborhood committees and would enforce laws, such as the one-child policy, with the help of citizens who informed on couples who already had a child but were expecting another baby. Post-Mao, the tradition of citizens snitching on peers remained strong. For example, during the outbreak of the COVID-19 virus in China in January 2020, the government imposed a lockdown on Wuhan, the city where the virus originated, and in the following two years implemented lockdowns in other Chinese cities with localized outbreaks, including Shanghai. Those who broke quarantine could be reported by neighbors.

There may have been another factor at play in the three women's motivation to tattle on Wang Gang: jealousy. When people are struggling to make ends meet, and they see someone else doing well — especially a hustler ripping off their employer — they develop a powerful resentment. Well, it seemed that Wang Gang and his crew were doing quite well. The women explained that Gang's operation was substantial in stealing BYC's most profitable products. Members of his ring would drive vans into our shops and load them up with unmarked fuel nozzles directly off our factory line. They would then ship the nozzles to a facility in Shenzhen in southern China, where they used a laser-marking machine to etch on them fake trademarks for the Bosch (German) or Zexel (Japanese) brands — both considered premium products worldwide. These counterfeit nozzles generated big sales in countries such as Malaysia and Thailand, earning Wang Gang and his collaborators what I estimated to be $3 million to $5 million annually in almost pure profit.

That night, I phoned Tim Clissold, president of Asian Strategic Investments Corp. — the U.S. private-equity fund that was the major investor in the Chinese-owned BYC — who'd hired me initially as the nozzle shop manager, then seen that I was promoted to GM, replacing the Chinese GM (whose performance was underwhelming). Tim said I should speak with ASIMCO'S chairman, Jack Perkowski, to formulate the best strategy for dealing with Wang Gang. I got hold of Jack on the phone, and we agreed we should discreetly "kill" (terminate the employment of) Wang Gang as quietly as possible, so as not to instigate interference from the former GM and his mafia, who likely were involved in the nozzle ring. Jack's and my plan was to get Gang out of the company as quickly as possible, and remove any ability for him to access the physical plant.

Jack and I knew that seeking police action against Wang Gang and his ring would have been complicated. It was not clear how many other managers were involved. It was better to choke the operation by removing its mastermind and all his information.

Now, in the meeting room, as I confronted Gang with a stolen nozzle, bearing a forged Bosch trademark, in my hand, I had to commend him on his extraordinary business acumen. He remained poker-faced. His cool confidence indicated to me that he knew the day would eventually come when his activities would be exposed, and he likely had a plan to continue the operation — regardless of whatever punitive measures I implemented. After all, I — a Westerner — had recently been made GM, replacing the Chinese GM under whose reign Gang's thievery had thrived. I could almost hear the gears humming in his head as he figured out how to continue ripping off BYC.

Gang asked me for a month's grace period so he could wrap up his office work and enable a smooth transition to whomever I named as his successor.

I said no.

"How about two weeks?" he asked.

"No."

"How about a week?"

"You don't understand," I said. "This criminal operation must stop, and you have to leave immediately."

He obviously wanted to buy time to download all of the logistical information of his operation and arrange for other insiders to continue the theft of our products. He left the meeting room, still deadpan, and I followed him back to his office. He sat at his computer terminal and immediately began downloading files onto floppy disks (the standard portable units for digital data storage in 1999). My temper rising, I reached over and unplugged his desktop computer and threatened to call security to get him to leave.

I'd refrained from summoning our gate security staff, so I could minimize the disruption and ease him out in a discreet fashion. But it was still an option. Faced with this ultimatum, Gang sullenly traipsed out of the building.

My next step was calling James Li on my cell phone. I told him to hurry over to seize all of Wang Gang's office computers. I instructed James to load them into his car, take them to his home and download their hard drives.

Next, I directed my company driver to replace all the office-door locks.

That night, I received a call from an irate Wang Gang on my unlisted home phone number. It was clear he had friends throughout our organization. He insisted that he had done nothing wrong and that I was unjust in firing him.

"You shouldn't treat me this way," he said, playing the part of a victim.

"You shouldn't have been stealing from BYC," I said. "We're done."

I hung up.

I didn't get a sense that Gang was threatening me with physical harm. However, I knew that had I been Chinese, retribution could have been quite possible. Gang could have threatened violence against members of my extended family, or personal property, that police would never be able to pin on him. That was the sort of retaliation the three women on the fuel-injector production line had to worry about. But not me. I had no extended family or other connections in China.

That surely was frustrating for Wang Gang. I was a foreigner, and to him that was like dealing with a Martian. He couldn't figure out how to manipulate me.

THIS EPISIDE WITH WANG Gang was a harsh lesson for me about the reality of doing business in China. I was now in my seventh year working with Chinese industrial businesses — first with machine tools, then with aircraft engines and parts, and now with automotive parts. I yearned more than ever to move into the financial field. But I had a tall task to attend to with BYC: turning it from a hemorrhaging loser in ASIMCO's portfolio, into a moneymaker.

BYC was based in a rundown neighborhood in the Fengtai District in southwest Beijing: the poorest of the four corners of Beijing. Fengtai District is an area of dusty, unpaved roads, ramshackle factory buildings and cracked concrete walls topped by broken glass. Tangles of telephone wires and power lines are strung overhead. Shantytowns pervade.

BYC's structure dated to the 1960s factory buildings: concrete plants with angled roofs and grimy skylights. In the nozzle shop, we had a production line of employees who were washing finished nozzles with diesel fuel, using their bare hands.

BYC, which had 4,000 employees, produced fuel pumps, injectors and nozzles, based on copies of 1960s-era Bosch technology, for multi-cylinder and single-cylinder diesel engines. Despite the distressed status of the business, BYC still captured about a one-third market share for fuel systems for all of China's midsize diesel engines installed in medium-duty trucks. Our parent company, ASIMCO, had injected almost $40 million of capital into BYC — a company carved out of the Chinese state-owned Beijing Automotive Industry Corp., to create a foreign-invested enterprise. BYC was among the distressed automotive-parts makers in ASIMCO's portfolio.

The most striking part of BYC's business was its nozzle operation. Nozzles are consumable high-precision products frequently replaced in diesel fuel-injection systems. Their economics resembled the razor-blade business, with 40 to 50 percent gross margins. Pumps and injectors, on the other hand, hovered around 10 percent gross margins. A sizeable portion of ASIMCO's injected capital had been invested in expensive German and Swiss grinding and honing machines to give BYC an early edge in nozzle product performance.

My first post at BYC was running the nozzle shop — which was the company's cash cow. I reported to BYC's Chinese general manager and his colleagues. This brought me up close to an unsavory reality. It was readily obvious to me that this mafia of insiders had exploited their positions to plunder BYC. From skimming off procurement deals signed with their friends and families, to taking kickbacks, to outright stealing from production and BYC assets, they had made off with millions of dollars in value. It was not hard to imagine that they maintained dual identities: at BYC, earnest socialist bureaucrats with threadbare clothes and modest cars; away from BYC, nouveau riche with fancy apartments, cars and clothes.

ASIMCO had tasked me with trying to unlock more value from our nozzle business. I could see that the configuration of the BYC manufacturing environment, and pressure from competitors, was causing BYC to drift continuously toward high-volume, low-margin nozzles for the domestic market. Returns on the BYC business were plunging. We needed to break out to more high-margin nozzle sales. I drove a painful re-arrangement of our production equipment into two separate production cells to cater for both low-volume, high-margin nozzles for export, and high-volume, low-margin nozzles for domestic consumption. Our export line boosted higher value sales to Southeast Asia, the Middle East and Europe.

ASIMCO's directors then exercised our fund's right as a major investor to replace the general manager at BYC. I was promoted to GM — to the chagrin of the existing management. As I took stock of the company I now was running, I found I'd been placed in charge of a business with $30 million of annual sales hamstrung with over $30 million of debt, 200 days of accounts receivable, large write-offs of scrap inventory, and corrupt sales and procurement organizations. Our sales team was taking kickbacks to accept delays in cash receipts for invoices. Our procurement team was taking bribes to overpay for materials. Our products were literally leaking out the door. Our cash flow was so anemic that we were continually seeking additional short-term financing for working capital.

Corruption is a people problem. The fastest way to solve the problem is replacing bad apples. And as I discovered, Wang Gang was just one of the rotten pieces of fruit in the cart . . .

I quickly arranged the removal and replacement of BYC leaders of finance and accounting, purchasing and sales departments. I brought in local Chinese staff from ASIMCO to take over these departments and to implement policies and procedures that included checks and balances on money collections and expenditures. Our first task was to stop the financial leakage by requiring everyone to comply with our new procedures. I then implemented a new set of incentives focused on conservation of cash. I instituted a rewards system. Sales representatives received bonuses for increasing collections from delivered goods. Purchasing staff got bonuses for lengthening payment terms with our suppliers. Finance accountants were paid to figure out how to monetize the assets where our cash was tied up in inventories and idle equipment.

Replacing people in production proved more complicated, due to the specialized nature of our production processes and the loyalties of our workforce to their shop-floor comrades. I resorted to identifying and promoting young, high-potential shop managers by conducting informal surveys of our employees. Establishing a reward system based on merit, rather than nepotism or personal favors, was a big step in leveraging capable in-house employees to making the biggest contribution to BYC's turnaround.

Orchestrating the turnaround involved liquidating assets, replacing multiple groups of management, and cutting costs. Among the cost-cutting moves were layoffs — which were also made for the psychological effect, to "kill some chickens to scare the monkeys."

The turmoil from these radical changes was palpable. Employees were angry, the union was causing trouble, and even the party secretary assigned to BYC — because BYC had been carved out of the mother company, which was state-owned — harangued me. All these enterprises had a Communist Party secretary — who had the same authority as the top business guy in the company, but didn't have the administrative responsibilities. That meant the party secretary technically had the same authority to make company decisions as I, the GM, did. If I got into an argument with this guy at a staff meeting, I could get nowhere. He enjoyed the same clout I did. (I can only imagine it was the same conundrum a captain on a Soviet submarine suffered, faced with the equal status of the secretary assigned to the sub by the Communist Party of the Soviet Union.) The party secretary often blamed me for failing to pay accounts on time — even though our cash-flow situation had been compromised by the corruption and mismanagement of my predecessor. My car tires were slashed.

It was hard to find capable confederates to help carry the banner of change. (James Li, whom I'll tell about more a little further on, was an exception.) Yes, it can be lonely — and stressful — at the top.

My duties as GM extended to comforting bereaved families of deceased employees. One day, I arrived for work and learned that a shop worker suffering extreme depression had hung himself in apparent suicide in the workshop below my office. His home was in an apartment building across the lot from the factory — on-site housing dating from the "iron rice bowl" policy in China, when the mother company provided for all the needs and services of employees. I climbed the steps to the apartment and joined three Chinese labor-union representatives in consoling the worker's widow. Their attitude stunned me. The gist of their comments was that her late husband had failed in his duty to take responsibility for his family and his life. His suicide, they declared, had been a desperate act of negligence.

I realized this was a classic Chinese response. What's more, their words may have been an attempt to cajole her to make a statement that her husband was irresponsible. That would've been important to them to use as ammunition to teach a lesson to other workers in the community. From my perspective, I didn't think there was a need to teach anyone a lesson.

I felt terrible for the grieving woman. She wept through the entire visit. I felt I had to say something to comfort her. I wanted her to have a positive view of her husband — not have her mourning tainted by a punitive view that he was a bad person.

"You should consider that your husband probably wasn't in control of his actions, because he was depressed and sick," I said, sympathetically.

My statement elicited howls of disapproval from the labor reps.

The widow continued weeping. She avoided any acknowledgement of my disagreement with the labor reps over her husband's motive for suicide.

Though I now had lived seven years in China, I still experienced the stings of culture shock. Fortunately, I had James Li to counsel me.

JAMES LI HAD BEEN hired by ASIMCO and begun at BYC the same time as I. I'd started as manager of the nozzle shop, James as assistant manager. Like me, he'd joined ASIMCO to learn about investment management — only to end up in the investment fund's manufacturing backwater of BYC.

James was a year younger than I. He was a bright and earnest self-starter who'd grown up in poverty in the waning years of the Cultural Revolution. James's neighborhood was the alleyways of Wuhan. Fortunately, he had a keen intelligence, an even temper and a tremendous work ethic. He'd lifted himself up academically, graduating from the China European International

Business School: one of the most prestigious business schools in China, with an English-language curriculum and courses run by visiting professors from the West.

James was, simply, a good, solid person. He had no political agenda in the workplace other than to do his job and make the company profitable. He was wise and not given to jumping to conclusions. He practiced measured speech and thought matters through. James proved to be an ideal collaborator for me in the intrigue-riven environment of BYC. We formed a bond as we jointly weathered the managerial upheaval at BYC, and we sought each other's counsel on solving people and business problems. I relied on him to help me assess situations with his local cultural perspective.

I admired James for his composed demeanor while helping me confront the local mafia of BYC. I knew that the day I resigned as GM from BYC, he would need to move on, as well, since he was a close ally of me — the chief making the unpopular decisions.

What James helped me understand about the endemic corruption in Chinese society — from the workplace to the offices of party officials — is that it springs from the survival instinct. After all, if you lived through an economy like pre-reform China's — in which resources were massively misallocated, and people were starving — you learned to do what you could to survive. That meant being outwardly charming in public, but inwardly committed to hiding from authorities, and to cheating and stealing. That was the reality of the common person's life in China before I arrived.

What I came to realize is that as China transitioned from the ironclad rule of Mao Zedong to a market economy under Deng Xiaoping, the public mindset didn't change. In fact, corruption — I saw — was not only widespread but expected and accepted, and not seen as a moral failure. Historically, governmental officials in China have been assumed to be leveraging their position for personal gain. In America, we have a fit over favoritism and graft. In China — in the absence of an independent media or watchdog groups — people with clout, such as political insiders, have been prone to exploiting state assets to get kickbacks, or to award procurement deals to friends or family. In fact, smart, capable people in China often have sought administrative power, because they could get wealthier that way than in starting their own businesses.

As James Li explained to me, those who operate or work in key positions at state-owned factories may very well siphon off products and sell them at below-market prices to friends or associates who otherwise cannot afford these goods, such as bicycles or televisions. Or the skimmers might sell pilfered products to black-market entrepreneurs, who will turn around and re-sell them at market prices. (That was Wang Gang's hustle — as it most certainly was for the former GM and his insider cohorts.)

A relatively different level of corruption — which had disappeared by 1999 — involved arbitraging prices for goods brought to market. Some items have regulated prices, some do not. You can end up with two prices for goods: the black-market price and the state price. What's more, not every product is available for every person. Some opportunistic people would procure a state product at the state price and sell it higher on the black market for those who couldn't obtain the product from the state. The Chinese government introduced foreign scrip that enabled the purchase of luxury items such as cosmetics and jeans, as well as scarce-in-supply electrical appliances such as color televisions and refrigerators. Chinese moneychangers on the street built up an active trade in acquiring foreign scrip from tourists and other visitors by trading for higher-than-official exchange rates for the Chinese yuan, then leveraging that scrip by acquiring the difficult-to-obtain consumer items and reselling them at inflated prices.

Today, as I write these words, the reality of corruption that permeates Chinese society is a cultural fact. Of course, it is not unique to China. It is surely a phenomenon of human society worldwide. However, when it comes to international business, the opportunistic impulse of getting what one can has harmed China's reputation. Nowhere is this more evident than in conflicts over the stealing of intellectual property. Chinese-made knockoffs of name-brand sneakers, or pirated movie DVDs or music CDs, or software technology, is of great consternation to companies and governments around the world. However, stealing intellectual property is supported by all levels in China, up to the top of the party leadership.

The notion of private intellectual property is simply not part of their mindset.

TURNING BYC AROUND PROVED exceptionally problematic. The company suffered from not having a technology pipeline for product development. Its financial hemorrhaging, in fact, left it nearly bankrupt, and ASIMCO was only a financial investor.

We managed by buying newer Bosch pumps in the open market in the United States, and then reverse-engineering them for localization at BYC. But this proved to be only a short-term solution. Fuel-injection technology was shifting to electronic systems and high pressure pumps known as common rail. Auto parts became increasingly dominated by foreign companies who had edges in technology and produced high quality.

I did not foresee a lengthy tenure for myself at BYC. I was nearing 40, and could see the younger Chinese generation rising as capable managers of industry. These people born in the post-Mao era rapidly absorbed factory and enterprise management knowledge. It was time for me to get out of manufacturing. The problem for a "manufacturing guy" — as I'd become — was how to re-define myself into some new sector.

Shannon had made the leap in 1999 from Pratt & Whitney's financial operations to International Finance Corp. IFC is an international financial institution that offers investment, advisory and asset-management services to encourage private-sector development in less-developed countries. The IFC is a member of the World Bank Group. As an investment officer, Shannon worked to close investment deals in multiple sectors in Mongolia, and later in China and other parts of Asia.

One weekend, I sat with an American businessman about my age named Tom Kirkwood, who had brought his 3-year-old son, Jack, to the Goose and Duck Farm outside Beijing the same day I'd brought my 3-year-old, Trevor. As we watched the boys playing among the trees, we struck up a conversation.

"Tell me more about what you do," I asked.

"We manage seed and early-stage investments in mobile-Internet businesses in China," Tom said. "It's a rapidly growing area with a lot of opportunities. Why don't you come talk with me and my partner about joining us?"

It was summer 2001. Although the Nasdaq exchange had started crashing from the implosion of U.S. Internet stocks — the bursting of the dotcom bubble — China seemed far away, and I considered that maybe mobile Internet was immune to the de-valuation in the United States. I knew that China was the world's biggest mobile market, and its 1 billion users were upgrading to more sophisticated phones with greater capabilities for m-commerce. Japan had led the way with value-added services offered by NTT Docomo, and Scandinavia was building mobile-service businesses partnered with carriers such as Telenor. Cellular phones were taking over communications in the business world, and in everyday life.

China Mobile and China Unicom seemed ready to offer revenue-sharing partnerships in an ecosystem for content developers and service businesses to expand their telecom offerings to include entertainment, interactive media, games, information services, and payments, among other offerings.

Investing in value-added services for mobile sounded substantially more interesting to me than managing the manufacturing grind of automotive. I was hooked. I decided to jump into the mobile-Internet industry.

And that's how I ended up co-founding a pioneer investment fund focused on seed-stage mobile businesses in China.

Goodbye manufacturing. I was going mobile.

Chapter Eight

Leaping into Risky Ventures

Wang Bin — a slightly pudgy and nerdy software developer with a receding hairline, wearing a ruffled suit — listened, eyes intent behind horn-rimmed glasses, as I explained in Chinese how my partnership, Mobile Internet (Asia) Ltd., could provide financing and coaching to his startup company.

It was August 2001. Wang Bin's operation of eight programmers was developing a web platform that would enable China Mobile — the enormous customer he was pursuing — to offer subscribers on its nationwide telecommunications network the option of downloading games and applications running on the Java programming language.

There at the start of the 2000s, this was a pioneering development in the mobile-phone industry. This evolution in value-added services for cell phones was transpiring in Japan and Scandinavia well ahead of what would end up taking place in the United States, China and the rest of the world as the century progressed. This technological leap would render smart phones as a constant and indispensable apparatus for the majority of people on the planet. But here in 2001, cell phones in China were already taking over communications in the business world and in daily life.

China Mobile and its main rival, China Unicom, were focused on establishing and exploiting this emerging high-tech ecosystem. These dominant corporations in Chinese telecommunications were eager to court software developers such as Wang Bin — and said they were open to sharing with these digital entrepreneurs the revenue streams to be generated in this emerging sphere of m-commerce. A bonanza loomed from the new-age applications and games, photo and video cameras, methods of sending payments, and other services marketed to China's 1 billion cell-phone users. Wang Bin's business plan called for not only collecting fees for providing the software for the web platform that would enable China Mobile's subscribers to download apps and games onto their cell phones, but also participating in the revenue share from those downloads.[18]

My two partners and I in MINT (the acronym we used for our company) recognized this early-bird opportunity in this cutting-edge industry. Thus, we were searching for opportunities to use our investment fund to finance and incubate seed-stage mobile-service businesses in China. We were building a portfolio of promising enterprises in mobile entertainment, interactive media, games, information services, payments, and technology. We were prepared to offer cash and backend support, and provide our business and managerial experience and our network contacts, to these businesses, in exchange for a minority share. Wang Bin's startup, indeed, seemed promising. As he and I met to explore an offer of seed money from us, I watched for cues indicating his receptiveness.

---

[18] Unfortunately, China Mobile never paid to Wang Bin's company a share of the revenue for downloads.

Wang Bin was in his late thirties, married with a child. (One child was all the central government would allow couples to have, in that period between 1980 and 2016.) He was earnest, ambitious, and hard working. To further himself, he'd worked for a time in Japan for Matsushita Electric Industrial Co. (aka Panasonic Corp.), where he'd learned about electrical engineering and sophisticated software programming. In this initial stage of launching his company, he'd already attracted an investor: a Chinese businessman, in whose office we were meeting. Wang Bin didn't reveal what stake this sponsor had in his startup. Nor did he share anything at all about him. I could only conjecture what ties this backer had to financiers — and what sort of financiers they were. I did get the sense, however, that Wang Bin was uncomfortable with the onerous indenture required by this businessman. He was dealing with a traditional Chinese business mentality regarding an investor's ownership power in an enterprise.

I continued my pitch. In addition to startup capital, I said MINT would sweeten the deal by offering free use of our offices for his team. Our offices were in the Kerry Center in downtown Beijing, in suites occupied by one of MINT's investors: PricewaterhouseCoopers Consulting. My offer meant that Wang Bin and his programmers could set up their laptops and work at a large table in the main room of the open-plan floor. There'd be back-office support with reliable wireless connectivity, telephone, accounting and printing services. It would be an ideal setup. MINT's offices were adjacent, and that would make it easy for my partners and me to schedule and conduct meetings with Wang Bin and his team, so we could keep abreast of his company's progress, and coordinate whatever guidance and support were necessary from our end.

Wang Bin's expression remained stoic, but I could tell these terms sounded attractive to him. He said he liked our proposal to work side by side with him as investors nurturing an entrepreneur and his team.

If I was reading him right, Wang Bin could see that MINT was going to be much more generous and transparent than his Chinese investor. And we were only asking for a minority share of his startup. He didn't have to fear he was building something that would end up stolen from him.

On my way out of the office building, Wang Bin followed me into the elevator and asked to meet with my partners and me at our office to learn more.

A tingle of excitement crawled up my spine.

I'D JOINED MINT IN summer 2001 as a partner with an American businessman, Tom Kirkwood, four years younger than I, and a Chinese businessman, Wang Xin, who was seven years younger. My partnering with these two had been consummated by my anteing up a high-roller check into the fund. That meant I had significant skin in the game. The early return on this investment was my elation at the opportunity it provided me for an exciting career change. This was my entry into a new world of venture capital, focused on tech, media, and telecom. This was a very different world from the production of airplane burner cans and fuel-injector nozzles!

I quickly became immersed in new venture deals representing a wide variety of business models and investment structures. The work was incredibly rewarding, particularly as we nurtured entrepreneurial teams to grow their businesses. It was fun for me to be in the glitz and glamor of the office environment we were in, working with investees in the sexy tech sector where the potential seemed limitless. This was the early 2000s. For foreign investors, backing startups that combined mobile and user content, data and gaming, information and entertainment, photography functions and payment services for the world's most populous and fastest-modernizing nation, was seen as a very hot sector. And this was even before the advent of social media!

Here in East Asia was where angel investors such as my partners and I needed to be. In America, mobile telecommunications was not yet a hot sector. In the States, mobile Internet was a person's laptop connecting to a wireless network. There was no general notion that it would involve people on their cell phones. (In fact, the ascendancy of cell phones and their value-added functions that would come to dominate the daily lives of billions would not become apparent to most Americans until after Apple Corp. chairman Steve Jobs led his company in developing its smart phone — the iPhone — and its introduction in 2007, setting off a lifestyle earthquake of young people going crazy with mobile games and cameras and an array of apps.)

The proliferation into everyday life of mobile phones — combined with Internet-connected, value-added services — really is an Asian story. It began with NTT Docomo's massive success in Japan at the end of the 1990s, and continued apace as the ecosystem quickly spread to China.

My new foray into mobile-cellular technology and venture capital excited me. I was reinventing myself in the business world from having been a general manager running manufacturing operations. This was a huge transformation for me — just as having dived into the worlds of metal-bashing, then aviation engines, then automotive parts, had been. Now I was getting my hands "dirty" handling all the tasks one must to invest in startup businesses and nurture them. It was highly stimulating and thrilling to be on the cutting edge of a new industry that was culturally transforming the world.

Doing angel investing is a people business. You have to treat entrepreneurs very carefully. After all, in the seed stage, they and their team comprise the entirety of their company's assets. The goose has not yet laid its first golden egg. It was being grown and groomed to do so. Each of us three partners in MINT had distinct responsibilities within MINT suited to our backgrounds, talents and skills. Mine was in dealing directly with Wang Bin, keeping him focused and encouraged. After all, Chinese entrepreneurs such as Wang Bin weren't well-rounded managers. They typically had technical backgrounds but no business and managerial experience. I was delicate in guiding Wang Bin to forge ahead with his business plan and make smart business moves. You must be very nice to the goose and hope it matures into a strong, consistent golden-egg layer.

My managerial skills were robust and well-rounded by now. My work experience in China — first with Cincinnati Milacron, overseeing the installation of heavy machinery at remote mining or factory sites, plus traveling to sell machine tools to other Chinese companies; then with Pratt & Whitney, leading efforts to forge a joint venture with Aircraft Maintenance and Engineering Corp. at Beijing Airport, and managing a crisis operation involving bringing in our own mechanics to improve the engine safety record; then with Chengdu Aerotech Manufacturing Co., overseeing construction of a factory making airplane parts, and then running that factory; and with the Beijing Fuel Pump & Fuel Injector Co., running a factory and stanching the hemorrhaging of employee theft — had given me significant operational experience in the industrial world. My positions as a general manager had trained me in everything from finance to sales to managing projects to supervising personnel. In addition, they had helped me hone my people skills.

I am essentially an empathetic person, but my years in China had given me a special interest in, and appreciation for, talented people dedicated to rising higher in their society, capitalizing on opportunities that were opening up in a growing economy embracing key principles of free enterprise. I was impressed with the Chinese entrepreneurs creating startups from their ideas for products and services. I knew they faced a challenging road in their nation's new economy. I respected their ability to be self-directed, motivated and market savvy. My role was as coach, guide, supporter.

I gently but firmly enforced a level of discipline to ensure that project schedules were being met, software being developed on time, company representatives making contacts with China Mobile and other prospective clients.

In sum, I was the "operational guy" in our partnership trio at MINT.

Tom Kirkwood was the "fundraiser guy."

Wang Xin was the "China guy."

Wang Xin was MINT's public face — obtaining licenses and all the other required legal documents and regulatory approvals that were needed, so that the companies in our portfolio could operate in China. Telecommunications was a restricted sector. That is, China would only issue operating licenses to domestic companies in such industries as the web, education, data center, and the media. Foreigners such as Tom and I were not supposed to be involved with telecom. So we used an investee structure for MINT that was adopted by most foreign-invested Internet companies in China.

For each startup we invested in, we established a local Chinese company referred to as a "variable interest entity" licensed by the government. The VIE would be owned by a Chinese national who was either a MINT partner or a trustworthy entrepreneur loyal to MINT. We would maintain control of the VIE's Chinese bank accounts, and sometimes even take title of the entrepreneur's apartment to safeguard the partner's trust. The VIE would contract to transfer all its economic value to an offshore entity — usually in the British Virgin Islands, a haven for foreign corporations taking advantage of the flexible incorporation rules and business-friendly regulatory environment. The offshore entity would be the vehicle for follow-on investments and exits.

Although we were operating within the letter of the law, for commonsensical reasons of decorum, neither Tom nor I ever showed our faces at China Mobile, much less attempted to secure legal documents for setting up VIEs. That was Wang Xin's role.

Wang Xin was a streetwise and shrewd man with a cautious and businesslike nature that led him to avoid small talking with strangers. He kept his cards close to his vest. When considering whether a startup would be right for MINT's portfolio, he began with a cynical viewpoint. Xin was clearheaded in his analysis of how a business was going to make money.

Xin stood about 5-foot-6, with short, closely cropped hair. He'd been born in China in 1970. His father had been a well-known star of movies produced by the People Liberation's Army; he was something like the Humphrey Bogart of China in the 1950s and '60s. Xin's mother was upwardly mobile and saw a much brighter future for her son and daughter and herself by moving to America, which the three did when Xin was 12.

Xin spent his adolescence in Palo Alto, south of San Francisco, where he attended Henry M. Gunn Senior High School, a large public school that by the 1980s already had a fair number of ethnic Chinese students. Xin wasn't a stellar student, though he earned passing grades. He had a mellow personality — very relaxed by American standards — and nurtured an avid interest in the outdoors, taking up cycling and snowboarding. Though he would end up in the corporate business world, his penchant was for a minimalist lifestyle. While studying at San Francisco State University, he'd worked for a time at The North Face, the outdoor-recreation products company. The attire suited him. He didn't own a suit or tie.

Being bilingual, Xin saw opportunities to further his business career in China. He moved there and worked at Mercer Consulting, a human-resources company and a subsidiary of U.S.-based advertising and marketing behemoth Marsh McLennan. He subsequently worked in China at an office of Ericsson, the Swedish multinational networking and telecommunications company. In these two positions, Xin learned the discipline of project management. This stood him in excellent stead as a numbers guy. The job with Ericsson also exposed Xin to the mobile-communications industry.

By the time the opportunity materialized for Xin to invest with Tom Kirkwood in MINT, he knew a great deal about the mobile industry in China, and had connections with the Chinese carriers. He and Tom may have appeared as opposites — Tom in his pinstripe suit, resembling an English banker, Xin in his T-shirt and blue jeans — but they were very suitable as partners, each bringing different skill sets to MINT.

Given his background in telecom, Xin proved instrumental in many of our dealings with China Mobile. When it came to developing our startups, Xin helped persuade local television and radio stations to sign service contracts by which our investee provided a texting platform to enable the media to interact with their audiences via mobile phones. He secured local licenses for Internet and mobile services for our variable interest entities.

Outside of work, Xin maintained his fun-loving, athletic side. In Beijing, he enjoyed exploring the wilderness beyond the Great Wall, and distance bicycling along country roads. At work, his frugal and prudent approach served as an example to Tom and me and our investees.

Tom Kirkwood — MINT's "fundraising guy" — was a funhouse mirror image of Xin. He stood 6-foot-3, was engaging, and exuded outward confidence. He also had a sixth sense for networking. This was partly due to his naturally gregarious nature, and partly because he was an eternal optimist. While Xin was reticent in public, Tom constantly struck up conversations with strangers. He was the type of guy who, standing in a Starbuck's line, talked to whoever was next to him. He could converse with sophisticated, high-level people or the man on the street, and make each person feel he was giving his full attention. Yes, it was a gift. So was his ability to manifest opportunities.

Tom might be at the airport to pick up someone arriving on a flight, bump into total strangers and chitchat. All of a sudden, a business prospect might pop out of the conversation. This was how he'd found out my business background when we'd chatted after randomly encountering each other at the Goose and Duck Farm, outside Beijing, a few months earlier, while taking our respective 3-year-old sons on an outing. That had led to Tom's invitation for me to talk with Wang Xin and him about joining MINT.

Tom had been born in Thailand, where his parents were working in the 1960s. His mother and father were trendsetters. Tom's father was a lawyer providing legal services in Thailand to everyone from the U.S. Army (which was engaged in a full-scale military effort in nearby Vietnam) to Thai citizens. Tom's mother was an early leader in the U.S. Peace Corps, which had been founded in 1961 at the onset of President John F. Kennedy's administration. The family later moved to Singapore, and then to Pennsylvania. Tom's parents sent him off as a teenager to attended Marlborough College: a fuddy-duddy, redbrick boarding school for ages 13 to 18 in England. There, Tom found himself to be the lone Yank — yet he thrived. He quickly absorbed the rules of cricket and the quirks of English boarding-school society. He was simply blessed with the gift of being a chameleon — changing his colors to what would best serve him in his surroundings.

(I witnessed myself, in business situations, Tom speaking with a full-on upper-class English accent, because he believed this would create the most advantageous image of himself to others.)

From Marlborough College, Tom matriculated at the prestigious University of Cambridge, where he majored in Chinese. His intellect for language was strong; he graduated from Cambridge with a knowledge of Mandarin, including traditional Chinese, superior to that of most native speakers. When we were waiting to board a flight from Narita Airport in Tokyo, back to China on a business trip courting investors, I'd watched Tom quietly pass the time by tracing a classic Chinese poem in Chinese calligraphy on a cocktail napkin. In addition to his college studies in Chinese, Tom had spent time working in Taiwan, and spoke Mandarin fluently. He'd put this language skill to good use when he had owned and operated a company, Cowboy Candy, making taffy in northeastern China. He'd also developed a metal-forging business in China.

Tom was finely suited to courting potential investors for MINT. He had a solid pedigree, based on his brief stint many years before in New York with the Wall Street investment banking firm of Wasserstein Perella & Co. Tom was self-assured and had a flair for peddling — and sometimes embellishing — our investment opportunities. We used to joke that Tom was sometimes wrong, but never in doubt. When it came to pitching investors for MINT, Tom put to good use his innate ability for hyperbole. His self-assuredness was unflappable. Tom could go into a sales presentation, deliver a message, be absolutely full of bull about certain points, yet be utterly convincing. Indeed, he was quite successful — to MINT's benefit.

I saw this firsthand when the two of us traveled to Japan to pitch a group of young, wealthy American investment bankers on investing with our venture-capital firm. Yet the way Tom got into the right mental zone minutes before the meeting impressed me even more.

We'd arrived at the Deutsche Bank office in Tokyo, where we were set to make our presentation to a group of young investment bankers. These guys, only a few years removed from their college days, were swelled with cockiness. They'd been sent by their employer to Japan to aggressively buy up distressed assets of failing Japanese companies hit hard by the brutal decade-long recession in Japan. Japanese banks were avoiding swooping up these distressed assets — given the resentment that would stoke in Japanese small investors who'd lost their money in the market — and the foreign banks were taking full advantage. These smug twentysomething bankers were making small fortunes. They could afford vacation homes in Maui. They threw boozy parties and tossed sushi around like frat boys.

As I focused on the presentation we were about to make, Tom suggested we walk out into the office's Bonsai Garden. There we were — almost ready to enter a room full of arrogant prospective investors, with the pressure on us to persuade them what a great opportunity MINT's portfolio was, and my mind racing about what we were going to say. Yet Tom was saying, "Let's stop for a moment."

The next thing I knew, we were sitting in this garden and reflecting on the beauty of bonsai trees set in a miniature landscape complete with a waterfall and trickling stream.

When it was time for our presentation, Tom's mind was clear, his tone controlled, his posture confident. On hearing his speech about the dazzling potential of China's ready-to-boom mobile-communications market, the young investment bankers were sold. And so we picked up additional investment capital for MINT. We also gained a lead on potential investors in South Korea. One of the investment bankers told us about some British nationals he knew who were investing in real estate in Seoul.

Off Tom and I flew to Seoul. The Brits' office was in a nondescript office tower. After we arrived, they directed us to wait for them in the first-floor lounge: a small disco bar. In these sorts of establishments, regular patrons store personal bottles of their favorite libations, with their names labeled on the bottles. The Brits instructed us to tell the bartender that, "Paul upstairs said we should have a glass of wine from his bottle of Château Talbot Eighty-five."

Tom and I each had a glass of the rich blend of Bordeaux reds, then another, then another. By the time the Brits joined us, we'd unwittingly drained the entire $2,000 bottle. They weren't happy about that!

But they did invest $1 million with us.

MINT ENDED UP ACCUMULATING 10 different Chinese startup companies. Eight of them ended up as strikeouts. One proved a base hit. And one — Wang Bin's — floated over the fence as a home run.

The day following my initial meeting, in August 2001, with Wang Bin about funding his efforts to develop a web platform to market to China Mobile, he met with Tom, Wang Xin and me at our offices in the Kerry Center. This was a snazzy business tower in the most prestigious location in Beijing, and automatically gave us credibility with Wang Bin. We briefed him on our fund and our approach. We said we would commit $100,000 for a 30 percent stake, but wouldn't write him a check for the whole investment all at once. We would pay out in portions — in what are known as "drip-feed payments" — over the course of the next 12 months, covering costs along the way that all of us would agree were necessary to successfully incubate his company.

Wang Bin saw this was quite a reasonable offer. In those days, programmers' salaries were very small in China. A team of eight people could be sustained for a year on $100,000. In addition, my partners and I would use our networking to attract follow-on foreign investors, who could invest in later-stage rounds: Series A — the serious venture-capital round, when the new company was generating revenues and scaling up — and Series B, when the company was so attractive as a moneymaker that a large, risk-averse investor, such as a multinational corporation, would acquire the company and take it all the way to a potential public listing. That was the ultimate goal, of course: the "exit" — selling the startup for a handsome profit to a larger company: likely a leading tech company in the United States.

Wang Bin shook hands with each of us. The unspoken words behind our agreement were that we were betting on him to accomplish what he said he would do, and betting that his company would perform. For his side, Wang Bin was taking a leap of faith that we were capable, trustworthy people. In addition, I knew he needed to disentangle himself from his current Chinese sponsor. I had to wonder whether this initial investor would be discontented upon learning that Wang Bin was parting ways with him. Would thugs show up at Wang Bin's apartment?

Fortunately, that never happened. I assume that since Wang Bin's operation hadn't progressed too far yet, the sponsor had felt no need to put the squeeze on him.

When MINT incorporated this startup as a variable interest entity, we changed its name from whatever bland, perfunctory name Wang Bin had initially given it, to "Awaken."

It would prove to be the best investee we had in our portfolio.

OUTSIDE OF WORK, MY family's life in China seemed far removed from events in the United States. On the evening of Sept. 11, 2001, I was socializing with colleagues at an outdoor café in Beijing when one of our American friends, Rich Robinson, received a long-distance call from his mother in the United States. According to the news, a plane had collided with one of the World Trade Center towers in New York City. Laughing it off as a probable freak accident involving a light airplane, we were soon stunned after she called back to report a second plane had crashed into the WTC. I jumped in a cab and raced home in time to catch the collapse of both towers on *CNN*. Shannon was traveling on business that night, and Lindsay, 6, and Trevor, 3, slept quietly upstairs, unaware of the malevolence of this dramatic terrorist event, and the upheaval in world events awaiting all of us.

The events were far from as destabilizing in China as they were abroad. There was no overt reaction to the attacks from the Chinese government in the sense of heightened public security. In Beijing, there was nothing noticeably different the morning after. However, at the PwC offices where MINT was set up, people were shell-shocked. And this trauma and trepidation persisted in our minds. In a sense, I was glad my family was living abroad. At least we Atkesons were prospering in China.

Shannon's and my third child, Caroline, was born the following spring in Beijing.

I reflected on my midlife transition. When I got involved with MINT in summer 2001, I was two years shy of 40. The following summer, I set a goal of running my first marathon (26.2 miles) that October, and of finishing in under three hours. As a runner at Yale, my race distances had been 5,000 meters (3.1 miles) in track, and 10,000 meters (6.2 miles) in cross-country. I followed a training program created by editors at *Runner's World* magazine and doggedly clicked off the mileage month after month.

The strenuous training regimen caused me to drop 20 pounds to 160 pounds. While achieving my marathon goal seemed like a healthy and fulfilling pursuit, I probably took several years off my total life expectancy by training in Beijing's polluted air. After practice runs, I noticed that my sinus passages were black. Indeed, I developed a chronic cough.

At the Beijing Marathon's starting line in Tiananmen Square that

October, it was a mob scene. The square was packed with runners in their racing gear, many of whom were college students who'd arrived in buses that entered the square. The airhorn blared. A couple miles into the race, I noticed a great many of these runners peel off the course. It turned out they'd been recruited by the government to make the race pool look enormous at the starting line. Another reminder of the Chinese Communist Party's interest in its world image.

I was unprepared for the mental collapse I experienced around the 20th mile. Marathoners call this "hitting the wall." I felt like a refrigerator was on my back. How could I keep my legs moving? I was ready to give up. But the sugary bottles of Tang passed to me by race aides at sideline tables revived my spirits. Thanks to this energy jolt, I staggered past the finish line in 2 hours 56 minutes. I'd reached the goal I'd set, but considered it a Pyrrhic victory. My lungs had suffered as if I were a chain smoker.

I will probably pay a high price for the damage done to my lungs.

AS TIME WENT ON, I knew I'd made the right decision to cast my fortunes with MINT. However, it could be nerve-wracking waiting for investees to mature as companies we could successfully sell. Success is never guaranteed in the venture-capital game. Still, I considered that my timing in joining MINT had been fortunate. Before I'd come aboard, there'd been a discouraging setback for Tom Kirkwood and Wang Xin. The first company they'd brought into the portfolio — Magus Soft — had blown up in their faces.

Magus was a developer of mobile games and entertainment applications. The company designed, developed, and marketed complete mobile-entertainment solutions to operators, handset manufacturers and phone users. While Magus accepted MINT's investment, its owners duplicitously set up a corporate double offsite. On learning of this deception, Tom and Xin had to unceremoniously evict them from the dignified offices of PwC. Having this fraud as their first investment and black mark on their early track record was not an auspicious start for MINT.

The rising-star portfolio company when I arrived at MINT was Mezzme Ltd. Mezzme was China's first wireless service provider focused on the media sector. Chinese TV and radio broadcasters could poll their audiences by inviting them to send text votes to the 8850 number, a short code linking mobile phones and carriers to media partners via Mezzme's platform. Mezzme earned revenues from the carrier charges paid by mobile users to vote via 8850. While Magus had been founded by a local Chinese team, Mezzme was the brainchild of Norwegian entrepreneurs who'd copied a similar business model from another Norwegian company. Wang Xin was instrumental in guiding the localization of Mezzme for China's market.

During Mezzme's early successes, my partners and I met with Fritz Demopoulos, a native of Los Angeles, to solicit his possible entry into MINT. Fritz already had a gunslinger reputation as a foreigner in China who had built a sports Internet business — Shawei.com — that was financially backed by Intel Capital, Softbank, and International Data Group (and later acquired, in 2000, by Tom.com). At the time of our meeting in 2001, Fritz was serving as senior vice president of business development at NetEase Inc. — one of China's largest Internet portals, and the largest operator of online multiplayer games.

Fritz chuckled at our proposal for him to join MINT, and countered by questioning us on why we didn't just invest in Sina Corp., Sohu Inc., and NetEase on the U.S. based Nasdaq. These three Chinese Internet giants were rehabilitating themselves after the dotcom bubble crash of 2001 by adopting aggressive texting businesses with exploding revenues from chasing Chinese mobile subscribers, sometimes with fraudulent billing schemes. From his position at NetEase, Fritz could see that the easy revenues generated by texting would rocket these Chinese Internet stocks up by many times their current market value within a year.

Fritz knew his stuff. In retrospect, if we partners had just parked all of MINT's capital in these three stocks, we would have quickly made a fortune without the headache of running local businesses. Fritz was that rare example of a man with the Midas touch. Every business venture he pursued turned to gold!

(Many years later, he founded Qunar.com, which was a prominent online discount-travel company in China. Qunar received financial backing from GSR Ventures, Mayfield, Tenaya Capital and Granite Global. Chinese Internet search giant Baidu acquired a majority stake in Qunar in 2011 and listed it on the Nasdaq in 2013.)

Mezzme turned out to be a strikeout for MINT.

Xel Ltd. was another bust. It had a clever Bluetooth hardware solution that never really found a market. Xel's CEO, Li Yang — a brainy engineering nerd from prestigious Tsinghua University in Beijing — was proud of his team's work on Bluetooth electronics. Bluetooth technology allows devices to communicate with each other without cables or wires. Bluetooth relies on short-range radio frequency, and any device that incorporates the technology can communicate as long as it is within the required distance. In 2001, Bluetooth was considered revolutionary. Our problem was that Li Yang lacked the selling skills to go out and find applications for his hardware. Xel would eventually disappear — starved of any licensing or revenue-generating opportunities.

YeePay fared better for MINT. YeePay offered payment solutions for e-commerce on Internet websites. Tang Bin, the CEO of YeePay, had experience in Silicon Valley and could see the need for payment solutions to support e-commerce. This sphere, however, already was a crowded space. The problem was that while the United States — with a much larger installed base of desktop and laptop computers than China — was more ready to adopt payments for e-commerce, China was more configured for mobile-phone connections to the Internet. Payments via mobile would be a carrier solution. Also, Chinese consumers lacked the credit and debit cards so common in America.

YeePay would eventually carve out a niche market but never play a dominant role in China. Nevertheless, it was a "base hit" for us.

One evening, my partners and I were invited to a reception in Beijing held by the Carlyle Group — one of the largest private-equity, alternative-asset management and financial-service corporations in the United States. Carlyle was considering an investment into Awaken. As I made the rounds during the cocktail reception, I found myself face to face with President George Herbert Walker Bush, now a strategic advisor to Carlyle. President Bush — who as a 20-year-old Naval aviator had bailed out of his burning aircraft in World War II — expressed to me his wish to skydive on his 80th birthday the following year. I wished him a safe jump and thanked Carlyle for its interest in our business.[19]

AS MINT'S PORTFOLIO MATURED, Tom Kirkwood, Wang Xin and I sought follow-on financings and exits. We successfully closed Series A financings from Carlyle, Draper Fisher, and Charles River Ventures. Our most

---

[19] Indeed, President Bush celebrated his 80th birthday by parachuting from 13,000 feet over his presidential library, on the campus of Texas A&M University, in College Station. It was a tandem jump, harnessed to a member of the U.S. Army's Golden Knights parachute team, because it was determined strong winds and low clouds made it too dangerous for a solo jump. President Bush also made a tandem jump to celebrate his 90th birthday, from a helicopter hovering at 6,000 feet near his summer home in Kennebunkport, Maine.

promising investee became Wang Bin's company: Awaken. But when it came to selling it off, it proved to be an emotional roller coaster.

The first suitor was Mforma: a leading global publisher and distributor of mobile entertainment. Mforma was shopping for an acquisition in China to grow its global footprint and justify a strong future initial public offering. Awaken's hold on China Mobile's infrastructure for Java content downloads to mobile phones seemed like a good fit. While Tom, Wang Xin and I excitedly pushed forward in negotiations with Mforma for the acquisition, Wang Bin held back out of some intuitive sense that he did not trust the CEO of Mforma. When the deal collapsed — largely due to Wang Bin's aversion to a union — we were crestfallen at the failure of our best company to successfully harvest the rewards of an exit. We would later learn that Mforma subsequently invested in the offensive Magus Soft in 2004. Mforma never succeeded in its IPO. Meanwhile, three years later, in 2007, we successfully sold Awaken to Glu Mobile LLC, a Nasdaq-listed U.S. developer and publisher of videogames for mobile phones and tablet computers. The sale price exceeded $35 million.

A summary of our track record at MINT over six years of active investing in our portfolio of 10 companies was eight strikeouts, one base hit — YeePay — and one home run: Awaken. Our total investment outlay, including cash and in-kind, added up to about $5 million. We had structured MINT as a corporation with equity in portfolio companies held as assets on MINT's balance sheet. As partners, we held equity in MINT alongside all our fund investors. We did not receive management fees or carry interest on exits. As a result, as our portfolio matured and we waited for exits, we needed to either raise new capital or find new work after placing all the money.

Looking back, I appreciated that Wang Xin and Tom Kirkwood each had proved to be a mentor and a colleague for me. We'd developed a close camaraderie, spending almost every workday shoulder to shoulder, facing setbacks, solving problems, celebrating successes. Yes, our trio worked very well together over the four years we ran MINT, investing our capital and nursing along our incubating investee startups.

AS THE COMPENSATION FOR my partners and my compensation from MINT dwindled, I again met with headhunters in China. The Korn Ferry firm referred me to Vesta Corp., a payments company for e-commerce merchants. Vesta was shopping for a mobile-payments business in China, and briefly considered MINT's payments business, YeePay. Eventually, Vesta decided to acquire a local business, Chinadotman, in early 2005, and asked me to join them as their representative on site in China, overseeing the Chinadotman operation and exploring other acquisitions.

And that is how I plunged into China's private-sector world of swashbuckling entrepreneurs, at the head of one of their bandit organizations. I would serve as liaison between Xiao Qingping — founder of our acquired Chinadotman — and Doug Fieldhouse, Vesta Corp.'s CEO in the United States. I would also become matchmaker between Lu Hongfa, founder of K-Pay, and Doug Fieldhouse.

I would directly witness private-sector triumphs.

With Vesta, I would encounter new business challenges in China. And I would discover there were limits for entrepreneurs in their competition with state-owned giants.

Chapter Nine

Chasing Pennies

The six beautiful young women stirred an uproar as they walked by our desks in the Chinadotman office in their miniskirts and bright makeup one afternoon in September 2005. Their faces were instantly recognizable to the twentysomething workers in our downtown Beijing office who had — along with hundreds of millions of Chinese viewers every week — tuned into the *Super Girl* vocal competition during its recently ended second season. They gasped with surprise and glee at the sight of these singing idols sauntering past their cubicles. Leading them was our smiling, swaggering, spiky-haired CEO, Xiao Qingping, who'd just taken them to lunch and now was parading them toward his office: a move obviously meant to impress the minions at his online and mobile-payments company.

Given the excitement their appearance generated, he'd definitely accomplished that. His stunt also underscored Xiao's clout in the nation's media industry. The astounding popularity of *Super Girl* had turned these singers in their late teens and early twenties into pop stars. The fact Xiao could take them to lunch indicated he had a special relationship with the executives at *Hunan Satellite Television*, which aired the series. A key element of the broadcasts was viewers voting for their favorite contestants via text message on their phones. Thanks to Xiao's masterful salesmanship, Chinadotman had secured the contract to provide the text-message service with the TV network. It was a business coup — as well as a sign of China's rapid embrace of Western entertainment models.

Hunan Satellite Television was the second-most-watched channel after *China Central Television (CCTV)*. *Super Girls* was similar to the global television franchise *American Idol* (United States) and *Pop Idol* (United Kingdom) and had become one of the most popular entertainment shows in China. The 2005 season — the show's second — had attracted more than 100,000 applicants during the preliminary selection rounds. Many of the aspiring vocalists had traveled great distances to audition for the competition, dreaming of stardom. Each hopeful was allowed 30 seconds to perform in front of judges and find out if she was selected for the regional rounds.

The final episode of the 2005 season, which aired on Aug. 26, was one of the most popular airings in Chinese broadcast history, drawing more than 400 million viewers — surpassing the audience for *CCTV's New Year's Gala* earlier that year. Perhaps it was no surprise that executives at *CCTV* criticized *Super Girl* as being "vulgar and manipulative."

Vulgar and manipulative — or not — *Super Girls* had claimed staggering viewership ratings. And one of the main factors contributing to its massive audience was that viewers were able to participate in the judging process by sending text messages with their mobile phones to vote for their favorite contestants, using Chinadotman's SMS platform. Millions of votes were cast to determine the top three contestants — each vote costing the voter a charge of 0.5 to 3 yuan. Jim Yardley of the *International Herald Tribune* wrote that viewer voting for *Super Girl* competitors was considered one of the largest "democratic" voting exercises in mainland China. (In fact, the following year, more than 800 million text messages were sent during the third season of *Super Girl*.)

The texting tallies thrilled me. I was vice president, China operations manager, with Vesta China Ltd., the company that owned Chinadotman. Vesta China was a subsidiary of Vesta Corp., a U.S.-based major-payments processor for e-commerce and prepaid mobile recharge. Vesta Corp.'s primary clients included mobile-communications giants such as AT&T, T-Mobile, and Verizon. Vesta Corp. had acquired Chinadotman early in 2005 and hired me in June. Now I was overseeing this operation, leading Vesta China in building commission income from mobile-value added services, online travel air-ticket purchases and pre-paid card transactions. *Super Girl* certainly contributed in a super way to Chinadotman's bottom line. The company chased pennies per vote — and earned millions of dollars in profits from the hundreds of millions of votes cast.

But not everyone was delighted with this phenomenon of hundreds of millions of Chinese viewers casting votes via text message. Mass voting, and the revolutionary widespread suffrage enabled by the lucrative texting business, could not escape the attention of officials high up in the Chinese Communist Party. (In 2006, Liu Zhongde, a delegate with the Chinese People's Political Consultive Conference — an advisory body with clout in the Chinese Communist Party's network of organizations and individuals that push the party's platform — would claim that the show was "poison for the youth" of the nation. Eventually, the central government's media regulator ordered that *Super Girl* be terminated without delay: killing a lucrative market for Chinadotman.[20])

---

[20] Martinsen, Joel, Laodanwei.org, Danwei: Chinese media, advertising, and urban life, April 26, 2006.

But there in late 2005, *Super Girl* was flying high. And no one could be prouder than Chinadotman's CEO: Xiao Qingping.

Xiao personified to me the new breed of maverick mogul driving China's new economy forward, with the spirit that his fast-modernizing nation was a Land of Opportunity, and boldness, creativity and political savvy would yield fortunes.

His was an interesting story itself.

XIAO QINGPING WAS A year younger than I, and a self-made multi-millionaire. He stood 5-foot-9 but carried himself with the presence of a giant in China's rising telecommunications industry. Xiao's mind was extremely quick with numbers, his business instincts keen like a professional poker player coolly calculating the playing cards and slyly sizing up his competitors.

Xiao hailed from Hunan Province, the land of Mao Zedong, and had a twinkle in his eye. Hunan natives have a reputation for mischievous personalities, and Xiao struck me as always being ready to do something daring or naughty. He always had a grin on his face. Sometimes I pictured him as a swashbuckling bandit, although he typically wore a nice suit without a tie, his dress shirt unbuttoned at the top, his feet in stylish but casual loafers. He sported a luxury gold watch surely purchased in Hong Kong, and drove a late-model Mercedes. He liked living well, although as a rags-to-riches success story, he was hardly one to pay more than the minimum necessary to his employees. He drove a hard bargain in business deals and as an employer.

A dozen years earlier, Xiao had left behind his poverty-stricken Hunan in central China to go to the southern island of Hainan to get rich during the go-go 1990s real-estate boom. He'd correctly sensed there were opportunities to be had. Back in the early 1990s, the Hainanese economy had liberalized, attracting economic migrants from elsewhere in China. Helped by a lack of central-government regulation and a flow of easy money, Hainan authorities encouraged property development; as a result, floor space under construction surged 750 percent between 1990 and 1995 (although admittedly from a low base). The boom market had promptly imploded after the central government in Beijing tightened monetary policy and prodded banks into canceling or calling in loans — triggering the collapse of numerous developers and credit unions.

Xiao, however, had kept a step ahead. He'd ridden the Hainan development wave, enriching himself, while dodging the worst consequences of the collapse. His next big move was to Beijing, seeking to exploit new opportunities in the expanding Internet market. He set up Chinadotman to capture revenues in both the mobile-phone and desktop-computer markets for web use — again, rightly gambling on an industry on the verge of booming.

In those days, mobile-phone penetration was high in China, but bank debit and credit cards were not common. Xiao leveraged premium text-messaging as a payment channel in which the carrier's texting charges covered payments for Internet content and services. Users would text a short code, 9588, used by Chinadotman and receive an activation code to pay for votes, downloads of videos, purchase of game credits and other content. While Chinadotman earned pennies per text charge, the company scaled up returns by attracting millions of users to consume the most popular content provided by Xiao's business-owner friends.

Xiao was the mastermind who'd maneuvered Chinadotman into position to connect viewer votes with *Hunan Satellite TV*, via our SMS platform. He simply was one of the best sales- and marketing-focused entrepreneurs I had met in China. The *Super Girl* phenomenon underscored this. Xiao had exploited the fact that he was a native of Hunan to win the contract from *Hunan Satellite TV* to provide vote-texting service for *Super Girls*. Xiao and his team were experts in leveraging the Internet in exploiting money-making opportunities.

I directly learned the power of Xiao's ability to manipulate the Internet via software that could swing user volumes to Chinadotman and other targets. In early 2008, prior to the Beijing Summer Olympics, the central government announced a competition to select three foreigners to participate in the Olympic Torch Relay across China. Interested foreigners could submit their candidacy in an online application, and the general Internet audience could vote for their preferred candidates. I figured I'd give it a shot myself.

Applying late in the process, I discovered that my ranking among candidates lagged near the bottom. I didn't have high hopes of winning a torch. I casually mentioned to Xiao that I had thrown my hat into the ring. He noted the details of my application and bade me be patient. The next time I checked my ranking, I'd shot up hundreds of places. Over the course of the final two weeks of the contest, I rocketed into the Top 10 and qualified to receive a genuine Beijing 2008 Olympic Torch and certificate!

I had to thank Xiao for the amazing contribution created by his mysterious computer manipulation.

IN ADDITION TO STEERING Chinadotman to massive success in providing payments via mobile texting, Xiao built an online travel business selling air tickets and hotel reservations.

This service was supported via a mobile-phone app, a website and a live-call center. Xiao had linked the service to payments via all major domestic bank debit and credit cards in China. Chinadotman typically earned 1 to 3 percent commission on processing purchases of air tickets and hotel reservations. As with our mobile-texting service, we were chasing pennies, so to speak, on the sales of plane tickets and room reservations, but hoped we would make money on volume. However, online travel is a marketing-intensive business requiring significant expenditure in advertising. This restricted our returns, so we looked for a competitive edge.

We embarked on building payments connections to international charge cards via our U.S. parent company, Vesta. This would differentiate us from other Chinese online travel companies who struggled with a cumbersome, high-friction payment process for international cards. Customers would have to provide a great deal of personal information, including driver's license copies, to complete a transaction. In contrast, we tried presenting a frictionless process for our customers, using systems Vesta employed in the United States. They would enjoy convenience in using their charge cards, and access to fully discounted air tickets.

One big challenge we faced was that online travel is highly susceptible to payment fraud. Scammers abound, seeking to steal credit-card information and other personal information via fake websites. When we launched payments with international cards, we exposed ourselves to the international world of fraud. Within months of offering services to foreigners, we began experiencing significant levels of chargebacks for fraudulent card use. Cardholders would notice unauthorized air-ticket charges on their monthly statements and report them to their credit-card company, who would then assess charge-backs to us on the fraudulent ticket purchases.

Recovering the loss on the face value of one ticket required us selling 50 to 100 tickets, given our tiny commission rate. We discovered that criminal insiders at banks in the United States were selling card lists to swindlers — who then used them to purchase easily fenced online goods such as airline tickets and mobile-telephone time.

As part of combating this problem, we resolved to organize a sting operation at an airport where the holders of known fraudulently purchased tickets would appear for check-in. We zeroed in on one particular case. The purchase had taken place but the boarding date for the flight at Guangzhou Baiyun International Airport, in southern Guangdong Province, had not yet arrived.

I proposed we send one of our employees to the airport to intercept the ticket holders. We also contacted the local Chinese police to help apprehend the criminals. However, when the police learned that foreigners were involved, and that the value of their crimes was relatively low, they declined to involve themselves.

I attribute this to Chinese law enforcement's general reluctance to interfere in foreign-affairs matters, and preference to investigate much larger-value crimes. That did not foster a favorable environment for free enterprise. At least, not of the legitimate kind.

Our employee did approach the fraudulent ticket holders in the airport — but without police present at the scene, the interdiction was ineffective. He was blown off.

ONE OF MY DUTIES running Vesta China Ltd. was ferreting out new opportunities to branch into.

During my nearly three years with the company, I met another entrepreneur, Lu Hongfa, who — like Xiao Qingping — had made money in the Hainan property bubble, then ventured into the Internet industry. Lu was now in Beijing, running a company called K-Pay. At my initiative, Chinadotman bought K-Pay.

Lu was about the same age as Xiao, yet very much his opposite. Lu was stoic and hardly hip. He was balding and sported a combover hairstyle. Instead of a flashy luxury car, he drove a boxy four-wheel-drive Land Rover. He did flaunt his wealth in one way: Like Xiao, he wore expensive watches procured in Hong Kong.

K-Pay's core business was selling scratch cards for mobile-phone time. As an authorized dealer for mobile carriers, K-Pay would distribute paper scratch cards to convenience stores for sale to mobile users. The mobile user would purchase the card, scratch it to access an activation code, and add credit to the mobile phone. K-Pay earned around 1 percent of the face value of the card. The significant effort and cost expended to distribute physical cards across Beijing limited returns on the business. Lu, however, hoped that the carriers might one day consent to K-Pay selling phone time online via its own website. This would offer K-Pay much less expensive distribution and a more lucrative business model.

We waited for several years in vain for dealer online distribution, which never was allowed by the state-owned Chinese carriers.

We helped Lu build a second business centered on payments using stored-value transit cards. Commuters could use their transit cards by swiping them in a K-Pay reader to pay for low-value items in convenience stores. We sourced a custom-designed card reader from a factory run by Blue Bamboo, a Shanghai-based manufacturer of point-of-sale terminals. We built a network of 5,000 readers in convenience stores across Beijing. To our dismay, the city's transit authority restricted K-Pay to commissions of less than 1 percent on the value of each transaction.

Again, we were stymied by a state sector that was too stingy and oblivious to the growth potential of the business that would have been possible from incentivizing its private-sector partners with reasonable revenue sharing.

"Chasing pennies" means to expend more money or effort in gaining something than it is worth. This was the essence of the low-return businesses of Chinadotman and K-Pay. They made money as sole proprietorships but not on a large scale. This was partly due to the limits on revenue sharing imposed on the private sector by the state-owned mobile carriers and Beijing's transit authority. The state kept the majority of the profits at the expense of limiting the overall growth of the pie shared with its private-sector partners. The state-owned enterprises were strangling their private-sector partners and sucking the oxygen out of the consumer ecosystem.

The few big private-sector winners in China often raised hundreds of millions of dollars from venture capitalists or via initial public offerings to build market share nationwide, while eking out relatively meager profits on pennies per transaction. But Xiao and Lu lacked the will and the resources to raise hundreds of millions of dollars to pour into building market share across China. Instead, they set their sights on relocating their families and wealth to the United States.

They had limited expectations for the Chinese government's approach to capitalism and how the economy should grow.

MANY OF MY CHINESE entrepreneur friends were busy plowing their wealth into real estate in Beijing and Shanghai — and also into houses in the United States or Canada. That's right: They were transferring their capital abroad. In addition to property, some wealthy Chinese were purchasing portable assets such as collectable art, fine wine, and even diamonds.

Precious stones were easily taken out of China: yet another way to carry wealth (literally) out of the country. Here's a little anecdote about the trade in gems:

Vesta's CEO, Doug Fieldhouse, was visiting China. A board meeting for Chinadotman was scheduled in Yunan Province, in southwest China. Xiao Qingping, Doug and I traveled to Yunan. In the provincial capital, Kunming, Xiao took us to a bar and met up with an advisor on the board: an older Chinese man who sported a gold tooth and a long pinky fingernail. He'd arranged for a ruby dealer to meet us.

At our table, the dealer produced boxes of the little red gemstones popular in jewelry. Xiao lifted a handful out and inspected them. A ruby fell from his hand and dropped inside his shirt, which was tucked into his pants. It slipped down into his pants. The dealer grew very agitated. Xiao impishly had to extract it.

(Chinese antiques were another commodity being smuggled out of China, but the government was watchful to stymie this trade, which had spurred a flourishing market of wealthy collectors buying these artifacts in Hong Kong. When my family prepared to move from China in 2015, a government inspector came to our home to check everything we were packing up.)

As China's modernizing economy spawned nouveau riche, the real-estate market in the early 2000s was booming in the major cities. On the recommendation of one friend, I purchased an apartment in downtown Beijing. The property value doubled within three years! But my friend — like so many prospering professionals and entrepreneurs — was planning a future outside of his native land. He and others had their sights on homes outside China. I asked him how he and his friends managed to purchase properties in America. After all, China maintains a closed capital account, and Chinese citizens are generally not permitted to move more than $50,000 out of the country.

He explained that Chinese who wanted to sneak out more than $50,000 to buy overseas assets — such as a house in New York, San Francisco or Vancouver, British Columbia — formed an investment pool with family members or friends, each person transferring the $50,000 limit out of China. The process is called "smurfing" in the banking industry; in Chinese, it's known as "ants moving their house." Chinese banks often turned a blind eye to these practices. At that time, the central government wasn't vigilant or skilled at monitoring bank transactions; smurfers were adept at evading the relatively lax governmental monitors.

Yes, the country's wealthy found inventive ways to bypass China's strict capital controls, and transfer money abroad. One method was using underground private banks, which are popular in China's southeastern provinces such as Guangdong. A Chinese resident can deposit 1 million yuan in his or her account in a domestic private bank and take out the same value of money in foreign currencies in the bank's overseas branches within hours.

Other methods for capital flight include overpaying for imports, and acquiring an overseas business at an inflated value. Using fake invoices, the wealthy can transfer capital overseas to pay for imported goods and deposit the surplus cash in a foreign bank. Many rich Chinese acquired businesses in Singapore and other safe-haven locations in which to park their capital.

CHINESE CITIZENS WERE NOT only getting rich as entrepreneurs; some did so in a more time-honored way: through exploiting political connections. This surely was the case with the person who bought my house in 2013.

In 2009, I'd purchased a detached stucco villa in a fancy residential compound called "Yosemite" in the northwest suburbs of Beijing. The development was deliberately designed (and named) to attract Western expatriates such as myself, as well as Chinese nouveau riche. I'd taken advantage of some creative financing to get into the multimillion-dollar home, by seeking a bridge loan from a couple of my old business partners in China. The Hong Kong-based Bank of East Asia, which was very bullish on China property, eagerly processed my paperwork and arranged a U.S. dollar loan to me in Hong Kong to pay my partners back.

Shannon and I renovated our villa. By 2012, its market value had doubled, and we decided to sell. Although the real-estate market was still rising, I'd started getting cold feet. I knew China's economy is unpredictable. I didn't want to risk a market crash. (As it turned out, this timing would prove premature. The property in Beijing continued skyrocketing.) I listed our house on the market. That was like pouring blood in shark-infested waters. Multiple wealthy Chinese buyers persistently contacted me, willing to satisfy one of my sales terms: paying me the entire sales price in U.S. dollars, to my bank account in Hong Kong.

Our home sale turned into a de facto auction. Our listed price was topped by one buyer, then topped by another in turn. Shannon and I held out. Then a mysterious young woman in her late twenties showed up with an extremely attractive offer. She worked at the Bank of China in wealth management, and would not have been able to afford the house on her salary. However, she was driving her elderly father around in a Porsche. That gave me a clue to her access to cash. I never did meet her father; while she met with Shannon and me, he remained in the Porsche's passenger seat outside.

One of my sales terms was non-negotiable: a lease-back option so that I could lease the home from the buyer for a year. My family planned to continue living in the home for that duration. The woman agreed to this term. With that, I had my Chinese lawyer arrange the transaction.

I supplied the woman with my account number in the Hong Kong and Shanghai Banking Corp. (the Hong Kong subsidiary of the London-based HSBC). By whatever means she had at her disposal, she successfully transferred the purchase price to my account in installments, notifying me each time a deposit was transacted. I then transferred the house's title to her.

I can only guess that her father was well-connected in the Communist Party — and therefore she'd had access to the capital to acquire our villa.

All this took place in 2013: a number of years in the future from my time at Vesta China Ltd. I would stay with Vesta for three years — 2005-2008 — during my time in China. It was during this period that Shannon and I added another child to our household.

IN 2006, SHANNON AND I decided to adopt a baby from China. We wanted another child, and decided to go the adoption route. Thus, we embarked on a complicated, multi-year adoption process.

First, we needed to satisfy China's adoption-eligibility requirements for age, family size, annual income, net worth, sexual orientation (no gays allowed as parents) and good health (AIDS victims were excluded).

The Chinese officials requested that we be vetted by a U.S. adoption agency before our application could proceed. We paid one such agency's fee, and an American woman who worked in China for the agency came to our house and interviewed Shannon and me and our three children. The agency helped us complete the adoption home-study process and guided us through the rest of the necessary steps for an international adoption — including getting finger-printed at the U.S. Embassy in Beijing, so that the FBI could run a background check on us, documenting our identities.

This whole process took more than a year. Then Shannon and I waited month after month, without any correspondence from Chinese authorities, for a referral to an infant up for adoption. It was as if our dossier had disappeared down a black hole.

In early 2008, I received an express-mail package at our house in Beijing. Inside the slim envelope was a photograph of a 6-month-old girl; her official medical record in Chinese, giving her a clean bill of health; and an official letter in English stating that this infant had been selected for us, and asked if we accepted or rejected adopting her. She was now 8 months old (the photo being two months old) and being cared for in a state-run orphanage in Nanning, in southern Guangxi Province. Should we decline adopting her, the letter explained, our position on the waiting list of parents seeking adoption would revert to the end.

Shannon and I let our Chinese friends peruse the medical report. They were skeptical of its accuracy. How could we be certain the report was factual, they said. The Chinese are naturally skeptical of official government reports. Shannon and I brought the report to a health clinic we used as foreigners and asked the physicians there to examine the report.

Their response? *The baby is healthy.* Shannon and I either had to believe the report, or not. We decided that the Chinese officials would never pass along a child who was physically or mentally disabled. So we went on good faith. We proceeded enthusiastically with the mindset we'd be welcoming a healthy baby girl into our family.

The next step involved setting up a visit to the baby girl in Nanning, and a court date in front of a magistrate to be questioned for final approval. This took another three months to be arranged. The only solace my wife and I took in this slow process was that Shannon had actually received favorable treatment in the Chinese system because she had a foreign-diplomat visa (not a visa as a U.S. citizen), as she worked for an organization that was part of the World Bank, which is part of the United Nations. Shannon was in China on a *laissez-passer* passport, which gave her special status, and afforded us special expediting in the adoption process.

In late 2008, Shannon and I checked into a hotel in Nanning to await the arrival of our baby, whom we'd decided to name Julie. We felt a strange anticipation. This was very different from how our two daughters and son had arrived. There would be no nine-month leadup of pregnancy and then delivery. We would be receiving a grown baby.

When Julie, now 11 months old, arrived at the hotel with her nannies from the orphanage, she slept while we drank tea and learned details about her. The nannies told us that she had been found left in a park. The backstory was that she'd likely ended up in the park because her mother had been a very young woman who lacked the means of caring for her. The police had picked up the foundling and followed procedure by posting a notice about her in the local newspaper. There were no claimers.

Shannon and I knew that an alternate explanation of the baby's journey to the orphanage is that poor families in rural areas sometimes sold newborns to baby brokers operating in a black market. This seems grim, but not as tragic as a mother and her family abandoning or killing an unwanted infant.

Later, after the nannies left, Julie awoke to find, to her fright, only Shannon and me. Two large, strange, white faces. She calmed down when she realized we were feeding her with a bottle. Over the course of cuddling and feeding, she warmed to us. The initial visit with the baby girl had gone well.

The next day, we appeared with Julie before a Chinese magistrate, who questioned us in Chinese about our family, our upbringing of our other children, and our intentions for Julie relative to our other children. Finding our answers satisfactory, she stamped our Chinese adoption papers with a big red chop. We were now the legal parents of Julie in China.

We then waited about a week while the local public security department created for Julie an official identity number (making her a citizen of China) and Chinese passport. While we waited, we visited Julie's orphanage — by Chinese standards, it was tidy and well run — and toured the sights of the southern city of Nanning.

Shannon and I joyously rendezvoused with our other children in Guangzhou. Lindsay, 13, Trevor, 10, and Caroline, 6, arrived in tow with their nanny. They got to meet their new baby sister. It was quite a moving scene. They were excited to meet Julie. Each wanted to hold her.

Shannon and I had another obstacle to clear with Julie: She needed U.S. citizenship. After all, our family eventually would be moving back to the States. Julie could legally leave China with us with her Chinese passport. But to legally live in the United States, she had to be a U.S. citizen. This proved to be another bureaucratic hassle.

Shannon and I went to the U.S. consulate in Guangzhou, where a service provided adopted Chinese children a special U.S. visa. We flew with her to Honolulu to engage in an expedited naturalization process at an office of the Department of Homeland Security. The "expedited process" involved federal agents interviewing our family and former neighbors and coworkers.

Somehow, it all got resolved, and within a couple weeks Shannon, Julie and I were reunited with our other three children in Beijing.

Julie fit in well. When Shannon and I took her in a stroller in public, we didn't get more than the usual odd looks from Chinese people seeing foreigners. As they eyed Julie, they quickly gathered that a Chinese child had been adopted by foreigners.

We were very happy. My wife always says the most important thing she and I got out of China — more than any of our work experiences, or friendships we'd made — was Julie.

Chapter Ten

Creating the People's EV

"Hi, Mark, I've got something that should be of interest to you."

It was the relaxed, confident voice of Kevin Czinger on the other end of the line. Bright, vibrant, and captivating — just like I remembered from the time we'd met, four years before. Kevin's tone was that of a gifted salesman, yet he was much more than that. He was an accomplished entrepreneur driven by a formidable will to succeed. That I remembered, too.

I was all ears.

"Mark, I've been riding around Los Angeles in an electric vehicle made by Miles Electric Vehicles," he continued. "These guys have a great future in sourcing electric cars from China."

Cars.

Instantly, my excitement wilted, replaced by a rush of nausea. I suppressed a groan. *Here we go again with another dud automotive venture . . .*

Like a post-traumatic stress reaction, my mind flashed back to my two-and-a-half-year tenure as general manager of the Beijing Fuel Pump & Fuel Injector Co.: coping with massive employee theft of products to sell on the black market, as well as China's lag in technology to foreign competitors.

I was absolutely the wrong person to entertain a pitch to get involved with a Chinese company having anything to do with manufacturing cars or their parts. But Kevin knew that. Sharp and focused as he was, he'd anticipated my mental reaction. And he didn't miss a beat.

"It's not what you think," he said with warm reassurance. "This is a whole new opportunity in automotive with a lot of potential."

It was early spring 2008. I was approaching my three-year anniversary as vice president, China operations manager, with Vesta China Ltd. Vesta was an innovative and aggressive company providing various web-based services in the mushrooming mobile-phone industry, yet it had smacked up against glass ceilings created by the stubborn, change-resistant regulation of China's central government. Needless to say, I was hungry for a new challenge.

But . . . an offer to plunge back into China's automotive industry?

Been there, done that.

If I was eager for anything in my professional life, it was to explore new industries, not backtrack into any type of manufacturing. And certainly not automobiles. But Kevin Czinger was persistent.

"Just think about it for a bit, Mark," he said. "We can chat again."

And so we did. And over the course of subsequent phone calls and emails, Kevin continued working to recruit me to a managerial position with the U.S.-based Miles Electric Vehicles, so I could help him build a business in electric cars sourced in China.

The concept wasn't bad. It was to manufacture low-cost, all-electric vehicles for the U.S. market. While I could see, as well as anyone, that EVs were certainly the future of automobile manufacturing — replacing internal-combustion engines — my reluctance to jumping back into the automotive industry, or even getting involved in *any* sort of factory operation in China, was profound.

However, the "Kevin Factor" was at play now. Kevin Czinger was the irresistible force to my immovable object. What's more, the fact he was involved in Miles Electric Vehicles was intriguing in and of itself. Here was a successful investment banker who'd helped score winning deals for Goldman Sachs, and he was impressed with Miles Electric Vehicles. I started entertaining the potential of this project. Maybe Kevin's willpower could drive Miles Electric Vehicles toward success in making low-cost EVs in China to sell in America?

What I knew of Kevin Czinger was that he was a man who could be brutally focused on the objectives he set for himself.

While I didn't say yes right away, I didn't say no, either.

I'D MET KEVIN in 2004, when he'd paid a visit to my office at Mobile Internet (Asia) Ltd. — MINT, for short — in Beijing. I was a partner in this investment fund developing seed-stage mobile-phone businesses in China. Kevin had been referred to me by my youngest brother, Jon, who'd attended Yale Law School, as had Kevin, and worked with Kevin on a charter school initiative in New Haven. Kevin was representing Yale's enormous endowment fund; he was in China ferreting out promising investment opportunities.

My first impression of Kevin was that he bore a striking resemblance to British icon James Bond as played by actor Daniel Craig. Kevin was about

5-foot-9 and all muscle. He wasn't a typical Yale alumnus. His background was a Horatio Alger story. He'd grown up in a working-class family in Cleveland. His surname is pronounced "Zinger"; it's Hungarian. His ancestors on his father's and mother's sides came from several different European countries before immigrating to America. Kevin was exceptionally ambitious. The youngest of five children, he became the first in his family to attend a private school — St. Ignatius, a Catholic Jesuit high school — where he excelled on the football field. While shorter than the typical football player, Kevin literally pushed himself to become physically powerful. His mother would sit behind the steering wheel of the family car while Kevin shoved it up a hill.

Kevin's gridiron prowess helped earn him admission to Yale, making him the first in his family to go to college. On the football field for the Bulldogs, he played linebacker — a position perfectly suited to an aggressive defender who acts like a self-guided missile, trusted by his coach to instinctively read where a play is heading, then rocket toward a bone-rattling tackle. Kevin set Yale team records for quarterback sacks, earned the Most Valuable Player honor in the Ivy League, and helped the Bulldogs win back-to-back league titles.[21]

After graduating in 1982, Kevin served as an infantry rifleman in the U.S. Marine Corps Reserves and worked for about a year as an oilfield roughneck on drilling crews. Then his thirst for knowledge and self-advancement, combined with encouragement from a Yale professor who saw his potential, led him to Yale Law School. In his third year, 1986, he worked as a summer associate at Goldman Sachs, the giant investment bank. After doing a stint as a federal prosecutor in New York City, Kevin was recruited by Goldman Sachs, where he learned firsthand how money makes the world go round. As a junior executive, he

---

[21] As a side note, I asked Kevin after I got to know him whether he liked watching football games on television. He answered in the negative, explaining that football was a violent experience for him where his objective at the start of every game was to inflict as much pain as possible on opposing players, to create intimidation.

worked with senior executives on major acquisitions brokered by his employer in Asia, including the purchase by global media magnate Rupert Murdoch of *Star TV*, the giant television network based in Hong Kong.

Kevin applied his now well-developed financial knowledge to building his own portfolio as a private-equity investor. When he contacted me in 2004 —exploring potential investments for Yale's endowment fund — he recognized that my company, MINT, was an early player in nurturing startups creating Internet platforms and applications for telecom customers to use with their mobile phones. These devices already were booming in usage in China and Japan, well ahead of the Western world, where ordinary consumers had little inkling their cell phones would evolve for usage as cameras, computers and music players.

Kevin was energetic and charismatic and forward thinking. But in the end, various deals we tried forging — including investing in a mobile-music service — didn't pan out. Nevertheless, I remained on his radar as a potential manager for whatever China-related enterprise he might get involved in down the road.

That had led him to contact me in 2008 after he'd embraced electric vehicles as the future of automobiles, as well as a way to reverse global warming, and wanted to mass produce them. And he wasn't one to take no for an answer.

KEVIN CONTINUED PITCHING ME on joining Miles Electric Vehicles to manage its Chinese manufacturing operation, which they were planning. Kevin was Miles Electric Vehicles' president and CEO. He needed an American manager who could bridge the communications and cultural gap between a U.S. company and Chinese partners.

I was used to that role by now!

Kevin sent me an investment report about EVs, from multinational investment bank Morgan Stanley. The report confirmed the capabilities and feasibility of new technologies — particularly, lithium-ion batteries and electric drivetrains — to power inexpensive electric cars with sufficient range and speed to compete with conventional cars. Surging oil prices above $140 per barrel in early 2008 made EVs a very attractive alternative to internal-combustion vehicles. Tesla was in the early stage of producing all-electric roadsters for wealthy buyers. Kevin approached the vision of producing electric cars as a crusade to end oil dependence, and to combat the harm from carbon emissions to our environment for us and our children. These objectives, he declared, should be shared by the United States and China: the world's two largest economies.

How could I not agree?

Even as early as 2008, China's government viewed the development of an electric-vehicle industry as a moonshot opportunity to leapfrog the developed world in automotive technology. China's automotive industry lacked core-design capabilities in conventional internal-combustion engine cars, including for the design of engines and automatic transmissions. Therefore, China's leaders hoped to leverage the nation's capacity for inexpensive car production (given its immense pool of cheap labor) with large-scale, cheap, lithium-ion battery production. Electric-car drivetrains based on motors and transaxles are significantly less complicated than those of gasoline-powered vehicles, and have many fewer parts than internal-combustion engines with automatic transmissions. China also happened to be the rising producer — behind Japan and South Korea — of lithium-ion batteries for consumer electronics and personal computers. The pieces of the puzzle fit very well together!

I realized Kevin Czinger was really onto something with this entrepreneurial idea. What's more, it was a crusade to save the planet for him. I could tell that was what motivated him even more than seeking profits.

I decided to learn more about Miles Electric Vehicles. I discovered that this company was the brainchild of Miles L. Rubin, a businessman approaching age 80 who'd founded the company in Los Angeles in 2004. Miles was a member of the so-called "Malibu Mafia": an informal group of wealthy American Jewish businessmen, Hollywood executives and intellectuals who'd donated money to liberal and progressive causes and politicians in the 1960s through '90s. Rubin, concerned by growing environmental problems linked to carbon emissions, drove a Toyota Prius hybrid. By founding Miles Electric Vehicles, he set out to make a difference by developing a line of safe, affordable, all-electric vehicles that produce zero emissions.

Miles centered the company's sourcing activities in Tianjin, China, where the battery industry had expert manufacturing experience. Miles Electric Vehicles began importing low-speed electric vehicles, which were exempt from the stricter U.S. safety regulations for regular gas-fueled vehicles, such as for airbags. Miles Electric Vehicles' cars and trucks were electronically limited to 25 miles per hour and were only street legal for use on roads with posted speed limits up to 35 mph. However, Miles Electric Vehicles aimed to build on its experience in producing low-speed vehicles to develop an all-electric, midsize sedan that could cruise at highway speed.

It could be a tremendous competitor in the U.S. car market.

Miles Rubin was working tirelessly in his advanced years to connect the dots among players in the Chinese auto and battery industries to source affordable all-electric vehicles for export to the United States. Miles Electric Vehicles gained prominence in 2005 when it began sales of the ZX40: the first street-legal Chinese-made automobile sold in the United States. The company offered a variety of compact utility cars and trucks available to fleet buyers in the United States. Security firms and parks management were typical fleet buyers. The EVs were used for onsite transportation for employees by entities such as NASA, the U.S. Navy, Yale, Rice University, Stanford University, UCLA, California Polytechnic State University, the San Francisco Airport Authority, Bennington College, and the city of Provo, Utah.

The low-speed vehicles offered a mix of older and newer EV technologies. They used wet-cell, lead-acid, deep-cycle batteries weighing around 100 pounds each. These batteries are similar to those found in older forklifts and vintage electric golf carts. For the 2008 model year, Miles introduced AC motors for its low-speed vehicles, offering four times the available power of typical DC motors. This increase in available power from the AC motor allowed the vehicles to come with options for air conditioning and heat: standard functions in traditional cars. Another innovation by Miles in its cars was the adoption of regenerative braking to capture kinetic energy from the vehicle slowing down; this energy was stored in the battery. In general, low-speed fleet vehicles sold for $20,000 and offered a driving range of 20 miles.

By 2008, Miles Electric Vehicles was contracting and sourcing low-speed cars and pickup trucks from China's state-owned Tianjin-Qingyuan Electric Vehicle Co. (TQEV for short). The pickup truck, called the "Minyi," was a small utility truck based on a Suzuki design from Japan, and produced by state-owned Hafei Motor Co. Meanwhile, Miles' mini-compact car was produced by a subsidiary of China's state-owned First Auto Works, which licensed the design from Daihatsu from Japan and sold the cars in China as the Huali "Happy Messenger." TQEV received bodies called "gliders," without drivetrains or batteries, and added the motor, battery and electrical components in their purpose-built assembly factory in Tianjin. TQEV exported finished vehicles in shipping containers to Miles Electric Vehicles' facility in Los Angeles.

Now — as Kevin Czinger recruited me to join the company — it was at a key juncture. Miles Rubin intended to join the automotive big league with his planned Miles XS500: a highway-speed, all-electric midsize sedan. The sedan would sport a top speed of 80 mph, and a range of 120 miles at 60 mph — which would make it an attractive option for many car buyers considering going electric to benefit the environment, as well as to save on spending dollars at the gas pump. The price tag of $30,000 ($23,000 after U.S. government rebates) for the XS500 would be kept down thanks to low Chinese manufacturing costs. Miles Rubin wanted TQEV to upgrade from low-speed vehicles to the XS500 within a few years. TQEV's engineers would be responsible for the design.

Maybe the XS500 could take market share from Toyota Prius?

Finally, I caved in and told Kevin yes. Though it meant returning to the automotive industry, in May 2008 I accepted his offer to manage Miles Electric Vehicles' manufacturing operation in China. I was the company's first hire in China.

Would it be like my other journeys in manufacturing in China? Would the drive be fraught with potholes, detours and wrong turns — a road trip to disappointment and failure?

Or would it be a cruise down a highway leading to great destinations?

In any event, my ride began . . .

MY TITLE WITH MILES Electric Vehicles was senior vice president, China Operations manager. My job focused on working with TQEV onsite at its 5,000-square-meter, 100-employee factory in Tianjin, to monitor the assembly operation for low-speed trucks and cars. The two-hour drive from my home in Beijing to the TQEV factory in Tianjin was not unreasonable. My strategy was to drive down and spend most of the week on site at TQEV, working long hours each day and staying in a local hotel at night, then return home for the weekend.

On May 12, 2008, my first day at TQEV, I walked through the factory following the progress of a line of low-speed trucks in a state of partial assembly. My mobile phone rang, and Wang Xin, my old business partner at MINT, greeted me on the other end.

"Did you feel it?" he asked. "There was a big earthquake in Sichuan, and we even had tremors here in Beijing."

Would the Sichuan earthquake, which killed as many as 80,000 people, become an omen for me of shaky times to come in our development of electric-vehicle sourcing in China? Well, it wasn't long before my initial enthusiasm and optimism were tempered by consternation and nagging pessimism. As Yogi Berra famously said, "It's like *déjà vu all over again.*"

State-owned TQEV's management team members came from automotive-research institutes in China and lacked experience running large-scale car-assembly factories. On the surface, this may not have seemed much of an issue, because the production process for the low-speed vehicles was quite simple. Gliders would arrive from Hafei Motor Co. The TQEV factory had an automated conveyor line. Robotic arms with overhead clamps would grab onto a glider, lift it off the floor and carry it on a straight line along the production line. At a certain point, the arms would raise the glider high enough so that workers could install the motor, transaxle and the lead-acid battery pack by pushing them up and fastening them into the bottom of the glider.

Bring the glider in one door and send the completed vehicle out the other door. That was the process. Where a major flaw existed was in the building of the gliders at Hafei Motor Co. TQEV's management had no presence at Hafei's factory in Harbin. There was no one from TQEV monitoring the glider production to ensure quality control. And as it soon became glaringly clear, the quality was inconsistent, to put it politely.

Gliders were arriving at the Tianjin factory eight or more at a time on vehicle-transport trucks. Unbeknownst to us in Tianjin, a fair number of the gliders were being negligently left out in the rain in Harbin. That led to them gathering rust under their beds. This rust could not be detected at our end unless we were to unbolt every bed to check for oxidation. That would have been impractical. But there were even more serious issues with carelessly produced gliders than rust. One such issue was poorly installed brake lines with high-pressure hydraulic fluid.

Gliders, of course, can't be test-driven, for they lack drivetrains and batteries. So if a brake line is loose fitting, you wouldn't know it until the entire car is assembled and then test driven. But TQEV's managers weren't interested in taking this extra step. Their viewpoint was that their company was only responsible for installing the drivetrains and batteries.

TQEV's general manager, Mr. Wang, was not a hands-on, production-minded manager, by any means. He was an academic who had industrialized some leading-edge ideas in electric cars. Even in the highly political world of Chinese business, he would not have been seen as qualified to run a car factory. I didn't trust him. I didn't see him as corrupt; he wasn't in the same vein, for example, as the original general manager at Beijing Fuel Pump & Fuel Injector Co., where products had been stolen off the floor and sold on the black market. But he was simply a political creature.

Mr. Wang wanted Miles Electric Vehicles to remain committed to TQEV, since his core business was winning money grants from the central government to pay for his pet projects. Assembling small batches of low-speed electric vehicles for Miles Electric Vehicles helped TQEV establish credibility in the automotive industry, but did little to help the company build a foundation of skills in car-making.

Mr. Wang would paint rosy pictures for Miles Rubin when Rubin paid periodic inspection visits to the factory to review recent shipments, price changes and contract details. And Rubin — a hands-off investor who was relying on Kevin to be the hands-on presence for the company's production efforts — remained sold on the health of the relationship with TQEV.

During summer 2008, Miles Electric Vehicles began wrestling with rising levels of quality issues from our low-speed electric vehicles shipped to the United States. Problems ranged from rust due to inadequate painting, to leaky brake fluid from poorly assembled tubing. That last was a safety issue and required Miles Electric Vehicles to recall batches of cars and trucks for rework in the States. The recalls created serious problems due to bad press and to Miles Electric Vehicles' lack of aftermarket support facilities stateside. Hafei produced gliders that could not be test driven. TQEV lacked experience in fixing quality problems beyond the electric drivetrain and battery.

Kevin did not shy away from tackling a challenge. As CEO, he charged right in and implemented an extreme measure for quality control. He called me from company headquarters in Santa Monica and directed me to begin inspecting and test-driving 100 percent of the vehicles in the TQEV factory.

"Reject any noncompliant vehicle for shipment," Kevin ordered.

I recruited my old trusted friend James Li, from our days at Beijing Fuel Pump & Fuel Injector Co. James was given the title of deputy operations manager. Together, we processed vehicle-inspection checklists and daily test drove hundreds of cars and trucks at TQEV. By now, my faith in TQEV was on the wane. And I was highly skeptical of TQEV's ability to transition from manufacturing low-speed EVs to highway-speed EVs. So was James Li.

I communicated our concerns to Kevin — relying on him to relay them to Miles Rubin.

Even Miles's visits to TQEV — to review quality problems, car shipments, price changes and contract details — seemed cursed. Nothing ever seemed to go smoothly on these visits. For one of them, I engaged a driver and car to accompany me in meeting Miles upon his arrival at Tianjin Airport. After I greeted him and grabbed his suitcase, the driver dashed off to retrieve the car from the airport parking lot. A comic scene ensued after the driver forgot where he had parked the car and returned empty-handed, convinced that the car had been stolen. Despite my embarrassment in front of Miles, I insisted that the driver persist in his search, and eventually he located the car.

Later that afternoon, as the driver and I were chauffeuring the fatigued Miles up the expressway to catch his flight out of Beijing, he shrieked that the driver was reckless. He screamed at him to stop the car and insisted on me driving the rest of the way. I had the driver pull over and shift to the front passenger seat. I got out from the backseat and took the wheel of the Buick LaCrosse. I drove for two hours to get Miles to the airport.

Needless to say, I was relieved when he safely boarded his flight for Los Angeles!

WHEN IT CAME TO our company's grand goal of producing a highway-speed sedan EV, the picture grew perfectly clear to me: Miles Rubin was not a car guy, period. He was too much in the trees and couldn't see the forest. He'd niggle over prices for the utility cars — haggling with Mr. Wang — and not focus on the elephant in the room: TQEV wasn't up to the task of producing highway-speed cars.

Slipshod production of the low-speed electric vehicles was one thing; inadequate engineering expertise for developing a high-speed EV was another. It presented a crisis for Miles Electric Vehicles.

Tension mounted as Kevin, and finally Miles, began realizing the limitations of state-owned TQEV in carrying us beyond low-speed vehicles to a real, highway-worthy electric car. The disillusion climaxed that October in a major meeting that Miles, Kevin and I held with Mr. Wang, to discuss the launch of the XS500. As Wang made a presentation about building the highway-speed car, Kevin began picking holes in the plan. We excused ourselves from the conference room and went outside for deliberation.

Two painful facts were clear. First, an affordable and safe, highway-speed, all-electric midsize sedan that could compete in the U.S. market presented enormous challenges to manufacture:

• The speed and range capabilities required a much bigger motor, drivetrain and battery.

• A sophisticated battery-management system would be needed to extend the car range in all kinds of weather and driving conditions.

• U.S. safety standards for a vehicle operated at highway speed called for additional front, rear and sidewall airbags, a re-design of the crush-zone structure of the front-engine compartment, and the application of high-strength steel in the auto body.

• The demanding quality expectations of U.S. consumers would require exacting standards for fit and finish for a car sold above $30,000.

The second painful fact that was clear to Miles, Kevin and me: TQEV would not be up to these challenges.

The Chinese company was entirely unready to produce a car satisfactory for the U.S. market. It lacked the engineering knowhow.

And so Miles and Kevin made a tough but necessary decision: They pulled the plug on building the sedan with TQEV.

KEVIN AND MILES WERE not people prone to tossing in the towel easily. They were not about to give up on their goal of producing a highway-speed passenger EV. So they determined to completely rethink their business plan for the XS500.

They decided to develop more self-reliance for technology development.

Since we could no longer rely on TQEV to engineer and produce the XS500 for us, Miles Electric Vehicles would need to design a new drivetrain, battery pack and battery-management system. This plan presented a formidable challenge. Miles Electric Vehicles had no engineers or car-design and manufacturing expertise. Choosing this path was a brave decision for Miles and Kevin, given the daunting capital requirements and technology-development challenges ahead. But they agreed that our new beginning should start with the launch of a new brand and a new corporate entity.

Thus was born Coda Automotive Inc., which Kevin and Miles founded in 2009. They settled on "Coda" as the name because they saw the company's electric-vehicle technology as representing an end for combustion-engine vehicles, and the start of the electric-vehicle era. Early funding for Coda raised $125 million.

Kevin quickly embarked on the development of an all-electric sedan. He engaged MillenWorks — a racecar-prototyping firm in Los Angeles — to produce a small number of drivable prototype Coda cars within three months. The prototypes were internal combustion engine cars from Hafei converted to all-electric. These cars would serve as the test vehicles for an engineering and development team Kevin put together, contracting with small design companies in Los Angeles, Detroit and other cities.

The production end of the cars would involve contracting with Hafei Motor Co. Coda would integrate our new systems into a re-designed Hafei glider based on a sedan called the "Saibao": a model updated from an old Mitsubishi design resembling a Nissan Sentra model. (We much later learned that J.D. Power & Associates rated the Saibao as the worst vehicle in its class in China.) I retained my role as operations manager, and James Li was deputy operations manager. The two of us began discussions with Hafei's management on the new concept that this highway-speed EV sedan would be constructed solely by Hafei Motor Co., which would be responsible for installing the battery pack and drivetrain.

James and I executed a purchase of a few Saibao gliders and shipped them to Miles Electric Vehicles' plant in Santa Monica, where the MillenWorks racecar engineers Kevin hired installed drivetrains and batteries and began refining the design.

Watching how quickly the engineers that were subsequently contracted by Coda became the alpha guys for electric-vehicle development in the world taught me about strengths of the American innovation environment. These engineers largely were young Americans and immigrants from China, India, Russia or South Korea who had attended graduate school in the United States. They were adept at innovating drivetrains for EVs and releasing working prototypes. Their passion and brilliance provided an epiphany for me: technical innovation is an American strength. Our nation draws the best and brightest from around the world, educates them and offers them marketplace opportunities.

Our Coda EV sedan was coming to life. On my visits to our company office in Santa Monica, I would sit with Broc TenHouten, our senior vice president for engineering, and Phil Gow, our chief battery designer, and watch them debate engineering solutions, using the back of a napkin to illustrate their ideas. As impressed as I was with these "alpha" engineers' dazzling ingenuity and energy in rapidly producing working electric cars, I would later come to understand that a different personality type — practical and workmanlike — was needed in the engineering team to provide the more subtle skills that were crucial to producing a mature product viable in the consumer market. These "beta" engineers would need to refine our designs for greater durability, reliability, and manufacturability.

OUR COMPANY'S MAIN TASKS in China were setting up a battery-manufacturing joint venture, contracting final-vehicle assembly, and developing a local-parts supply chain. Coda Automotive had determined to invest in Lithium-ion battery-pack production in Tianjin in a joint venture with state-owned Lishen Power Battery: a Chinese firm that supplied batteries to Apple, Samsung, Motorola and others. Kevin led the negotiations to close the joint-venture contract.

Coda and Lishen agreed to invest $100 million into the joint-venture company, alongside local bank lines of credit for working capital. The JV would produce battery cells, assemble them into packs, and install a U.S.-made battery-management system. Kevin came up with the name for the JV — LIO Energy — by spelling "oil" backward. LIO Energy would ship the completed battery packs to Hafei for installation into Coda cars.

Our in-house legal counsel, Alan, and I then hunkered down in the cold city of Harbin in northeast China to negotiate a direct sourcing contract for vehicle assembly with Hafei Motor Co. The biggest hurdle was working out how to make an affordable electric car. Hafei produced the dated Saibao sedan with an internal-combustion drivetrain, and sold it in China for $12,000. Our battery pack alone cost nearly $20,000, given the Lithium-ion battery-manufacturing costs at that time. However, Coda's re-design of key parts and systems of the Saibao resulted in expensive tooling, materials, and parts-sourcing costs.

Hafei's outdated production line needed significant capital improvements to meet Coda's quality standards. To our dismay, Hafei's managers stubbornly refused to share the burden of investments geared for the electric Saibao, even though they would benefit in the future from higher quality and an early start on electric-vehicle production. The lack of concessions from state-owned Hafei put significant upward pressure on the Coda car-sourcing cost, bringing us nearly to an estimated $45,000 retail price, after options, in the United States. This ridiculously high price (in 2008) for an imported, unglamorous sedan — albeit all-electric— from China was at the limit of feasibility for our business plan. I couldn't fathom a large market of consumers for this EV at that price.

Still, I was excited. I believed the battery joint venture was a real asset. I felt optimistic that we could overcome quality and negligence issues at Hafei. Kevin and I shared an enthusiasm that we were taking the right steps to make it work. I began recruiting engineers and other staff in China to fulfill our sourcing mandate, drawing candidates from other foreign-Chinese joint ventures who responded to my placements on job-recruiting websites.

My Chinese team grew to 70 members as a local-parts supply chain grew and our operation became more complex. We had to localize as much content in China as possible to reduce costs. In many cases, my team translated U.S.-language designs and specifications into Chinese drawings and supply contracts for alternative parts made locally in China. We had engineers and designers focused on car parts, electrical systems, body stamping, structural welding, painting, and final assembly. I had quality inspectors, safety engineers, procurement managers, production supervisors, logistics experts, human resource managers, and accounting staff. Our team basically operated as a double for Hafei management, bolstering them in areas where they lacked the resources or motivation to perform.

I was gratified by this team James Li and I assembled. Our young Chinese engineers had the skills to work with sophisticated digital designs and figure out how to realize them in factories in China. Our procurement managers cleverly sourced tooling and parts at reasonable prices across China in the indigenous automotive industry. Our production supervisors spent countless weekends in Hafei at all hours supporting the assembly of Coda cars. In every case, they made valuable contributions toward the launch of the Coda car.

We worked with great urgency to meet our project schedule, but experienced disheartening delays. The Coda car design required much unanticipated work for comprehensive upgrades to the Saibao, in addition to the development of the drivetrain and battery pack. In China, we formed a local entity to pay salaries for our employees, as well as cover payments for buying parts in China. We managed the procurement of hundreds of parts from numerous suppliers. Designing and producing molds and dies was time-consuming and complicated. Fine-tuning body stamping, robotic welding lines and paint-shop robots required booking spare time in the Hafei production schedule. And that proved to be a major source of frustration.

Hafei's managers were not responsive to our requests for access to equipment on their line. They often initiated work stoppages and insisted on payments from Coda before starting up again. The delays and friction with Hafei took their toll. Meanwhile, Kevin faced ongoing pressure to raise money to keep our capital-intensive business afloat. His travel between Los Angeles and China became a slog. One trip stood out in particular.

One evening, James Li and I met Kevin at Beijing Capital Airport on his arrival from a 13-hour flight from Los Angeles. The three of us immediately boarded a local flight to Harbin and settled into our seats. Two hours later, the plane began its descent. However, the captain announced over the intercom that due to adverse snowy weather, we would abort a landing and return to Beijing. After a long flight back, we landed in Beijing and sat waiting onboard for news of clearing weather in Harbin. Again, we took off bound for Harbin. Another two hours clicked by. To our astonishment, the pilot came on the intercom and announced that we would abort our landing and return to Beijing a second time. By the time we arrived back in Beijing in the early morning of the following day, we resolved to take a break at my house before venturing a third time to Harbin.

Yes, Kevin put up with a lot of adversity. Fortunately, he had an unbelievable ability to sleep anytime and anywhere. He was able to keep his energy and mental clarity in good shape. But even herculean powers couldn't withstand the twin pressures from impatient U.S. investors demanding tangible evidence of progress in producing Coda cars, and the intransigence of state-owned Hafei's managers — who simply were disinclined to cooperate with our needs to access their production facilities, and our initial state of illiquidity.

ONE NIGHT LATE IN 2010, Kevin phoned me to say he was stepping down from Coda after pushing back the car launch date into late 2011. He had driven Coda forward in capital raising and engineering development by sheer force of will. However, he and the board disagreed in their strategic outlooks for the company. Kevin would be missed! I thanked him for bringing me into Coda, and I resigned myself to dealing with whatever outcome the new management might have in store for our China operation and me.[22]

In January 2011, Mac Heller, interim CEO of Coda, called me to say that Phil Murtaugh would take over as CEO. Murtaugh had launched General Motors' joint-venture car factory with Shanghai Automotive Industry Corp. On a visit to China not long thereafter, Mac and Miles introduced Phil to the managements of Hafei and Lishen. Phil had exceptional experience and credentials in working with Chinese joint-venture partners and building world-class cars in China. The SAIC-GM JV was ranked in the No. 2 spot in China, behind the FAW-Volkswagen JV, with more than 1 million cars produced and sold annually.

Phil was a car guy at heart. He represented a balance of "alpha" innovation focused on rapid creation of first-release products, and "beta" industrialization geared to refining the product for durability, reliability, and manufacturability. He immediately understood our challenges of stamping and welding body parts, achieving perfect coating surfaces in the paint shop, and assembling all the components, trim, glass, plastic, rubber and other parts with perfect fit and finish.

I introduced our China team to Phil, who made a point of meeting each member and learning about the person's work. Phil made sure to express his appreciation for the contributions of our employees. He was a good listener, and he welcomed frequent visits to the production line so he could determine firsthand how to solve problems. He also instinctively knew when

---

[22] Kevin Czinger continued in the automotive industry. As of this writing in 2023, his company, Czinger Vehicles Inc., based in Los Angeles, has developed and built the 21C: a 3D-printed car that reportedly can go from 0 to 62 mph in 1.9 seconds and has net-zero emissions when operated on carbon-recycled methanol.

to forge ahead when faced with a multitude of challenges. His motto might be summarized as: "Move the metal!"

Unfortunately, Coda was not General Motors, and we were outsourcing the car to state-owned Hafei, a third-tier car partner from hell. Other than working to cajole Hafei management to respond to our resource and schedule needs, Phil did not have much other leverage to work with. We were aware that state-owned Chang'an Automobile Group had purchased Hafei's assets, prompted by a Chinese state policy aimed at consolidating the nation's domestic automobile manufacturing industry. Chang'an is the smallest of the Big Four automakers in China. Given Phil's background in having partnered with another Big Four automaker — SAIC — he attempted to gain access to, and lobby, Chang'an's leadership to support Coda's production at Hafei.

Unfortunately, Chang'an's managers were unhappy with the government having forced the adoption of Hafei into its fold, and they were hostile to supporting production of Hafei cars or a partnership with Coda. The relationship with us grew toxic.

Chang'an's leaders attempted to extort us to obtain our electric drivetrain and battery technology by threatening to shut down the production of our Coda car. They requested a renegotiation of our sourcing contract. Our internal legal counsel and I met with them at a hotel to discuss their proposed changes. They wouldn't budge from their demands. The counsel, Chris, had previously been employed with the prestigious White & Case international law firm. He was savvy and worldly. He saw the writing on the wall. So did I. It was a no-win proposition for us.

If Chang'an shut us down, Coda would be dead in the water. But if we agreed to transfer to them our technology — which our U.S. investors had paid for — we also would be dead in the water.

After silently listening to their demands for us to hand over our electric-vehicle intellectual property as a price for doing business, Chris and I excused ourselves and quietly exited the meeting room.

"Let's just leave," Chris said. "Let's not even tell them we're not coming back."

So we did.

I figured the probability of Coda succeeding now was less than 50 percent.

CRASH TESTING IS ONE of the most important methods of validating a car design. Unsatisfactory results of Coda crash tests mandated time-consuming changes to the car design, and created significant delays for car launch. These tests included front-end collision, side-barrier collision, side-pole collision and a rollover test. Each test was conducted on multiple Coda vehicles, and the tests were meant to simulate real-world conditions, including dangerous speeds and road conditions. It was imperative to identify any design that could potentially cause serious bodily harm or death, and correct it.

Late one weekend night at my home in Beijing, I received a phone call from our head of vehicle integration, based in Los Angeles, regarding the results of a recent Coda crash test in China. There had been a fire at the Chinese company where our crash tests were being conducted. He wasn't more specific about the fire. He didn't know how it had started. But he needed me to travel as soon as possible up north to our crash-test provider to assess the situation.

I immediately called James Li, and we bought tickets on the morning express train to Jinzhou to get to the Jinheng Automotive Safety System Co.

Upon our arrival, Jinheng's general manager, Mr. Zhang, led us into the test cell and closed and locked the garage doors behind him. The three of us walked alone along the dark shed interior to an illuminated front area where the collisions took place. What we saw was a nightmare. The Coda test car was completely incinerated. The exterior paint had blistered and blackened where it had been exposed to the fire. Interior trim and seat coverings had melted and burned to a crisp and emitted a foul, sooty plastic stench. Most unsettling, the remains of the crash-test dummy, slumped in the front driver seat, looking like a ragged metal-skeleton "Terminator" with metallic skull and ruby eyes. The dashboard and console were a mess of melted plastic.

Here's what had happened. In a side-pole impact test, the car is propelled sideways on a sled at 20 mph into a bone-crunching impact with a rigid, narrow pole: simulating the type of blunt-force collision one might suffer skidding a car sideways into a telephone pole. When the Coda car began wrapping itself around the pole, the car floor had suffered severe crumpling forces and pushed into the battery pack. The battery module's rigid connections had cracked, creating electrical short circuits. The arcing had produced intense heat, which had ignited the semi-inflammable ducts above the battery pack. The fire had moved along the ducts up into the front-motor compartment and into the passenger space.

Zhang informed us that the fire had taken time to reach the passenger space, but the damage in the end was complete. His immediate concern was for us to remove the car and dispose of it before Jinheng employees might snap photos with their phones of the burned Coda for uploading to social media. I saw the wisdom of that.

Zhang assisted James and me in loading the carcass onto a flatbed truck that was driven into the darkened test tunnel by a driver Zhang provided. We pulled a tarp over the reeking wreck and climbed into the truck with the driver. Zhang waved goodbye as we departed into the city of Jinzhou with our vehicle's charred remains.

We directed the driver to a local garage Zhang had contacted. We offloaded the dead Coda for disposal. Getting rid of the car body was relatively easy, as the garage staff — per James' directions — reduced the car body and interior remains to small pieces with the use of electric saws, crowbars, and hammers.

After documenting the configuration of the scorched battery to feed back to our U.S. design engineers, James and I mulled over how to discard the charred array of battery modules and cells. We found to our amazement that despite exposure to an inferno, most of the battery still sparked with a full electrical charge. We couldn't send a fully charged battery to a landfill. It could electrocute whoever might handle it there.

Our only option was spending hours squatting on the dirt floor of the garage, laboriously disassembling more than 700 cells — each about the size of a large cigarette pack — and individually placing them in plastic bags.

Finally, we drove them to a local dump and discarded them there.

I was relieved when James and I wearily boarded the night train out of Jinzhou heading home to Beijing. Our clothes and skin smelled like a burned-down house: melted plastic and steel and burned rubber.[23]

THE LAUNCH OF THE CODA CAR continued suffering significant delays and cost overruns. Designing and manufacturing, from scratch, an electronic sedan imported from China for sale in the U.S. market was a

---

[23] After the car fire, the design issues were addressed, and there have been no fires since with the model.

risky bet for a brand-new car company. Outsourcing all the production to China increased Coda's challenges. Outsourcing is commonly looked upon by management as a convenient way to keep costs low. But the unresolved question is: "*Which* costs?" In addition, there is the matter of, "What is the effect on overall costs?"

The cost reductions of localizing content and sourcing assembly labor in China were offset by additional costs in long-distance travel, inefficient communications, partner issues, poor quality, scrap production, lengthy lead times, complicated logistics and delayed deliveries.

What if Coda had acquired an inexpensive car factory in Michigan during the financial crisis, and built the car in the United States? (General Motors, for example, was looking to sell its Saturn division with tooling, factories and several models included.) Would the launch have been sooner? Would the overall project costs have been less? I often wonder!

Coda car deliveries to retail customers in the United States began in March 2012 after being rescheduled several times. The retail price of the 2012 Coda began at $37,250 (before any electric-vehicle federal-tax credit and other state and local incentives to be applied). The car was sold exclusively in California, and only 117 units had been delivered by April 2013. Time and money were running out.

On May 1, 2013, Coda Automotive filed for bankruptcy.

In postmortem, sourcing the final assembly from state-owned Hafei had been a major blunder that ultimately proved fatal for Coda. Apple Inc. is a prime example of a U.S. company successfully outsourcing in China by choosing a capable and collaborative, privately owned partner: Foxconn, an electronics contract manufacturer. But Hafei was no Foxconn.

Phil Murtaugh had realized early in his tenure as CEO that although we were yoked to Hafei in the short term, Coda needed to find an alternative final-assembly partner that would be responsive. Having met chairman Wei Jianjun, of Great Wall Motors, several times over the years, Phil had proposed a partnership with privately held Great Wall in Baoding, Hebei Province.

We'd visited Great Wall Motors and immediately noticed a difference. Wei, already a billionaire, could be seen personally leading the company in the factories and offices and sharing mealtimes with employees in the company cafeteria. He'd quickly assigned a young team of engineers to work with us on a feasibility study of converting Great Wall's mini-compact car to all-electric. Great Wall Motors reminded me of Sony Corp. when I'd worked there in the 1980s. Wei's employees were proud, disciplined, and enthusiastic about building more than 600,000 cars annually that were very popular among Chinese consumers.

The outcome for Coda might have been different in a marriage with Great Wall Motors.

Unfortunately, we ran out of time.

I WOULD BE REMISS if not sharing that Coda did enjoy success in sourcing lithium-ion batteries in China. This was an entirely different experience than our fiasco in sourcing the car manufacturing.

Chinese state officials recognized the urgency in creating batteries for electric vehicles, and invested in developing lithium-ion batteries for transportation. The state-owned Tianjin Lishen Battery Joint-Stock Co., Ltd. (Lishen), responded by adding capabilities to build battery packs for electric-commuter buses in China.

Coda presented Lishen with a well-timed opportunity to enter the EV battery market. Lishen had grown from a small research laboratory in 1997 into a major producer of Lithium-ion batteries by 2008, becoming a global battery-cell supplier to Samsung, Motorola, and Apple for consumer electronics and other device applications. Lishen produced a wide variety of battery cells at its massive campus in an industrial district of Tianjin. Lishen's automated factory mixed powdered graphite for anodes and powdered metal oxides for cathodes into slurries in huge vats, spread them into finely uniform coatings on electrode sheets made of aluminum and copper on machines resembling printing presses, wound anode sheets around cathode sheets and separator materials, robotically assembled and welded the windings into cells, and packaged and tested the cells prior to shipment to its customers. Lishen's production line represented the state-of-the-art for the battery industry worldwide.

Qin Xingcai, the general manager of Lishen, had energetically led the company from its humble beginnings to becoming a major producer by 2008. He had broken out of the bureaucrat mold and driven the growth of Lishen like a zealous entrepreneur making deals to build his business. Although Lishen was state-owned, it incorporated many of the attributes of a foreign multinational company.

Coda had wisely recognized the strategic value in owning lithium-ion battery production for its cars. Lishen wholeheartedly welcomed Coda as a partner, primarily because Coda's plan to source electric vehicles in China would help Lishen enter the electric-vehicle battery business. Thus, Coda established a joint venture — LIO Energy Systems — with Lishen, for the design, manufacture, and sale of battery systems.

The planned investment into LIO Energy Systems was $100 million for a manufacturing facility co-located at Lishen's facilities in Tianjin. Initially, the Coda car was to be the primary recipient of the battery systems produced by LIO. LIO's production capacity was targeted to grow to a total of 1.4 billion amp hours in Tianjin at full scale.

Coda's team of battery engineers in Santa Monica designed the battery pack from the ground up, starting with individual power-cell specifications. Cells were assembled into modules, and the modules — all interconnected with a spiderweb of conductors — were loaded into a large aluminum tray forming the pack, which was to be bolted beneath the Coda car. Coda designed the configuration of cells and modules, the connectors across all the units and the overall packaging of the pack. More importantly, Coda designed a battery-management system to monitor the battery pack, to optimize voltage and current against expected load scenarios and deliver the range required for the vehicle.

The basic Coda car model was powered by a 31 kilowatt-hour, lithium-ion, iron- phosphate battery system that was substantially larger than that of other vehicles in its class at that time. Iron phosphate chemistry was chosen for its longer lifecycle and its safety characteristics. The Environmental Protection Agency rated the Coda car as the most efficient among all electric cars available in the United States by early 2012. Coda estimated the range of its car to be up to 125 miles under favorable operating conditions.

The Coda had a top speed of 85 mph. The battery system featured an active thermal-management system, which would give the vehicle a more dependable range than other electric vehicles and improved battery-system durability.

It was a shame that this early mass-produced EV had its life cut short by a dysfunctional relationship between its parent company and its outsourcing partner. We at Coda had earnestly tried salvaging this relationship.

As we encountered difficulties with Hafei, we asked Lishen's managers and its state shareholders to influence Hafei's managers to be more supportive of the car development. We pointed out that delays in the launch of the Coda car would directly harm our joint venture with Lishen. Sadly, we never experienced a case of Lishen or its shareholders lobbying on Coda's behalf with Hafei or Chang'an.

A sign of the Chinese government's prioritizing Lishen's role in the battery industry was its transfer of ownership of Lishen to the giant China National Offshore Oil Corp. Kevin and I met even met with Fu Chengyu, chairman and CEO of CNOOC, who'd listened quietly while we described our challenges with Hafei and appealed for his help.

Then he proceeded to lecture us about how the United States needed to re-industrialize.

I DID APPRECIATE THAT key U.S. leaders at the federal level endorsed companies such as ours.

In May 2010, Coda had hosted U.S. Secretary of Commerce Gary Locke on his visit to LIO Energy Systems facility in Tianjin, a trip that was part of the Obama administration's first cabinet-level trade mission to China. Commenting on the visit, Locke said, "International green technology partnerships can produce rapid job growth back home and deliver energy solutions abroad, and Coda's venture proves it."

In 2012, I'd escorted former Treasury Secretary Hank Paulson on his visit to Lishen. Paulson was an investor in Coda. As treasury secretary from July 2006 to January 2009, Paulson had negotiated economic reforms with China. As head of Goldman Sachs, he'd helped major state-owned enterprises with public listings of their shares. He created the Paulson Institute to focus on China's environmental and economic challenges. We hoped that Paulson's visit would draw Chinese state officials' attention to Lishen and Coda.

Wasn't to be!

On one of my regular visits to Lishen to check up on the joint venture in 2012, I received word that an important visitor would be coming the next day. All employees of Lishen, including JV staff, would be required to gather in the parking lot outside at the appointed hour to greet our visitor. I shuffled down the stairs together with a horde of Lishen workers and joined the edge of the crowd of nearly 1,000 people standing outside. A convoy of official vehicles appeared with a Toyota Coaster Minibus in the center. Out stepped Premier Wen Jiabao, China's second-most-powerful man at the time. Premier Wen accepted the crowd's greeting cheerfully. And then, spotting me — the only foreigner —in the distance, he began wading through the crowd in my direction. He came right up to me and extended his hand, repeatedly saying, "Thank you!" in English.

It was a moving moment!

In 2013, as Coda's money ran out, our CEO, Phil Murtaugh, directed me to liquidate our holding in the JV to generate cash. I negotiated with Qin Xingcai for Lishen to buy back our shares in LIO Energy Systems. It was a sad, yes, coda to our story in China.

IN HINDSIGHT, WRITING THESE words in 2023, I marvel that of all the industries China is excelling in at the moment, making electric cars is at the top of the list.

China had the world's largest market for EVs, and the big automakers were privately owned Chinese companies such as BYD and Li Auto, XPeng and Zeekr. *NBC News* reported in a story in July 2023 headlined, "China's Rising Dominance in Booming Electric Vehicle Market," that Chinese EVs were sleek and high tech, and had helped China overtake Japan as the biggest exporter of automobiles, largely due to Chinese sales in Europe. (Most Chinese brands were unavailable for sale in the United States, because of steep trade tariffs put in place during President Trump's administration.)

The *NBC News* story also reported that Chinese automakers had a strong hold on the supply chain for raw materials for the lithium-ion batteries used in EVs, since China's mining interests across five continents represented 28 percent of the world's supply of lithium and 41 percent of the supply of cobalt.

It is obvious to me that Coda Automotive was ahead of its time. We were about a decade too early in the game. And we'd made a big misstep in partnering with the state-owned Hafei Motor Co. Had we instead partnered with the privately held Great Wall Motors, a joint venture could have worked. I say *could*, rather than would; Great Wall's owner was a keen follower of Toyota, and in 2013 he likely would have preferred making a hybrid vehicle like the Toyota Prius rather than an all-electric car. But in time, his vision could have changed . . .

Despite the dashed dream, I am proud that Coda Automotive was focused on producing a viable, marketable EV. It was capable of providing this solution for the automobile industry — if only it had found a conducive Chinese partner! In 2023, when I look under the hood of my Chevrolet Bolt EV, I see an electric powertrain design Coda had produced more than a dozen years before.[24]

I don't regret having jumped back into the automotive industry. But as Coda came to its premature coda, I once again found myself in a position where I had to reinvent myself in my business career.

---

[24] Lishen continues to produce Coda-designed cells and batteries. Coda technology has made its way into Chinese EVs.

Chapter Eleven

Salvaging the Good

Once again I was looking for a job.

"What does a foreigner do in China?" I asked the man with whom I was meeting over coffee.

His name was Davin Mackenzie, and I trusted he would have an accurate answer about where I now fit into China's evolving job market. Mackenzie's title was "consultant, Greater China" for Spencer Stuart — the global firm specializing in placing upper-management executives. In other words, he was an expert headhunter for this part of Asia.

His answer was blunt, and not entirely unexpected:

"Nothing. You're done."

"There must be *something* for me to do," I replied, halfheartedly.

There I was in January 2013: 27 years into my business career, with 22 of those years in managerial posts with Chinese-based companies. Each time I'd made a move to change employment, I'd readily found opportunities, since I was someone whom foreign companies coveted to manage their joint ventures with Chinese companies. I served as a sturdy bridge between the Western co-owners or investors and their Chinese partners. I was a Chinese-speaking American with an MBA and a master's in engineering, and a solid track record as a general manager for companies in manufacturing, mobile technology and startup investing.

But there in 2013 — after a third of a century of China's fast-paced modernization — a young generation of capable, well-educated Chinese had flooded the managerial ranks in companies across the spectrum of industries. This new guard had been born and raised during China's dizzying leap forward to industrialized prosperity from an impoverished nation with an antiquated, agrarian-oriented economy. A foreigner like me — despite my experience — suddenly wasn't a valued commodity anymore.

And Davin Mackenzie confirmed this for me as he explained that his employer's recruiting practice in Beijing no longer saw people like me as marketable in the Chinese business world. Spencer Stuart, he explained, had pivoted away from placing foreigners and ethnic Chinese born overseas into managerial positions in China. The firm was now purely focused on placing local, native Chinese candidates who had lucrative personal connections: a social advantage known as *guanxi*.

I left our meeting deflated, but not defeated.

Once again, I had to reinvent myself. I resolved to figure *something* out . . .

AS I CONTEMPLATED WHERE an experienced 49-year-old American business executive fluent in Chinese might find his niche in China's radically changing business landscape, an idea popped into my head. *As the*

Swiss are to watches, Americans are to airplanes and jet engines. That is, the United States has the foremost designers and manufacturers of aviation products. China was the fastest-growing market for aviation, but the Chinese lacked the capabilities to produce their own planes.

Surely, there must be a role I could play in China's aircraft industry. There had to be some angle for me to parlay U.S. aviation supremacy to something of value to Chinese companies. To be a middleman connecting the makers or owners of U.S. planes and parts to buyers in China.

Perhaps I could work for a large bank as an executive brokering financing for the buyers?

I stumbled across a three-day crash course in air finance offered by Citibank in Hong Kong, and enrolled myself. Attired in a business suit, I joined my air-finance class of bankers at Citibank's headquarters in Hong Kong. The course would cover all aspects of financing — from operating leases to securitized approaches. We were to learn about asset valuations, maintenance reserves and residual values.

The first day of class, I looked around the room at my classmates and realized I didn't fit in. The vast majority were Hong Kong-born Chinese in their mid-twenties to mid-thirties and already employed by multinational banks such as Citibank, Standard Chartered or HSBC. I would be turning 50 in November. I was too old for these banks to hire. Nor was I attractive as a job candidate to a major foreign manufacturer that had facilities in China or was considering opening such facilities, such as Airbus or Boeing.

During a break, I bumped into a fellow classmate, a Frenchman named Laurent Biousse, who was closer to my age than the other students. We chatted about our work experiences. And an intriguing lead popped up. Laurent shared an alluring story about his aviation-asset trading. He had been an independent securities trader who had discovered the profits to be reaped from buying old airplanes and disassembling them to sell their valuable parts. He became an asset trader and organized the purchase of a mature and aging European Airbus A320 aircraft. Laurent's strategy was raising funds from investors to take title to individual aircraft. Each fund would own a specific aircraft identified by a serial number. Laurent would then organize the teardown of the aircraft and the sale of salvageable parts. It was all perfectly legal and safe, because before the plane's parts could be sold on the aftermarket, they were re-certified by shops licensed by the U.S. Federal Aviation Administration. The investors enjoyed positive returns on their funds if the cumulative cash proceeds from sales of used serviceable materials exceeded the purchase price of the aircraft. That was the case with the Airbus A320. Laurent had founded the Aeronautics Fund to invest and trade in used commercial aircraft in the mid to end-of-life market.

This was the high-end junkyard business!

I decided this could be a hot tip, indeed.

I QUICKLY GREW CONSUMED with the idea of starting an aviation asset-trading business in China. It struck me as a golden opportunity. China, after all, was the largest commercial-aircraft market outside the United States. Although China's large fleet of aircraft was relatively young, the sheer size of that fleet offered ample numbers of aircraft for retirement each year. If I could raise capital to acquire mature aircraft in China, I could ferry them to the United States for teardown and the sale of the used parts on the world market.

I researched the market thoroughly, compiling statistics, and created a prospectus to pitch to U.S. investors. I then traveled to San Francisco and New York and made presentations to aviation-related funds such as Vx Capital Partners and Fortress Investment Group. But my project wasn't an easy sell.

While my investment proposal generated mild interest to my audiences, their primary concern was my lack of experience in trading aircraft and spare parts.

Then, another hot tip . . .

"Have you talked to Abdol yet?" one of the New York investors asked.

"Who is Abdol?" I asked.

"He owns GA Telesis, which just signed a joint-venture agreement with Air China to start an aviation asset-trading business in China."

I confirmed this news with an Internet search.

I could not believe my lucky timing!

"Abdol" turned out to be Abdol Moabery. Despite his foreign-sounding name, he'd been born in the United States and did not look Middle Eastern, were that his ancestry. He had a degree from Florida Atlantic University, in Boca Raton, but his real education — which qualified him as a self-described "serial entrepreneur" — was learning the principles of selling by working in the Women's Shoes department at Nordstrom's. From there, he'd moved up the salesman ladder to eventually selling and marketing aviation assets at companies in New York.

Then he'd sold an aviation legend on taking him into a partnership to trade in aviation assets. The legend was George Edward Batchelor, and the company they cofounded was named GA Telesis. "GA" stood for George and Abdol. "Telesis" means progress that is intelligently planned and executed. Batchelor was 81 by this time, but still a household name in the flyboy fraternity. The Oklahoma native had learned to fly at 16 and gone on to graduate from the Aeronautical Institute in California. By the time he was in his early twenties, he'd helped design the P-51 Mustang single-seat fighter-bomber: a key aircraft in the Army Air Corps during World War II. After serving as a pilot in the war,

Batchelor had launched his first aircraft company by buying a DC-3 in Hawaii, flying it to the mainland and selling it — and using the profit to purchase more aircraft. Batchelor became wealthy owning or investing in passenger and cargo airlines, aircraft maintenance and overhaul, aircraft leasing and insurance. He certainly was intrepid. I even heard a story that he would fly down to Latin America to personally repossess aircraft from deadbeat airlines. Batchelor would sneak into those foreign airports, climb into the aircraft in question, and take off before he could be apprehended.

The same year, 2002, Batchelor and Abdol cofounded GA Telesis, Batchelor passed away. Abdol took over the startup, organization and development of the company, and GA Telesis slowly took off. Beginning with the purchase and disassembly of an old Boeing B737 aircraft, it grew — deal by deal — to ever-greater opportunities, until it became a full-service aviation asset-trading house: buying, selling or leasing aircraft, engines and used spare parts.

I introduced myself via email to Abdol and submitted my candidacy for general manager to run his new joint venture with Air China. He suggested I interview with his trusted deputies, Alex Tuttle and Lynda Cheng: a married couple who were in Beijing to set up the joint venture. I agreed.

We probed each other's backgrounds and outlooks for the JV. Alex, a native Floridian, managed aircraft and engine teardowns and used-parts sales for Abdol in Florida. Lynda, a native Taiwanese, ran business development in Asia for GA Telesis. Abdol had tabbed Alex to run JV operations, and Lynda to manage sales and marketing.

Air China — as the JV partner — wanted to vet me prior to selecting a GM for the company. I met with Zhang Yang, general manager of corporate planning at Air China, and we conversed in Chinese for about an hour regarding my working experience in China. Zhang Yang was on the cusp of retirement: a female success story in the Chinese business world. She double-checked my references with her contacts at Pratt & Whitney Aircraft Engines in China. (My lengthy résumé, after all, listed my job as a project manager in China for Pratt way back in 1993-95.)

In the end, Yang and Abdol agreed to me becoming the GM of the JV. I would be in charge of getting this business off the ground and then managing its daily operations to turn a profit. My initial task as I began in March 2013 was setting up the office and warehouse operations, and hiring and training a local staff of some 20 employees. Our core business was acquiring decommissioned aircraft and engines, disassembling them for their parts, and selling those surplus parts worldwide.

Despite what obviously were very steep odds, I'd managed — once again — to successfully reinvent myself to become the manager on the ground for a foreign partner in a foreign-Chinese JV.

THE JV, CALLED GA Innovation China, set up its office at a site all too familiar to me: in a dilapidated administrative building adjacent to the campus of the Aircraft Maintenance and Engineering Corp., a stone's throw from Terminal 2. Yes, AMECO: the joint venture between Air China and Germany's Lufthansa Technic that maintains, repairs and overhauls aircraft and their engines and components. My first work assignment in China after moving there in late 1993 (nearly 20 years earlier) from a job in Europe had been to manage the development of a joint venture that my employer, Pratt & Whitney Aircraft Engines, was trying to forge with Air China and Lufthansa, to create a facility at the Beijing Airport to overhaul and repair aircraft engines.

On my first drive to the office of GA Innovation China, I experienced a powerful flashback. I navigated my Buick LaCrosse onto the two-lane road of cracked concrete that was the very same one I remembered my parents, siblings and I being driven on from the old airport in Beijing on my first-ever visit to China: as a 19-year-old taking a Christmastime vacation in then-exotic China in 1982 — wide-eyed to see what this Communist country that had previously been closed to Western visitors looked like. Then my eyes fell upon AMECO's drab and rusty hangar buildings, with steam billowing out of the ancient, Stalin-era pipes. Just like I remembered them from my time with Pratt.

I had come full circle. I was now commuting to work next to AMECO, where I had worked decades before. GAIC was focused on retiring aircraft purchased by Air China 20 ago, back in my days at Pratt.

I was gratified that our JV's partner, Air China, didn't saddle us with top executives who were solely political appointees or corrupt opportunists. Air China placed several very capable employees in the JV. Our chief financial officer, Lu Lingfei, came from Air China's finance department and had useful experience with aircraft financings. Our asset-trading manager, Hou Runxiu, had more than 10 years of experience in the Chinese aviation industry — with Air China, and with SkyWorks Capital Asia Ltd. (a Hong Kong-based joint venture between Air China Development Corp. and Swire Pacific Ltd., a British investment holding company). Our component sales manager, Zhang Kai, had more than 15 years experience in China's maintenance, repair, and overhaul industry. Together with us who came from GA Telesis — Alex and Lynda and our sales manager, Jade Mitsongkroh — our team was well staffed to trade aviation assets.

What a difference from my maddening experience at Beijing Fuel Pump & Fuel Injector Co.!

I WORKED AT GAIC from April 2013 through February 2015. I am proud of the results. In our first 18 months, we generated sales of surplus aircraft parts totaling more than $10 million, achieving profitability.

During my tenure, we acquired two aging Boeing 747-400 aircraft from Air China, and several engines on the open market. After our first 747 purchase, we held a large ribbon-cutting ceremony at the big AMECO hangar to show off the jumbo jet. Business dignitaries were in attendance, and I made a speech about how exciting it was for GA Innovation China to be working with Air China. AMECO, Air China's maintenance arm, would be tearing down the plane, and we at GA Innovation would be selling the parts.

And so it went with each of the 747s. AMECO removed the four engines and all the salable components from each 747 — which made up almost 90 percent of the salvage value — and we sold them on the worldwide aftermarket. We also sold the airframe from one of the 747s to the Beijing Airport authority for use by its security unit for anti-terrorist training, and sold the second airframe to a creative entrepreneur from Hunan Province. He had the airframe disassembled at the Beijing Airport for conversion into a restaurant destined for some remote location in China. His workers built a bamboo scaffolding around the jumbo jet and proceeded to saw the fuselage into sections and remove the wings. The sight of the huge 747 torn down into large chunks resting on the ground resembled a shattered giant toy.

Of course, our JV weathered challenges. As we identified mature aircraft for purchase from the fleet in China, we encountered a major obstacle to closing deals. In one deal, Alex and I made a pitch to acquire several Boeing 777 aircraft from Air China at a fair-market value of $12 million per aircraft. However, Air China carried these aircraft at a $40 million book value each on the company's balance sheet. The over-valuation was a legacy of loose accounting practices and a balance sheet inflated to increase Air China's stock-market value. Alex and I quickly realized that the leaders of the state-owned airlines would be unwilling to take personal responsibility for asset-value write-downs associated with retiring their older aircraft and absorbing the difference between inflated book values and much lower fair-market values. Nobody wanted to be blamed for such large losses! In many cases, the airlines would hold onto the aging aircraft and delay retirement until the current management could move on. We tried piggybacking on leasing deals with Chinese banks, who could help resolve the valuation issues. In the end, the aircraft purchase opportunities were many fewer than we had hoped for.

Another daunting hurdle was the cumbersome bureaucracy of Chinese customs bureau officials tasked with regulating the import-export aspect of our used-parts trading business. For us to effectively support airlines in China with discounted used parts for sale, we needed to process significant volumes of imports and exports of these parts in and out of China. That is, we had to ship the used parts (which we removed from planes) out of the country to be repaired and worthy for sale, then bring those refurbished parts back into China as we put them up for sale. But the officials with China's General Administration of Customs did not look favorably on the importation of used aircraft parts — as the government frowned on importing used equipment into the country — and were prone to assessing a barrage of duties on them. This complicated the logistics of our parts trading and compromised our competitiveness.

At one point, a high-level customs official in Beijing discreetly advised me that we should relocate our parts trading to free-trading Hong Kong, to eliminate Customs problems. His point was that China's customs officials were not that sophisticated, and simply could not grasp that our business needed to export and import the same used parts. The high-level official suggested we should base our shipping and receiving in Hong Kong: a duty-free port.

GA Innovation ran into yet another snag due to a very human emotion: jealousy. After Zhang Yang retired as general manager of corporate planning at Air China, she joined GAIC as its chairwoman. That seems to have bred resentment in managers at Air China who saw her as feathering her nest after leaving their company. The impact for GAIC was that we sometimes had difficulty getting deals from Air China.

As of this writing in 2023, China has not yet developed an aircraft-junkyard industry on the scale that it exists in the United States. In America, we can park aged aircraft in remote places such as the Mojave Desert. When we need parts, we use cheap labor to disassemble the aircraft and salvage what is salable. Costs are low because non-licensed mechanics can do the work. Airlines in the U.S. are the biggest consumers of used parts. China one day will develop teardown locations like our deserts, but as of 2023, China's facilities and labor costs at existing airports are too high.

AMECO — I should note — made much progress since my days in the early 1990s negotiating for Pratt & Whitney to take over its non-performing engine shop. AMECO capably overhauled engines, taking only a few months. It dramatically expanded the scope of its maintenance services to include passenger-to-freight conversions of aircraft and comprehensive repairs capability for components. Even United Airlines chose AMECO for heavy maintenance of its Boeing 747 fleet.

China's commercial aircraft fleet continued growing faster than any other country's, including the United States'. Chinese consumers drove demand for both domestic and international travel. As of this writing in 2023, China is working hard to develop a locally made airliner, the COMAC 919, to compete with Airbus and Boeing in China.

I KNEW MY TIME in China was running short. One key factor that added to my unease about prolonging my family's stay transpired in winter 2013. That was when Beijing and the rest of China suffered an "airpocalypse" of a massive toxic haze. It covered more than 500,000 square miles and affected 800 million people — 60 percent of China's population — according to Chinese researchers.[25] Visibility declined to about 60 feet. The U.S. Embassy in Beijing recorded a fine-particulate matter reading that was 40 times the World Health Organization's recommended upper limit for breathable air.

China's government has since worked hard to improve air quality, in part by encouraging the switch from coal to natural gas and renewable-energy sources. Indeed, China reportedly reduced the amount of harmful particulates in the air by 40 percent from 2013 to 2020.[26] But the heavy smog we encountered in 2013 only spurred Shannon's and my plans to relocate our family back to the States.

In 2012 — as I described in Chapter Nine — Shannon and I had sold our villa to a wealthy Chinese woman, but leased it back from her for a year to continue living there. After that year's lease ran out, my wife and I decided to stay on in China a bit longer. We found another villa, close to the one we'd sold in Yosemite, which we could rent. It belonged to a friend of Xiao Qingping, the dynamic entrepreneur who'd founded Chinadotman, and whom I'd befriended as the manager of China operations for Vesta China Ltd., which had acquired Chinadotman.

We ended up living there a year before we Atkesons finally decided to return to the United States. I resigned from GAIC in February 2015.

---

[25] Wong, Herman, "2013 will be remembered as the year that deadly, suffocating smog consumed China." *Quartz*, Dec. 19, 2013.

[26] Jayaram, Kripa; Kay, Chris; Murtaugh, Dan, "China Reduced Air Pollution in 7 Years as Much as US Did in Three Decades." *Bloomberg*, June 14, 2022.

I'd left America as a young college graduate. I now was a middle-aged husband and father who'd built an expatriate business career in China that had paralleled that nation's dramatic economic rise. Now I was returning to my home country to savor the fruits of those labors — and to reinvent myself once again.

This time, in history's greatest Land of Opportunity.

Chapter Twelve

Coming Home to America

S hannon and I realized by 2014 that China was hitting the hard part of sustaining economic growth and development. We knew a slowdown was inevitable, as it is with any booming economy, even if indicators were not statistically evident yet. We'd ridden China's wave of modernization but anticipated that as growth slowed, prospects would dwindle. Already, we felt diminishing lifestyle returns. Traffic congestion had thickened in Beijing, air quality was abysmal, and the central government's crackdown on Internet access rendered foreign news and websites inaccessible without a virtual private network to circumvent the blockage.

We knew the government was quite capable of slamming the brakes on economic growth by clamping down on opportunities for Chinese entrepreneurs and investors whose rising wealth might appear to party officials to threaten their control. We'd seen a fair number of our foreign and Chinese friends not only spirit assets out of the country to park them abroad, but physically leave China.

I feel no need to criticize China for this or hold a grudge against its leaders. China simply was, and is, progressing to having a mature economy

— and the progress is not a consistently upward trajectory. There are plateaus and troughs.

On a personal level for Shannon and me, by 2014 we felt the encroachment of our fifties and the pressure to move back to the United States to start the next chapters of our family's life. That always had been our plan. Our children would be attending high school and college in the United States. Indeed, our eldest — Lindsay — the year before at 17 had chosen to enroll in a boarding school in the United States, to play ice hockey and prepare for college. It made perfect sense for the rest of our family to move back to the States sooner rather than later. Delaying the decision would only make it harder for us to adjust to the transition. We'd settle down and invest ourselves in new friends and communities somewhere in the country.

In 2015, we did exactly that, buying a house in Marin County, California, north of San Francisco. I enthusiastically planned to establish my own startup Internet business, while Shannon arranged to work remotely for her longtime employer, International Finance Corp., managing investments in tech ventures located in California and aligned with IFC's development mandate, such as new online education, green energy, and agriculture technology businesses.

Our son, Trevor, enrolled in high school; our daughters Caroline and Julie enrolled in middle school and grade school, respectively. We reacclimated to American life, transforming from expatriates to suburbanites.

THERE WAS, NATURALLY, A great deal we instantly missed about China, beginning with the friends we'd made.

The luxury of having an affordable housekeeper/nanny wasn't something Shannon and I missed. We had no trouble making our beds, washing our clothes, vacuuming our floors, cooking our meals. Our diets, however, went through a radical adjustment. We'd eaten Chinese food every day, three meals a day, with lots of cooked vegetables and spices. We discovered that Marin — despite its plethora of excellent restaurants, including Japanese cuisine — isn't abundantly blessed with good Chinese restaurants.

A startling revelation for Shannon and me was how our daily moods were affected by the pace of American life — all the stresses of the so-called rat race. While in China each of us worked and raised our children and tended to their needs. The very fact we were living in a foreign and slightly exotic country, communicating in a foreign language and being mindful of foreign customs, had distracted us from the grind and headaches of daily life. But in America, back on familiar ground, our minds shifted gears and we felt the stress and exhaustion of work, meals, getting kids to and from school, getting them to their after-school and weekend sports and other activities, and socializing in our new circle of friends and acquaintants — who largely were the parents of our kids' friends and classmates.

We were swept up into the hectic routines of American parents with school-aged children. *Get so-and-so to a dental appointment. Soccer practice. Get the car's oil changed. Yard work. Vacation planning. Bills.*

Then there were aspects of life in our new home in the north San Francisco Bay area that we appreciated more than ever. The shocking beauty of a sky that was blue not yellow, air that was breathable, trees that were green. I logged onto the Internet and no websites were restricted.

As for missing the friends we'd made in China, to our surprise, a fair number of our fellow expats relocated to Marin County. In fact, about 20 in all.

We hardly were making a clean break from China. The language and culture were too embedded in us. Shannon kept up her Chinese study, taking lessons from a Taiwanese teacher at the College of Marin. Our four children had little need for their Chinese skills, but did flex those linguistic muscles when we vacationed in China at Christmastime 2018. On that trip, we reunited with Quan, the woman who had been our "ayi" (nanny/housekeeper) our last five years in Beijing, and to whom our children were very attached.

Quan's husband had been a driver for a wealthy family while she had worked for us and her mother cared for their young child. Now they had two more children (though it was still illegal in China to have more than one child, the law wasn't enforced), and their family had moved to Quan's hometown in Shandong Province. That's where we visited them. They were living well in a high-rise apartment equipped with three bedrooms, a refrigerator and television. They were middle class. Quan took us to see the small brick house she'd grown up in. It had a woodburning stove and an outhouse. Her employment with us had helped her and her husband get ahead. In fact, they owned a small retail outlet in their town, selling dried fruit and nuts. Quan had gone from being a maid for expats to being a business owner.

At the end of our visit, Quan invited us and her extended family to a banquet in a restaurant. We sat at a large round table in a private room, savoring Moutai and various Chinese delicacies. Shannon, our children and I then gave short speeches in Chinese.

I snuck out before the end of the meal to pay the bill at the register. Quan and her husband caught wind of this. They raced across the restaurant, tore the bill from my hand and paid for the meal.

I DID NOT EXPECT after moving back to America that my business career would end up closely tied to China again.

In spring 2015, as we settled into our new life in California, I founded a new venture called Airline Buyer LLC. My objective was to disrupt the aviation used-parts industry by creating a price-discovery Internet platform for these parts. The platform would provide pricing history and sourcing transparency for airline buyers, to allow them to gain leverage over parts sellers. I employed very capable student programmers in San Jose, California — the heart of Silicon Valley — at a coding boot camp that charged fees competitive with programming services from China. The kids did an impressive job in building my marketplace, using an agile process for software development.

I uploaded a massive database of parts transactions I sourced from vendors worldwide to enable online demos of the platform. I then contacted heads of procurement at Delta, American, Southwest, Alaska, FedEx, United Parcel Service and United Airlines. While the chiefs of these departments were interested in adopting my platform, their buyers —the ones meant to use the platform in their daily work — surprisingly resisted.

I discovered that the buyers all had personal relationships with parts sellers; they didn't want my platform to interfere with their choice of preferred sellers — who obligingly treated their customers to dinners, golf excursions and other pleasures. These buyers unanimously voted not to adopt my price-discovery platform, thereby terminating Airline Buyer's business.

Thus, I learned that America and China are very similar in terms of personal relationships driving business!

My next move was setting up China Aviation Partners LLC, to help U.S. businesses entering the China aviation market recruit local Chinese staff to represent them. When I failed to generate any interest in the recruitment business, I sought partnerships with Chinese businesses in aviation-asset trading. The Chinese were beginning to salvage serviceable parts from their end-of-life aircraft, and they needed help in selling these surplus parts to customers outside China.

In one engagement, I escorted a Chinese maintenance-company CEO, along with a half-dozen Communist Party leaders from Gansu Province, to visit U.S. aircraft boneyards in Victorville, California, and Marana, Arizona. The Chinese were interested in learning about setting up an aircraft storage and disassembly business in their own western deserts in Gansu. The plan was for them to engage my business to sell parts outside of China. However, during the trip the provincial party leaders became distracted by their yen to take a gambling weekend in Las Vegas, a three-hour drive from Victorville. They peeled off and did just that. The maintenance-company CEO and I stayed behind to discuss business opportunities. Ultimately, the party officials lost interest in my business plan, and did not proceed with establishing an aircraft-teardown facility in Gansu.

China Aviation Partners hasn't fared too badly, though. As I write this in 2023, my company represents a U.S. software company, Aeroxchange, to connect Chinese airlines' procurement systems with their global supplier networks. This saves the airlines time and cost when procuring spare parts. As China's aviation sector matures and China's domestic travel recovers in the post-pandemic period, Chinese airlines are aggressively seeking to adopt the sophisticated management practices of their U.S. counterparts. Everyone is concerned with controlling costs and preserving cash.

One of my Chinese clients for China Aviation Partners wants to support China's national objective of developing a Chinese designed and built commercial aircraft engine. The client engaged me to help source and develop a test aircraft that can convey the Chinese prototype engine for testing up to actual flight altitudes and speeds. My role is to source a jumbo 747 aircraft wherever I can find one worldwide, and to coordinate the modification of this aircraft with an engineering firm in Seattle. The Chinese prototype engine will be installed on the wing of this 747. This project is furthering China's desire to become self-reliant in aviation technology.

IN 2022, A DATA-insights company, Pacific Epoch, engaged China Aviation Partners to help it sell its data and insights on Chinese consumers to foreign investors, retailers and restaurateurs eager to improve returns on their investments and businesses in China. Pacific Epoch gathered both online-shopping and foot-traffic data to create comprehensive profiling of Chinese consumers and track the performance of foreign and domestic brands in the China market.

One major insight from their data is that younger generations in China, such as Gen Zers (born 1997-2012) and Millennials (born 1981-1996), drive a disproportionate share of consumption in the Chinese economy, with tastes and preferences for local brands that differentiate them from older generations such as Gen Xers (born 1965-1980) and Baby Boomers (born 1946-1964). The younger generations are clearly spending and behaving differently from their parents. They represent a distinct break from the past.

I personally experienced this divergence between younger and older generations when I entered new-economy businesses in China, such as mobile Internet, mobile payments, and electric vehicles described in preceding chapters. My Chinese colleagues in these ventures were significantly younger than I. I was excited by their creativity, education, skills, openness, and intellectual curiosity. I wondered what impact they could have on China's future.

All this is to say that as China's economy matures, and as the younger generations born and raised in a technologically modernized nation — in a prosperity their grandparents and great-grandparents could not have imagined, and that still may amaze their parents — gain greater economic clout and influence, China's future could increasingly grow in new directions. Those who live to create — entrepreneurs and engineers, artists, inventors and investors — may gain increasing sway over those who live to control: change-resistant government leaders. The young understand, embrace and create fast-changing technology. They reinvent an economy, change a culture, point the way to a nation's progress.

They are an irresistible force. They drive the future.

While I have no desire to return to live in China — not at this stage of my life — I remain excited that my company's fortunes are tied to this great, growing, sometimes frustrating, but endlessly fascinating nation's fortunes — just as my own livelihood, prosperity and professional fulfillment were harnessed to China's modernizing economy for the majority of my adult life.

In retrospect, it was risky business for me to place my faith in forging a career in rising China. But it was more than worth it.

The gamble paid off.

Afterword

The Youth Are Key to China's Prosperity

As I write these words in summer 2023, U.S.-Chinese relations are at their lowest point since diplomatic relations were established in 1979. Flashpoints reminiscent of 20th century Cold War tensions are flaring on fronts across global economic, political and military spheres.

The downslide began under the Trump administration. Friction ranged from a trade war (the White House canceled negotiations on the bilateral investment treaty, and imposed tariffs and other trade barriers on Chinese goods) to military posturing (the United States pressed ahead with defense commitments to Japan, South Korea, and Taiwan, and vigorously patrolled shipping routes in the South China Sea; China reacted with defiant statements and increased patrols of its own), to discord over human rights (the United States labeled China's persecution of ethnic Uyghurs as a genocide, and also revoked preferential treatment of exports from Hong Kong after China's central government, cracking down on pro-Democracy protests by Hong Kong residents, imposed China's National Security Law in the special administrative region).

The increasingly adversarial relationship bodes ill for the rest of the world. The need for mutual cooperation by the two nations with the largest economies and greatest military might is obvious. A world roiling from climate change needs a joint approach to cutting greenhouse gases. The same is true for the need to control and curtail the spread of weapons of mass destruction, and to manage other existential crises — from pandemics to environmental catastrophes.

Do I see an eventual thaw in the icy U.S.-China relationship of the present? Not, perhaps, in the near future. However, my long-range forecast is much more optimistic. This hopefulness is tied to China's younger generations and my expectation that when they finally assume control of the central government, they will plot a different course for their nation than the old-guard authoritarians currently wielding power.

I see a great positive change in China's governmental direction taking place in 10 to 15 years — meaning, sometime in the mid to late 2030s. That is a timeframe for when China's paramount leader, Xi Jinping, 70, can reasonably be expected to step down from his seat of power (or, perhaps, expire in office). At present, Xi has served as general secretary of the Chinese Communist Party since 2012, and president since 2013.

Xi, born in 1953, is noteworthy as the first CCP general secretary born after the People's Republic of China came into being in 1949. His autocratic style of rule has much in common with that of his predecessors. While continuing China's swift rise as a military superpower and economic powerhouse increasingly engaged in geopolitics around the globe, Xi has maintained the CCP's central control and its aim to keep China's economy firmly under the party's thumb. He has aggressively pushed the modernization of China by supporting investment in infrastructure, industrialization, and education, but his domestic policies have not enthusiastically embraced markets and entrepreneurialism as drivers of China's economy. Xi has asserted state control of industries from high tech to even the private tutoring parents pay for school-aged children to help them advance in the nation's highly competitive educational system. The CCP has continued favoring state-owned entities over private firms. That has cost Chinese companies investment capital and hampered their growth. In October 2022, Xi — his government padded with loyalists — was awarded by the ceremonial National People's Congress a third five-year term as president. This triggered a stock-market selloff that cost Chinese tycoons more than $35 billion, according to reporting by *Bloomberg*.[27]

Xi's grip on power is very tight. In 2018, term limits were removed for the presidency, meaning he could continue winning five-year terms as long as he was alive. But no reign lasts forever. After Xi no longer is China's leader, younger generations — the current Millennials and Gen Zers — will step up to run China. They represent their nation's longer-term future.

It is useful to consider how China will resolve its most pressing challenges, by hypothesizing how the younger generations will respond and lead the reforms required to deal with these challenges.

My prediction is that these children of post-Mao China — progeny of history's greatest national rise from poverty to relative prosperity — will complete China's transformation from a communist-oriented autocracy (which reestablished China's national sovereignty by forming a strong central government after a century of foreign domination) to a government more like Singapore's one-party republic — adherent to the fair rule of law, transparent in its dealings, and committed to the primacy of a market-driven economy, not one hobbled by the state. This would help China — one of the oldest civilizations — realize its vast economic potential in the modern world.

---

[27] Feng, Venus, "China's Richest Lose $35 Billion Following Xi's Reshuffle." *Bloomberg*. Oct. 24, 2022.

MUCH HAS BEEN WRITTEN profiling China's Millennial and Gen Z generations, and I will attempt only to summarize their future influence on China's direction. My perceptions are strongly informed by my three-plus decades living and working in China as an eyewitness to its breakneck modernization. My views also are influenced by my deep and abiding wish that in the future, Chinese-U.S. relations will shift to collegial, focused on the security and prosperity of each nation — and, by extension, the world.

That said, allow me to outline the differences in experiences and mindsets of China's older generations raised in poverty and totalitarianism, and younger generations raised in rising prosperity and increasing economic and educational freedoms, and with exposure to cultures outside of China.

Older and younger generations in China grew up with radically different experiences in terms of historical events, social changes, and economic development — a divide much more pronounced than that of older and younger generations of other countries. In 1978, there was a distinct break in China's development path between Mao Zedong's draconian collectivist policies and Deng Xiaoping's open-market economic reforms: a change that defined a strikingly new identity for younger generations.

The older generations had suffered from the brutal policies of Chairman Mao's leadership: from the post-civil war establishment of the People's Republic of China in 1949 to the mass-starvation years of the Great Leap Forward (1958-62) to the chaotic era of the Cultural Revolution (1966-76). They experienced the consequences of failed policies — including collective destitution, widespread chaos and lost opportunities to chart their individual futures. In utter contrast, younger generations fortuitously grew up during Chairman Deng Xiaoping's period of economic reform and opening up (1982-97) and the extension of these policies by Deng's successors. China's Millennials and Gen Zers witnessed China's transition toward a more market-driven economy. They experienced rapid economic growth, urbanization and globalization. Their memories are not haunted by China's past.

Older generations lived in a highly collectivist and centrally planned economy. The state controlled most aspects of their lives — from education to employment to social welfare. They were taught what the government wanted them to learn, worked in jobs the government assigned to them, received healthcare the government administered to them. They had limited opportunities to pursue personal and economic freedoms. But younger generations witnessed the expansion of private enterprise, foreign investment, and market-oriented reforms. These generations, by in large, have enjoyed more opportunities for education (including to study abroad), career choice and advancement, and freedom to dress as they like and buy what they want.

Many of the younger generations in the post-Mao era have emerged into a middle class and experienced a higher standard of living than their parents could have imagined. They have grown up in the comfort of their parents' modest prosperity. As a result — in comparison to Chinese who remember the Mao era — they are less willing to work long shifts in factory jobs, and more interested in leisure. Most younger Chinese, especially those born after 1990, have been raised to expect only ever-growing national wealth and strength. Therefore, they are predisposed to believing that China succeeds because of the firm leadership of the central government, not despite it. They are proud of China's economic achievements and more patriotic than their elders.

However, in the eight years since I left China in 2015, the weaknesses in the four-decades-long Chinese economic boom have jarringly slowed growth — and, indeed, have darkened the rosy optimism of young Chinese born in the 1990s and 2000s. When my family and I relocated to the United States in 2015, the decline in China's economy was not yet evident. The young Chinese working for me in the joint venture I managed for a foreign company, selling surplus parts from decommissioned jetliners, were brimming with the self-assuredness that they were upwardly mobile, that their salaries would continue rapidly rising, and that the job market was robust and would continue yielding ever-more opportunities.

But the Chinese economy of 2023, as I write these words, is headed the other direction — and fast. Chinese in the age 18 to 34 demographic — analogous to younger Millennials and Generation Z "Zoomers" — are being hammered by a shrinking job market, rising costs of living (especially in housing prices), a central government increasingly inhibiting free-market principles and impeding the growth opportunities for entrepreneurs, and an aging population that will require younger generations to work harder to provide for the older generations' welfare, while seeing less return for themselves.

An article in the Aug. 17, 2023, issue of *The Economist* zeroed in on two catch phrases these younger Chinese have added to their generational jargon: *Tăng ping* and *Băi lan*. Translated, they mean, respectively, "lying flat" and "letting it rot." The phrases refer to their dashed expectations for financial opportunity — and their gloom and malaise. While their generational peers in the United States have made popular the workplace term "quiet quitting" to characterize that they simply put in the minimum of expected effort in their jobs — seeing no benefit for working hard, since advancement and income boosts are not in the offing — young Chinese are simply surviving with no expectation of thriving. While paramount leader Xi Jinping touts their parents' and grandparents' sacrifices for the good of the nation, and instructs younger Chinese to "eat bitterness" for the benefit of the whole, a great many of the youths don't care for his dietary advice, though they aren't eager to declare this publicly.

The Economist article shared statistics showing that urban Chinese ages 16 to 24 have experienced unemployment rates exceeding 20 percent for months — a rate about double that of the pre-pandemic level in 2018-19. The article also reported that between 1998 and 2021, homes in Chinese cities became four times less affordable — gauged by the ratio of average house prices to median disposable incomes. To quote from *The Economist* article, which relied in part on interviews with young Chinese about how they feel: "Plenty still have faith in the party and support Mr. Xi's calls to make China strong. But many are suffering a deep sense of angst. University graduates are finding that the skills they spent years learning are not the ones employers want. Scarce jobs and punishing property prices have dashed their hopes of buying a home and starting a family."[28]

In addition to the gloomy economic present and forecast, even the pre-downturn, sustained boom in the economy was accompanied by a sense that livability had been compromised by the breakneck industrialization. During my time in China, I understood that many in the younger generation were bothered by the high price that had been paid for the new era of economic prosperity, in terms of environmental degradation and a growing income gap between urban and rural Chinese. Since they will have to live with these consequences, they will consider them as problems that must be addressed. When it comes to the compromised environment, I'll never forget the yellow haze of thickly polluted air in Beijing; but a distinct image in my mind are the piles of Styrofoam boxes and plastic bags in the streets, discarded from takeout Chinese food. No wonder that in the years since, biodegradable boxes and packaging are on the rise in China: the world's largest producer of plastic waste.

A great tragedy for older generations of Chinese was the significant disruption in their education due to Mao's Cultural Revolution. Schools and universities were closed, and many intellectuals were sent to the countryside

---

[28] "China's defeated youth." *The Economist*. Aug. 17, 2023.

for re-education — including, by the way, China's current paramount leader, Xi Jinping. Opportunities for higher education and professional careers were limited during this period. But younger generations benefited from China's rapid expansion of its education system. They had access to improved educational facilities, and the number of universities and colleges significantly increased. This generation had more opportunities to pursue higher education, and had a wider range of career choices. Equipped with modern skills and exposed to foreign ideas, they are comfortable with change and technology — and capable of imagining a new future for China. I'll always relish my memories working alongside Xiao Qingping, the self-made multimillionaire who bootstrapped his way out of poverty in Hunan Province and ended up founding and running Chinadotman — service provider of text messaging to millions upon millions of Chinese consumers. This texting service helped propel the television show *Super Girl* into the ratings stratosphere before the central government stepped in, fearful of the precedent of so many Chinese casting votes for *anything*, not just beautiful singing contestants. (I recounted this in Chapter Nine.)

The older generations grew up in a relatively primitive environment lacking many modern amenities. Their daily lives were impacted by limited technological advancements in China, and isolation from the global community. China had negligible exposure to international influences and technology. But the younger generations experienced an era of rapid technological advancements and globalization. China became more connected to the world, and there was a significant increase in the availability and adoption of modern technologies such as the Internet, smartphones, and social media. This generation has been more exposed to global influences, trends, and ideas. And they have been adept at "leapfrogging" ahead of long-industrialized nations, such as the United States and those in Europe, when it comes to adopting new lifestyle technologies. While citizens of Western nations in the 20th century got used to standard telephones, and eventually mobile phones — China's 20th century generations had no phones, or need of them in their daily lives. But in the 21st century — with their booming prosperity — the Chinese quickly brought mobile phones into their everyday lives. And they were using payment features on their smart phones while typical Americans were still using credit cards and debit cards. Perhaps it will be the same with electric vehicles.

Finally, older generations were subjected to strong communist ideology and collectivism. Loyalty to the state and revolutionary ideals were emphasized. Traditional values and cultural practices were often suppressed during the Cultural Revolution. As a result, older generations are more cynical than their descendants. But the younger generations experienced a shift in cultural and social values. While communist ideology still has a presence, individualism, consumerism and materialistic pursuits have become more prominent. Younger generations never experienced poverty and psychological hardship the way their parents did. And so they are generally confident of China's culture and economy, optimistic about China's prospects, and drawn to things Chinese.

I marvel when I read about such phenomena as digital influencers on the Chinese-specific short-video app Douyin — the counterpart to the TikTok app (also created by a Chinese company) used in the United States and most of the rest of the world. One of the most popular has been an influencer named "Liu Yexi." To quote from an article from *China Daily* — an English-language newspaper owned by the Chinese Communist Party — in Liu's first video clip "the virtual beauty blogger sat in a neon-lit alley and did her makeup in a mirror while dressed like a Taoist priest." The kicker: Liu is a "virtual avatar."[29]

---

[29] Feifei, Fan," Digital influencers captivate Gen Z attention." *China Daily*, Sept. 21, 2022.

One of the greatest influences on younger generations (Millennials and Gen Z) was the one-child policy, a population-planning initiative in China implemented between 1979 and 2015 to curb the country's population growth by restricting most families to a single child.[30] These single children grew up lonely, highly pressured, and well-educated with no siblings with whom to play or compete. They bore the heavy weight of parental expectations — from performing academically, to finding a good job, marrying and having children, and taking care of their parents and other elderly relatives.

How will younger generations deal with China's challenges? Let's consider a few major challenges that China is facing:

Will China grow old before it grows rich?

China's population, which has already started declining, is aging faster than populations of other major countries. China's demographic outlook is much bleaker than leaders earlier projected. A shrinking workforce, coupled with more resources allocated to care for the elderly, will detract from economic growth. Young workers, who are crammed into apartment housing, are not willing to produce multiple children while still working and taking care of their parents and grandparents. The cost and sacrifice of raising children discourage younger generations, who are expected to have decreasing fertility rates in the next decade.

This indicates that China will age faster than it gains wealth.

---

[30] The one-child policy ended in 2016, as families were allowed to have two children. In 2021, the government passed a law allowing married couples to have as many as three children. Pletcher, Kenneth (fact-checked by the editors of *Encyclopaedia Britannica*), "One-child Policy, Chinse Government Program," *Encyclopaedia Britannica*.

Will China be able to leverage private consumption to drive the growth of its economy?

China's private consumption amounts to less than 40 percent of nominal gross domestic product — compared to more than 70 percent of GDP in the United States.[31] As the contributions to economic growth from the property, export and infrastructure sectors decrease, China must rebalance its economy toward private consumption. However, China needs to spend more on its people if it wants its people to spend more. At present, too much income accrues to the state, and not to the people. This is a result of the central government adopting a policy of directing as much resources as possible toward producing exports and toward investments in infrastructure and state-owned enterprises. This policy was partly funded by a form of financial repression in which interest earned on consumer bank deposits was held artificially low. That restricted Chinese average incomes to anemic levels. In turn, that meant average citizens have not been able to accumulate leisure dollars — and therefore their consumption beyond the staples of daily life and mortgage payments is limited.

As a result, China today has a very lopsided economy — one still very much based on exports and on state-run investment in infrastructure. The central government directed the pool of money in citizens' bank deposits toward loans for infrastructure or to finance operations of state-owned companies. If there was one area to which Chinese wage earners directed excess income, it was investing in real estate. And — as I write these words in 2023 — property-asset values are starting to decline. A negative wealth effect will cause Chinese citizens to pull back even further in purchases of consumer goods.

In the United States, private consumers earn enough income to drive

---

[31] CEIC, "China Private Consumption: Percentage of GDP, 1952-2021."

about 70 percent of the nation's economy. In China, private consumers cannot pick up the slack in a slumping economy.

Normally, young workers do the consuming that generates economic growth. They save less and borrow and spend more than do older generations. However, in China the burden of having to financially support their elderly relatives has a catastrophic impact on young workers' professional and financial development, gutting consumption. In addition, urban youth unemployment of more than 20 percent (as of 2023), and adverse wealth effects from the slump in property prices, further discourage consumer confidence.[32]

Youth unemployment could lead to social instability in China's future. Also, a generation of young people is faced with a significant gender imbalance. The shortage of females could also lead to social unrest.[33]

The nature of consumption in China is changing due to the distinct characteristics and preferences of younger generations. As with their U.S. generational counterparts, they are tech-savvy and rely heavily on smartphones, social media, and e-commerce platforms for purchases. Chinese Gen Z consumers focus on lifestyle and experiences, such as travel, dining out, entertainment, gaming, and wellness, rather than material possessions. They are socially conscious and concerned about the environment, sustainability, and social justice. Gen Z consumers rely heavily on local influencers, who are active on platforms such as WeChat, Weibo, and Douyin. They prefer online

---

[32] *Statistica*, July 17, 2023. "Monthly surveyed urban unemployment rate of people aged 16 to 24 in China from June 2021 to June 2023."

[33] In 2021, the male-to-female ratio of China was recorded at 104.61 to 100. Researchers attribute the gender disparity to a combination of causes, including a cultural preference for sons, the government's one-child policy from 1979-2015, and easy access to sex-selective abortion. Chi, Zhou; Dong, Zhou Xu; Xiao Lei, Wang; Wei Jun, Zheng; Lu, Li; Hesketh, Therese (February 2013). "Changing gender preference in China today: implications for the sex ratio." *Indian Journal of Gender Studies*. 20 (1); 51-68.

shopping on Alibaba's Tmall and JD.com, and making mobile payments via Alipay and WeChat Pay. Gen Zers seek fitness apps, organic foods, and clean beauty products. They are driving a major volume of food delivery nationwide. This bodes well for the growth of services in China.

However, Gen Z's minimalist approach to work and income will not be enough to drive the animal spirits of the overall economy.

Chinese Gen Z consumers exhibit a strong sense of national pride and are supportive of Chinese brands. They appreciate domestic products and services that reflect Chinese culture and heritage. Gen Z is building its identity around re-invented Chinese tradition and style in fashion, food and the arts. They increasingly prefer Li-Ning and Anta sportswear over foreign brands such as Nike and Adidas. They eat at Haidilao Hotpot rather than McDonald's or KFC.

But it is hard to see how China's younger generations will have the income to consume in China at a level required to replace the decline in income from exports and property investment, to continue China's vigorous economic growth.

Will property continue to be China's primary store of wealth — and a driver of economic growth?

The property sector in China accounts for about 30 percent of GDP.[34] This includes land purchases, construction, and related industries such as materials (cement, steel, glass, plastic.), interior decoration, furniture and more. All this activity is not sustainable at its current scale, and the state needs

---

[34] De Matos, Luis Pinheiro, "China's real estate sector: size does matter," CaixiaBank report, Jan. 17, 2022.

to find new engines for growth.

Residential property accounts for 70 percent of Chinese household assets.[35] This is due to Chinese citizens having few other investment options in China. The return on their bank savings deposits is very low, and the volatile return of China's stock market scares them away. Housing prices relative to incomes in Beijing and Shanghai are already three to four times higher than in comparable cities in the United States. China has an oversupply of unsold apartments, equivalent to around 4 million homes.[36] Existing floorspace is sufficient for the 65 percent of the population already urbanized. The remaining rural population cannot move to the cities without a big increase in urban job opportunities and a change in China's household-registration system.

Young people struggle to pay for apartments with the help of their parents and in-laws. Single men who want wives must first acquire a property. This is leading to fewer marriages and fewer children. A decreasing population lowers the demand for housing. The central government cannot afford a loss of confidence in the property market. There are too many spillover effects, including a loss in consumer confidence, and defaults on local government debt. A housing slump could result in greater capital flight, and increasing Chinese purchases of property outside China. The Chinese already represent about 15 percent of all foreign-buyer purchases of houses in the United States.[37]

Local governments in China derive the majority of their funding from land sales. As this diminishes, China needs to move toward a system of property taxation to fund local governments. However, the adoption of

---

[35] Yu Xie and Yongai Jin, "Household Wealth in China," *Chin Sociol Rev.* 2015; 47(3): 203-220

[36] Xie, Stella Yifan, "China's Housing Market Has Plenty of Space but Not Enough Buyers," *Wall Street Journal*, April 4, 2023.

[37] "Foreign Purchases of U.S. Homes Fell in the Past Year," *The Business Journal*, Aug. 3, 2023.

property taxes will have a major negative impact on property values. The reasons may surprise those unfamiliar with China. For one, there are many absentee owners who cannot afford to pay annual property taxes. For another, a nationwide system of property taxation would identify all the government officials who obtained titles to multiple properties as favors from real-estate development companies over the years!

The housing boom has likely come to an end, and house prices have nowhere to go but down.

Will the private sector continue to provide jobs, economic growth, and dynamism for China's economy?

Private enterprises in China produce 60 percent of GDP and 80 percent of urban jobs. They are led by Chinese entrepreneurs who are market savvy, have an appetite for risk, and know how to efficiently allocate and leverage their resources.[38] They embrace market discipline rather than seek protection from it.

In 2021, China launched a regulatory crackdown on formerly high-flying sectors dominated by private companies that previously attracted ambitious young people. Internet companies were hit with fines for monopolistic behavior, real-estate businesses were starved of financing, and the private-tutoring sector was almost entirely shuttered. Employment in these sectors has dropped. China's central government does not want private firms to get large enough to challenge the power of the state, and therefore has caused them to be reined in.

---

[38] Cunningham, Edward, "What is the future of China's private sector," John F. Kennedy School of Government, Harvard University, summer 2022.

This crackdown was headlined with the saying — describing a policy direction — popularized during President Hu Jintao's tenure, which preceded Xi Jinping's: "The state advances, the private sector recedes."

China's private sector, the biggest source of jobs for its 1.4 billion people, continues to struggle — partly explaining record-high youth unemployment and calls for more action to boost investor confidence. The younger generations are increasingly disillusioned, losing faith in private companies, and more willing to accept lower pay in the state sector. The state sector cannot absorb all the unemployed youth. Foreign investors are growing wary of China, and foreign investment is drying up. Lower income expectations, and talented employees and foreign capital shunning the private sector, are likely to lower economic growth in the long term.

The structural adjustment by China's economy as I write this in 2023 actually needs more young people to become entrepreneurs and strive. Being ambitious in China often entails having to cultivate ties with the Chinese Communist Party — a step many young people are reluctant to take. They are wary of inviting another level of interference into their lives. They know that participation in the CCP can help them get ahead in their careers, but they also would be scrutinized by party officials to toe the party line.

Some entrepreneurs are unconvinced by Beijing's expressions of support for private business owners, and are worried about a loss of their civic freedoms. Conflict between China and the United States only exacerbates the problem. Some Chinese tech-business owners say they need to gain permanent residency or citizenship abroad to avoid the trade curbs imposed on, and the biases held against, Chinese companies by the U.S. government and U.S. companies. China cannot afford a brain drain of its most entrepreneurial people.

The private sector's future prospects remain uncertain.

Can China create technologies to drive productivity growth?

Since ancient times, China has been a world leader of inventing new technologies, such as the compass, papermaking, gunpowder, movable type, silk, iron smelting, acupuncture, porcelain, bronze, the kite, paper money, and more. These achievements placed China in the top tier of innovative nations.

China has continued this tradition in the 21st century with world-leading development of applications in artificial intelligence, clean energy, green technology, electric vehicles, social media, online shopping, and digital payments.

China is gaining a reputation for controversial applications of AI. TikTok — the social-media video platform — is China's best-known AI export, leveraging proprietary algorithms to optimize the video content presented to its users. It is so effective that the app has become addictive for a significant number of Americans, who squander many hours a day mesmerized by TikTok. China is a leader in facial recognition (another AI technology) and has built the world's most sophisticated surveillance system. China utilizes its access to the private data of its citizens, together with its foundation in AI, to build China's social-credit system. This system expands on the idea of combining a credit score with purchasing profiles and social-media activity to all aspects of life — judging citizens' behavior and trustworthiness. China's social-credit initiative calls for the establishment of a record system so that businesses, individuals, and government institutions can be tracked and evaluated for trustworthiness. Individuals with low trustworthiness might be blacklisted and denied access to some services.

China already is the world's largest producer and user of clean-energy technologies such as wind turbines, large-scale solar-panel arrays and a new generation of nuclear reactors. China's greentech industries include the world's largest production of lithium-ion batteries and electric vehicles.

China boasts the world's largest standalone mobile app — WeChat, from Tencent — with more than 1 billion monthly active users. WeChat has been described as China's "app for everything" and a "super-app" because of its wide range of functions. WeChat provides text messaging, hold-to-talk voice messaging, broadcast (one-to-many) messaging, video conferencing, video games, mobile payment, sharing of photographs and videos, and location sharing. The Chinese have leapfrogged beyond bank and credit-card payments and enthusiastically adopted mobile-payment apps such as AliPay and WeChat Pay. They use their mobile phones to swipe QR codes for everything from wet-market goods to durables to online services.

In 2015, Chinese Premier Li Keqiang launched "Made in China 2025" — "MIC 2025" — an industrial policy of the Chinese Communist Party that sets out to modernize China's industrial capability. This 10-year, comprehensive strategy focuses heavily on intelligent manufacturing in 10 strategic sectors: information technology, robotics, aerospace equipment, high-tech ships, railway equipment, green energy and green vehicles, new materials, medical devices, agricultural machinery, and power equipment. MIC 2025 has the aim of securing China's position as a global powerhouse in high-tech industries. The plan involves replacing China's reliance on foreign-technology imports with its own innovations, and creating Chinese companies that can compete both domestically and globally. This research-and development-driven plan is seen as a critical element in China's sustained growth and competitiveness for the coming decades, as the nation transitions into a developed economy.

The most substantial tool of China's central government is financial support for key initiatives. Funding from state banks naturally leads to preferential treatment for Chinese state-owned businesses. However, government initiatives that try to pick high-tech industry winners has a history of mixed results both in China and abroad.

A question arises over whether China's technology inventions are fundamental breakthroughs or are creative adaptions of basic technologies. China does seem to excel in rapidly applying technologies to maximize their commercial returns. China is endowed with a large, competitive private sector and a huge population of engineers and programmers capable of developing and adapting technology for rapid market introduction. China also has a large-scale domestic consumer market. I would argue that China's technology adaptations already contribute to higher productivity and improve the quality of life for users. Up to now, reverse engineering and incremental improvements have been cheaper and faster than basic research and innovation.

As China reaches the boundaries of many technologies, is it prepared to create fundamental breakthroughs on its own? China's youth grow up in school with rote learning and a focus on test taking. Does this limit their imagination and creativity? They are exposed to widespread copy culture driving a get-rich-quick ethos. Does this signal a fragility of Chinese technological strength?

In my latter years living in China, the central government began restricting access to Google, Facebook, YouTube and Western media such as *Bloomberg* and *The New York Times*. However, creativity and inspiration are best nurtured by the free flow of ideas and knowledge, and full transparency. China's government has turned away from openness — which will likely affect the pace of technology development in China.

Can the central government improve its governance and accountability for greater transparency, fairness and efficiency — before the inevitable economic slump shakes confidence and sows discontent among the general populace?

The Chinese Communist Party absolutely controls the government of China, with the CCP constitution outlining the party as the "highest force for political leadership." The CCP controls appointments in all government bodies, with most senior government officials being CCP members. All government bodies, as well as state-owned enterprises, have CCP committees, and these panels often supervise and lead the decision-making in such bodies.

The CCP claims that it deserves to rule because it governs well and efficiently, resulting in greater economic growth and national strength. The CCP justifies single-party authoritarian rule by pointing to China's extraordinary historical economic growth — making the claim of "performance legitimacy."

China's domestic media is state-controlled, and widespread censorship of social media is often used to suppress negative stories or critical coverage. The nicknamed "Great Firewall" separates the nation's Millennials and Gen Zers from banned Western websites, and restricts them to a local Chinese ecosystem of blogs, messages, social media, and video downloads, where content is subject to state censorship and has helped foment the rise of youth nationalism (per the CCP's wish). Chinese citizens can use social media to express opinions — up to a point. Foreigners in China seeking objective news rely on foreign journalists, who brave China's censors and police to investigate and interpret China's affairs. The Chinese government responds by expelling overly inquisitive foreign journalists.

Chinese regulators have urged financial investors to avoid reading foreign news reports about China, while analysts and economists have been suspended from social media for airing pessimistic views.

There is no check on China's government by independent news media or an empowered legal system.

Since Xi Jinping's rise as paramount leader in 2012, China has been regressing from CCP collective rule into an authoritarian strongman regime. Xi's authoritarian approach has been accompanied by widespread crackdowns on corrupt officials and the construction of the world's most sophisticated surveillance system. China spends more on domestic security than on its military defense.

The power of the state provides China's greatest potential — and its gravest inherent risk for prosperity.

The CCP still enjoys the support of the overwhelming majority of the Chinese people. Chinese citizens accept limitations on their privacy in exchange for the sense of safety provided by a highly organized, capable, and paternalistic CCP. They value security over freedom and personal liberty. Anti-corruption campaigns are popular, even when they are implemented to purge rivals of Xi. Most Chinese like the surveillance cameras. They admire the stability of Singapore — the prosperous island state in the South China Sea, with its restricted freedom of press and limited civil and political rights — over the chaotic democracy protests of Hong Kong. Young Chinese see Hong Kong as cosseted and spoiled. China's central government responded to protests in Hong Kong in 2019 by imposing its National Security Law — killing democratic opposition.

Chinese youth have been brought up on lofty expectations, and they have been accustomed to unprecedented opportunities on the back of China's economic boom. Incredibly, many have U.S. educations and understand the virtues of open society. However, China's Millennial and Gen Zers have enjoyed the opportunities of steady economic growth and are not as keen to confront the government as are their social-justice-obsessed counterparts in the West. Young Chinese are far more nationalistic, and broadly view criticizing their government as akin to betraying their country.

Is there any demand for greater individual self-determination in China? It's important to remember that China is still a relatively poor country. More than 600 million (43 percent) of its population have a monthly income of $140, according to a statement issued by Chinese Premier Li Keqiang in May 2020.[39] The wealth divide between rural and urban Chinese is a great source of instability. The urban middle class has a vested interest in CCP rule preventing an adoption of democracy, which could lead to wealth redistribution via policies enabled by majority vote. The CCP is mindful of maintaining middle-class support from the cities.

The CCP cannot afford to have people lose confidence in their government.

The CCP can take temporary comfort in the fact that China has not gone through an economic downturn in the past few decades — the last dating to the international fallout from the Tiananmen Square anti-democracy massacre in 1989. The central government has not experienced major economic hardships, which seems to have fostered a stay-pat approach. In other words, the CCP's mindset for running the economy is still more or less stuck in the past. Because of this, economic reforms are stagnating.

When economic hardships inevitably emerge for the Chinese people, they will challenge the broadly held notion of the citizenry — particularly its younger generations — that government knows what is best for its people.

---

[39] Banyuetan.com, June 22, 2020.

As of 2023, China's slowing economy, slide in house prices and lack of job opportunities is undermining the population's confidence in the CCP. The economy is losing steam. The CCP bungled the implementation of its draconian zero-COVID policy and undermined public confidence in the health of the economy. China's young people are facing record-high unemployment as the country's recovery from the pandemic is floundering. They're struggling professionally and emotionally. Yet the CCP and the country's top leader, Xi Jinping, are telling them to stop thinking they are above doing manual work or moving to the countryside.

The party's propaganda machine spins stories about young people making a decent living by delivering meals, recycling garbage, setting up food stalls, and fishing and farming. It's a form of official gaslighting, trying to deflect accountability from the government for its economy-crushing policies, such as cracking down on the private sector, imposing unnecessarily harsh COVID restrictions, and isolating China's trading partners. As economic growth slows and employment opportunities dwindle, will youths struggle with disillusionment and rebellion in a system that tries to keep them in line? Will civil discontent grow as incomes stagnate?

Due to the inevitable economic slowdown, could the CCP become a victim of its own success? That is, its ability to instill patriotic pride in younger generations? What happens if economic growth falters? How will the people respond to the financial decline? There is a risk that Chinese nationalism — originally nurtured by the CCP — will turn against the party. Meaning, there could be a widespread change in the population toward a belief that what's best for China is *not* the sole party that has ruled since 1949. Already, citizens who have prospered in the economic boom of the past four decades are sending a no-confidence vote by transferring their assets out of China to Singapore, Australia, Canada, the United Kingdom, and the United States —

despite governmental controls in place to prevent capital flight. The rest of the population faces coming to terms with diminishing opportunities in China. This is a bitter pill to swallow.

The CCP's leaders may come, in time, to realize that safeguarding their rule will require a shift in strategy — from suppressing the financial success and power of its nouveau riche, entrepreneurs and business moguls, to focusing on the nation's economic growth via market-oriented reforms. This is still the best option to ensure the legitimacy of one-party rule. Reforms should focus on re-balancing the economy away from reliance on exports, property and infrastructure investment, and toward more private consumption. The government should increase support for the innovative and efficient private sector and downsize the inefficient state sector. This will, of course, result in a loss of direct control and wealth generation for the CCP. But the alternative — massive, widespread, riotous dissent — surely is less desirable to leaders.

Fiscal policy should consider the greater allocation of national income to consumers, including distributing stimulus payments directly from the government to the people. A massive redistribution of income away from party members toward ordinary citizens would be necessary to spur more private consumption — but this is unlikely to happen.

Chinese people often remark that China is not well-suited to democracy. However, as CCP rule stumbles in its management of the economy, China's rulers must be held accountable by the people. Transparent rule, free speech and independent courts are not unique to the West. Accountable governance is a public good that all deserve. Chinese people want fair outcomes and the efficient allocation of resources that only accountable governance can provide.

Will the Chinese government's adversarial relationship with the United States change to one that is collegial and mutually beneficial to both nations?

China's government has alienated the United States — the one power that had created the very conditions by which China had depended for its impressive growth: access to global resources and markets. Despite rifts in our nations' relationship, the United States needs to partner with China to resolve most of our major global challenges that transcend national borders. The United States and China can have a great future as partners working to solve global problems such as climate change, nonproliferation of nuclear weapons, pandemic threats, and development of clean-energy technologies. More importantly, trade between our two countries is mutually beneficial.

We in the United States should avoid demonizing China and recognize its preferences for governance. Also, we should consider how the American approach to international relations can alienate non-aligned countries.

In one sign of how strained U.S.-China relations have gotten in recent years, though the COVID pandemic has also played a role, there are just 350 American students studying in China, down from 15,000 a decade ago, according to U.S. state department figures. About 300,000 Chinese nationals are enrolled in higher-education courses at U.S. colleges, and China remains the top source of international students in our country, but these numbers, too, have been falling sharply in recent years, according to U.S. embassy and consulate figures.[40] Yet some U.S. and Chinese experts, and at least one Chinese official, say that more, not fewer, civilian-to-civilian contacts in the form of student exchanges, cultural link-ups and business cooperation is precisely

---

[40] U.S. Mission in China, "China remains the top sender of international students to the United States in 2020/2021."

what is needed to put relations between the two economic, technological and military superpowers on a better footing, and for these relationships to thrive. They will be a vital component of rapprochement and cooperation. There is only so much that relatively brief, high-level contacts between governmental diplomats can achieve.

Young people from the United States and China "need to have a familiarity with each other," said Nicholas Burns, the U.S. ambassador to China, in an *NBC* interview in Beijing in June 2023, related to the network's coverage of how deteriorating international relations between the U.S. and Chinese governments is impacting U.S. students seeking to study in China. "You want the two countries' people to be talking to each other, and twenty-year-olds probably do that best," Burns said. "They achieve a degree of familiarity and expertise in a country that is lifelong."[41]

There are a tremendous number of very smart and talented people in China who continue to show the remarkable drive that has taken China from an impoverished nation to where it is today. With the help of a new generation stepping up to positions of leadership in China and the United States, we can find ways to thrive together.

That is my great hope, and prediction, as the 21st century unfolds.

To repeat what I said in the preface of this book: China's destiny, welfare and prosperity are inextricably entwined with that of the United States. One might say that the fate of the entire human race depends on these two superpowers working as partners. We are not so different — and we share similar aspirations and desires as nations and individuals.

---

[41] Frayer, Janice Mackey, and Jett, Jennifer, "How the U.S.-China Clash Is Being Felt on Campus." *NBC News*, June 2, 2023.

Appendix A

Uncle Ted's Prologue

The following text is my Uncle Ted's prologue to his book, The Final Argument of Kings: Reflections on the Art of War, *published in 1988 by Hero Books. My Uncle Ted was Maj. Gen. E.B. Atkeson, United States Army (Ret). He was my father's younger brother and became a career Army man. While my father, Timothy Breed Atkeson, served briefly in the U.S. Marine Corps, he ended up attending Yale Law School and pursued a legal career. As I mentioned in Chapter One, their father — my paternal grandfather — was Clarence Lee Connor Atkeson, a career Naval man assigned in 1938 to serve as lieutenant commander on the USS Marblehead: a cruiser with the U.S. Asiatic Fleet, based in the Philippines.*

Early Impressions

It may have been a youthful rebellion that led me into the Army, in defiance of a naval tradition established by my father, four uncles and a grandfather. That as a young boy in the late 1930s I would be interested in one of the armed services was never in doubt. World War II was getting under way as I came to grasp what was happening about me. Germany's invasions of neighboring countries electrified the world. My father was stationed in the Far East, and the trappings of the Japanese conquest of China, which had been underway for half dozen years, were in evidence at the front gates of our home. Living abroad as cataclysmic events crashed into the headlines on a daily basis, I could hardly remain aloof from the realities about me. What might have been a boy's mock battles with toy soldiers gave way to watching real soldiers at Camp John Hay on central Luzon in the Philippines (even if they seemed largely engaged in fatigue details maintaining the golf course). During the summers, which my family spent on the Chinese mainland under Japanese military occupation, we had virtual ringside seats to the history of the day.

My father was assigned to the cruiser *USS Marblehead* with the Asiatic Fleet in 1938. Later he became the skipper of the *USS Pope*, one of the old "four stackers" of the "Pifteenth Division" (so known because three of its four ill-fated destroyers had names beginning with "P." None of the four would survive the war). My brother and I, in boarding school in the Philippines for most of the year, found our own way each summer to Tsingtao on the Shantung Peninsula, joining our parents there while the fleet was in Chinese waters. We usually took a small Dutch steamer from the Philippines to Hong Kong, and from there to Shanghai. These ports were in Western hands, but the air was tense with premonitions of the storm which was soon to break out over the entire Pacific.

Hong Kong was already dressed for war, with elaborate camouflage over its oil tanks and warehouses and other vitals. Long antisubmarine booms in the harbor would slowly swing open, allowing ours and other ships gathered at the gate to enter or leave. It was a city preparing for siege.

Shanghai was important on our journeys because it was only from there that we could obtain passage on one of the Japanese troop ships which carried passengers further up the coast. Even before our first visit in 1938 Shanghai had received its baptism of fire. My brother and I gazed in wonder at the handiwork of modern military aircraft as our ship eased into the port. The Chinese sector was a shambles from Japanese bombing, with pitiful people stumbling about in the wreckage.

The International Settlement in Shanghai had not been touched. It was a well-developed metropolis with tall buildings and bustling crowds. We were happy that the French had fine looking armored cars and the British a Scottish garrison with a splendid full-dress band to soothe our apprehensions about the terrifying conqueror from the islands to the north.

Our apprehensions would reach heart-pounding proportions as we boarded one of the Japanese vessels, walked up the first class gangway, and saw the little brown-clad soldiers with their huge backpacks crowding across narrow planks into the hold below. We traveled not uncomfortably. I usually preferred sleeping on the carpeted floor to one of the catcher's-mitt bunks, but the food was palatable and there were always a few other Western passengers on board. It would be some time after we left the mouth of the Yangtze that the toilets would stop flushing with the muddy river water and finally go clear. From then on the purser would carefully post our progress on a wall chart as we proceeded up the coast.

Our curiosity about the troops below sooner or later would stiffen our courage sufficiently to lead us down the ladders into the bowels of the ship. At first we would attempt to stay out of sight, daring each other to step into one of the troop compartments. And sooner or later we would be discovered and coaxed with toothy smiles, and a little physical pulling, into a mat strewn room. The soldiers wore little more than loin cloths, but were clean and friendly and had fascinating rifles and packs and little white slippers with a separated big toe. We supposed the peculiar footwear was for climbing trees to snipe at the enemy. The soldiers seemed pleased to see us and must have made great jokes at our timorousness because there was always great laughter when our courage would cave in and we would scramble off up the passageway.

Traveling with us in first class were the staff officers with their elegant boots and spurs, aiguillettes and samurai swords. Most were preoccupied with their own concerns, but one or two professed a desire to learn English. One was particularly persistent, and once he had cornered one or the other of us, was disinclined to release his reluctant tutor until he had added a dozen or more words to his vocabulary. In return he would give us unintelligible lessons in a game played with different colored kidney beans on top of a chopping block.

Most terrifying was the night my brother lost our passport. The purser solemnly advised us that no debarkation would be possible at any mainland port without it, and that we could expect to remain on board until the ship returned to Japan. "There," he announced somewhat officiously, "your case will be resolved by Proper Authorities." We knew all about arrival formalities in Japan. Bowel specimens were required of all foreigners, and adults were limited to 14 cigarettes each. Neither of these rules would have pertained to us: we didn't smoke, and we both developed acute constipation until the passport was recovered some days later. Had it not been, we might well have remained in that uncomfortable condition throughout the remainder of the voyage.

Tsingtao, our destination, was one of the few Chinese cities that had not suffered extensive damage. It had been the capital of the German fortified colony on Kiaochow Bay from before the turn of the century. The Japanese captured it during World War I in the name of the Western Alliance, and then returned it to China in the 1920s. In January 1938, about six months before I first saw it, the Japanese stormed ashore again, this time under cover of the

Berlin-Tokyo Anticommunist Pact and Japan's efforts to build a "Greater East Asia Coprosperity Sphere." The German residents ostentatiously draped their houses and stores with swastikas and pretended to enjoy the protection afforded by the troops of an ally.

Our first summer we lived in the relatively modern Edgewater Mansion Hotel. While the building was given over primarily to Western guests, members of the higher echelons of the Occupying Authority were often in evidence in the common rooms. They were splendid in their gold braid and steel-heeled boots, which snapped smartly as they strode about on the ceramic floors. They always had gleaming staff cars with pennants on the fenders waiting for them at the front door. The cloak room looked like an arsenal, with swords and pistol belts hanging in little groups on the walls.

The hotel had a fine beach, but one had to be careful to avoid the dreaded "Tsingtao tummy" to which each of us succumbed at one time or another. While I never heard a satisfactory explanation, I understand it had something to do with the sun and microorganisms in the water. A swim followed by a period of relaxation on the beach was sure to produce a violent personal plumbing disorder the next day. The same activities in reverse order, followed by a shower and dressing, would usually permit one to escape the disease. We would take secret delight in pointing out newly arrived Japanese officers pursuing the former regimen and imagining their discomfort on the morrow.

Adjacent to the hotel grounds were the largest of the city's elaborate fortifications, somewhat the worse for wear under successive Japanese assaults. I suppose that sections of the Maginot Line must have appeared much the same after the fall of France two years later. There were large steel turtle-back gun emplacements, underground ammunition railways, searchlight hangars, troop barracks, and kitchens. We imagined that the barbed-wire entanglement had been electrified, and believed the tale about a street car in downtown Tsingtao which had caved in a tunnel leading from these fortifications to the hills behind the town. We clambered everywhere, cranking the guns, imagining that we were the defenders, holding off the very foe who had so recently triumphed for the second time.

Seldom, however, were we able to get away without becoming self-conscious subjects for Japanese propaganda photographs. Soldiers would gently insist that we pose beside the useless bunkers holding banners with Japanese characters and smiling as though we understood what it was all about. I suppose they mistook us for Germans and thought that we should show some appreciation for our liberation from the "criminal" Kuomintang (Nationalist Chinese) regime. I often wondered who might read the banners I held and what conclusions they might draw from my squinting grin.

The next year we settled in an Irish boarding house just across the inlet from the fortifications. The proprietress, a friendly woman of substantial proportions, managed the staff: a Number One Boy, a Number Two Boy, and innumerable coolies. The nameless but numbered "boys" appeared to be real people with thoughts of their own and a sense of identity. The coolies seemed a faceless group of Chinamen with sinewy muscles in blue pyjamas who opened their mouths only in an occasional grin, displaying their crooked dentistry.

Seewah, our rickshaw "boy," was the exception. Seewah had a name and the sinewest muscles of all. He also had a cricket in a wooden cage hanging on the back of his rickshaw. The cricket was a theft alarm. It would chirp merrily while alone, and stop suddenly if someone approached the vehicle. Seewah kept the rickshaw in immaculate order and the brass lanterns highly polished. No Westerner ever rode in a public rickshaw; the local wisdom was that the Chinese hauled their dead to the burial grounds in public rickshaws, and one was bound to contract cholera or dysentery from a ride-for-hire.

Life and death never seemed very far apart in the native population. One day I had to dismount my bicycle to steer around an elderly beggar who had seen his last just a short way from our front gate. I was relieved to note later on in the day that his body had been removed from the curb where he had left it.

The balcony of the Erin House afforded a much better view of the routine of the garrison troops than we had had before. The barracks were situated about half a mile to the north, while the training ranges were about the same distance in the opposite direction. Small detachments would march past according to some unpredictable schedule. The soldiers would carry their full field gear with greasy bayonets attached to their rifles and little white napkins buttoned on to the backs of their caps to ward the sun off their necks.

The soldiers traveled the same road that was occasionally used by Very Important People, come to the occupied territories to inspect the troops. On such occasions we would be cleared from the street by the police as part of the customary sanitation precautions so that we would not foul the air to be breathed by the visitor. Even the police and military route guards would turn their backs to the high speed motorcade so that they would make no contribution to whatever pollution there might be in the air.

There were few restrictions on our movements about town. Occasionally we would pedal over to the training area to watch the soldiers in their battle drills. No one seemed to take much interest in us. Only when a roadblock or checkpoint was established was there any cause for alarm.

A checkpoint could mean that something was in the wind. It was a regular part of the buildup for an anti-British day, a poorly disguised attempt at stirring a "spontaneous" protest among the Chinese against Japan's leading trade competitor. Give-away signals that the British were in for it would be

Seewah's unexplained absence for a day or two, or the closure of some stores. All doubts would vanish the day before the event. Posters depicting the Union Jack as a tentacled octopus enveloping the world would go up on every lamp post and wall, and inebriated locals would aimlessly ignite fire crackers and yelp at each other in the side streets.

On the day there would be a staged incident or two: chanting crowds, a grenade over the British Consul's wall, possibly a desecration of the British colors. I can't remember anyone being seriously hurt in any of the shows, but we were careful to stay indoors while a huge Irish flag swayed in the breeze over our gate. The next day the poster and roadblocks would be gone, and sweepers would have passed by before dawn, collecting the rubbish left by the crowds. The troops would be on their way to the training area on schedule.

My regard for the Japanese Army was an odd mixture of fear and fascination, a little like the way one might contemplate a cobra in a basket: timorously, but unable to resist a peek. Never was this paradox more plain than the morning a squad of little Mitsubishi tanks came coughing and clattering up the street. The tanks had mean little treads that dug into the pavement, kicking the stones about. Following the tanks were a dozen or more coolies, bent double, picking up the stones and packing them back into place. Something must have happened to irritate the leading tank commander; at one point he started shouting and waving his arms, apparently ordering a reverse course. His vehicle stopped with a lurch, turned around in its own length, and clanked back fifty yards in the direction from which it had come, scattering the terrified coolies to the curbs like chickens. Having made whatever point he had in mind, the commander again reversed course and resumed his deliberate advance up the street. The coolies stoically gathered themselves up and fell in behind the tanks again, picking up stones and patting them back into place.

I was fascinated by that army. Its strength, its order and its military panoply were stirring and oddly attractive. I also felt its menace. And even at my tender age I sensed the absurdity of the imbalance between that Japanese Army, with its tanks and battle drills, on the one hand, and the American soldiers on fatigue details at Camp John Hay and the parading British in Shanghai, on the other. A most elemental misgiving told me that something was dreadfully amiss. I was uneasy then, and would come to understand much more clearly as the terrible events of the following years unfolded, that this imbalance would make possible the most blatant military aggression and infliction of human misery over thousands of miles. I could not have had the necessity for adequately prepared defensive forces imprinted more clearly upon my mind or at a more impressionable age.

Years later, when I entered West Point, I had a feeling of confidence that I was joining a profession absolutely vital to the nation. I had early gained some idea, and later, in the Army, became well aware of the many weaknesses of that institution, but I never doubted its legitimacy, its purpose, or its devotion to the highest principles of the people it serves.

This book identifies a number of weaknesses in the Army, but the reader should understand that in my opinion the defects of the organization are far less than its strengths. Its faults are much more of the head than of the heart. That the US Army makes mistakes is a commonplace. That it sincerely desires and strives to improve should be similarly accepted. Warts and all, the Army deserves the attention, support, and honest commentary of a caring nation. I take great pride in having been a member of the institution for thirty-three years, but I share with equal enthusiasm the goals of those who would improve it.

In the following chapters we will examine three areas of military endeavor meriting special attention. The first two, military theory and strategy, need no increase in financial commitment, only a greater effort to think through our problems in an organized way. The third, the defense of Western Europe, will inevitably demand additional resources in order for us to keep abreast of the march of technology in weapons design in the decades to come. In return for this investment there is ample promise of reward through increased security and diminished likelihood of nuclear war. But here, too, the financial investment must be matched with more imaginative and disciplined thinking. If there is a central theme to this book it is a call for greater and more thorough exercise of our intellectual talents in pursuit of our security.

* * *

As a postscript to this appendix, my Uncle Ted visited China with his wife in 2007 and said, "Let's go to Tsingtao and find where your father and I stayed in Nineteen Thirty-eight."[42] I was interested in accompanying him, to get a glimpse into his and my father's boyhood.

We kicked off the morning walking around the city with map in hand. It took most of our day, but we found the art nouveau building that had been the Edgewater Mansion Hotel — the swank 88-room resort that had opened in 1934, and where my uncle and father had stayed as boys in 1938, nearly 70 years before. It now was the Donghai Hotel, owned and operated by the Chinese Navy. We went inside and Uncle Ted showed me the dining hall and the main area where the Chinese manager paid him and my father to swat flies. He guided us to the anteroom where the Japanese officers hung their swords.

Uncle Ted also spoke about the fortress positions next to the hotel grounds, where he and my father liked climbing around, cranking the now-abandoned and empty guns and imagining they were holding off an invading army. We walked over to what was now a tourist destination known as the Qingdao Canon Fort Site, on Mount Jing. The Fort Site Museum, at the foot

---

[42] The more common spelling of the city is now Qingdao.

of the mountain, provided an overview of the city's history from the turn of the 20ᵗʰ century — including its occupation by the Germans in the late 1800s (who'd built the fortifications) through the first Japanese conquest during World War I, its return to Chinese control, and its occupation by a second Japanese invasion in the years leading up to World War II. That last was the period in which my uncle and father had spent two summers in Qingdao, living innocently yet with a strong premonition that danger hung in the air for America from the fiercely disciplined Japanese military whose garrison officers and troops in the seaside town exuded confidence and belligerence in their drills and parades.

Appendix B

Timeline of Mark's Life in China

December 1982 to January 1983
China Christmas Trip

Visited China for first time, age 19, with parents and siblings, on guided tour of Beijing, Xian, Shanghai, and Guilin.

September 1982 to May 1986
Yale University

Awarded bachelor's degree in electrical engineering.

June 1986 to June 1988
Project Manager – Cincinnati Milacron

Managed Cincinnati Milacron's first technology transfer project in China. This project consisted of transfer of intellectual property for a machine-tool product line to a Chinese partner in Wuxi, China. Traveled across China for machine sales and installations.

July 1988 to May 1989
Marketing Manager – Sony Corp.
Developed marketing strategies directed at Greater China market and managed distributors in Hong Kong for Sony Corp.'s Semiconductor Components Division, located in Tokyo. Traveled to Hong Kong, Macau, and across China for chip sales visits.

June 1989 to June 1991
Massachusetts Institute of Technology
Awarded master's degrees in management and in electrical engineering.

August 1991 to October 1993
Project Manager – United Technologies Research Center
Managed sourcing of services and funding of R&D in 3D printing (stereo-lithography, laser sintering, etc.) for UTC Divisions in Europe. Supervised technology transfer of prototyping technology from U.S. to European businesses. Led successful bid for $1 million industrial research grant from the European Union.

April 1992
Marriage to Shannon Wells

November 1993 to December 1995
Project Manager – Pratt & Whitney Aircraft Engines
Managed joint-venture project development for an engine overhaul and repair facility for aircraft engines at the Beijing Airport. Negotiated with Air China and Germany's Lufthansa airlines on a JV feasibility study and contract. Supervised mechanics in direct support of Air China's flight operations. Prepared business plan investment analysis.

August 1995
Birth of daughter, Lindsay Atkeson

January 1996 to November 1998
General Manager & Director – Chengdu Aerotech, Sino-U.S. joint venture
Led new company greenfield start-up from construction to successful product launches and Federal Aviation Administration certifications for Chengdu Aerotech Manufacturing Co., Ltd., a joint venture between Pratt & Whitney and Chengdu Engine Co. Supervised a staff of more than 150 employees tasked with factory construction, manufacturing process development, equipment procurement, and raw materials supply. Total capital investment in the project was $22 million.

April 1998
Birth of son, Trevor Atkeson

December 1998 to July 2001
General Manager of BYC – Asian Strategic Investments Corp.
Directed the turnaround of ASIMCO's diesel-fuel injector/pump investee company BYC with $30 million in revenues. Captured market share of 30 percent for products installed on mid-size diesel trucks.

August 2001 to June 2005
Co-founder & Partner – Mobile Internet Asia Ltd.
Co-founded MINT, a pioneer investment fund focused on seed-stage mobile businesses in China. MINT used a hands-on management approach to develop portfolio companies through participation on boards and direct involvement in day-to-day management. Key limited partners/ co-investors included IBM, Carlyle, Draper Fisher and Charles River Ventures. MINT's exits included the sale of one of its portfolio companies to Nasdaq-listed Glu Mobile, Inc., for $35 million.

March 2002

Birth of daughter, Caroline Atkeson

June 2005 to April 2008

Vice President, China Operations Manager — Vesta China Ltd.

Supervised the China subsidiary of Vesta Corp., a major payments processor for e-commerce and prepaid mobile recharge, whose primary clients included AT&T, Boost Mobile, T-Mobile and Verizon. Led the development of Vesta's China operations including building commission income from mobile value-added services, online travel air ticket and hotel room bookings and commuter stored value card transactions.

March 2008

Adoption of daughter, Julia Atkeson

May 2008 to March 2013

Senior Vice President, China Operations Manager —Coda Automotive

Led the China operations of Coda Automotive, a startup focused on the design and manufacture of low-cost all-electric vehicles for the U.S. market, as well as power-battery systems for transportation and utility storage applications.

April 2013 to February 2015

General Manager – GA Innovation China

Managed GAIC, a joint venture between Air China and Florida-based GA Telesis LLC. Oversaw the launch of the new company's organization, operations and trading business in China and Asia.

March 2015

Moved from China back to the United States

February 2018 to Present (as of November 2023)

Managing Partner – China Aviation Partners LLC

Supporting airline operations, software services, asset trading, technology development, consumer spending data analytics, and other consulting for China-related businesses.

Further reading

Books

Atkeson, Maj. Gen. E.B. (1988) *The Final Argument of Kings: Reflections on the Art of War*. Fairfax, Virginia: Hero Books.

Clissold, Tim. (2004) *Mr. China: A Memoir*. London: Constable & Robinson.

Clissold, Tim. (2014) *Chinese Rules: Five Timeless Lessons for Succeeding in China*. Glasgow: William Collins.

Dikötter, Frank. (2022) *China After Mao: The Rise of a Superpower*. New York: Bloomsbury.

Fish, Eric. (2016) *China's Millennials: The Want Generation*. New York: Rowman & Littlefield.

Garside, Roger. (2021) *China Coup*. Oakland, California: University of California Press.

Hessler, Peter. (2010) *Country Driving: A Chinese Road Trip*. New York: Harper.

Hua, Yu. (2011) *China in Ten Words*. New York: Anchor Books.

Hung, Ho-fung. (2016) *The China Boom: Why China Will Not Rule the World*. New York: Columbia University Press.

Jaivin, Linda. (2021) *The Shortest History of China: From the Ancient Dynasties to a Modern Superpower — A Retelling for Our Times*. The Experiment. New York.

Jin, Keyu. (2023) *The New China Playbook*. New York: Viking.

Kissinger, Henry. (2012) *On China*. New York: Penguin Books.

Lee, Kai-Fu. (2018) *AI Super-Powers: China, Silicon Valley and the New World Order*. Boston, New York: Houghton, Mifflin, Harcourt.

Midler, Paul. (2010) *Poorly Made: An Insider's Account of the China Production Game*. Hoboken, New Jersey: Wiley.

Osnos, Evan. (2014) *Age of Ambition: Chasing Fortune, Truth and Faith in the New China*. New York: Farrar, Straus and Giroux.

Pan, Philip P. (2008) *Out of Mao's Shadow: The Struggle for the Soul of New China*. New York: Simon and Schuster.

Paulson, Jr., Henry M. (2016) *Dealing with China: An Insider Unmasks the New Economic Superpower*. New York: Twelve.

Pei, Minxin. (2016) *China's Crony Capitalism: The Dynamics of Regime Decay*. Boston: Harvard University Press.

Platt, Stephen R. (2019) *Imperial Twilight: The Opium War and The End of China's Last Golden Age*. New York: Vintage.

Rosling, Hans. (2018) *Factfulness. Ten Reasons We're Wrong About the World – And Why Things Are Better Than You Think*. New York: Flatiron Books.

Rozelle, Scott and Hell, Natalie. (2020) *Invisible China: How the Urban-Rural Divide Threatens China's Rise*. Chicago: University of Chicago Press.

Shan, Weijian. (2023) *Money Machine: A Trailblazing American Venture in China*. Hoboken, New Jersey: Wiley.

Shum, Desmond. (2022) *Red Roulette: An Insider's Story of Wealth, Power, Corruption, and Vengeance in Today's China*. New York: Scribner.

Zeihan, Peter. (2014) *The Accidental Superpower: The Next Generation of American Preeminence and the Coming Global Disorder*. New York: Hachette Book Group.

Zhang, Xin Xin and Sang, Ye. (1987) *Chinese Lives: An Oral History of Contemporary China*. New York: Pantheon Books.

Periodicals

"Xi's Failing Model." *The Economist*. Aug. 25-Sept. 1, 2023.

"China's Disillusioned Youth." *The Economist*. Aug. 19-25, 2023.

"China's economy is way more screwed than anyone thought." *Business Insider*. By Linette Lopez. June 14, 2023.

"Why China Doesn't Have a Property Tax." *The New York Times*. By Keith Bradsher. May 16, 2023.

"Peak China. A Special Briefing." *The Economist*. May 13-19, 2023.

"America V China." *The Economist*. April 1-7, 2023.

"The World According to Xi." *The Economist.* March 25-31, 2023.

"The World China Wants." *The Economist*. Oct. 15-21, 2022.

"China's Slowdown. The Trouble with Xi's New Economic Model." *The Economist*. May 28-June 3, 2022.

Research paper

Trinkwalder, Michael. (2020) *China under Xi: Moving Beyond Performance Legitimacy?* Mapping China Working Paper Series, 2020, No. 1. Brussels: NATO Parliamentary Assembly.

Subject Index

About the Author

Mark Atkeson is a foremost expert on doing business in China, having managed, partnered in or provided services to Chinese-based companies for more than three decades, in industries ranging from machine tools to aircraft engines, automotive manufacturing, mobile technology, startup investing and asset trading.

A graduate of Yale University and the Massachusetts Institute of Technology with graduate degrees in electrical engineering and business administration, Atkeson resided in China for 22 years and is fluent in Mandarin. He continues participating in the Chinese economy as founder and managing partner of China Aviation Partners LLC, which provides software services, market research and other consulting for China-related businesses.

A father of four, Mark and his wife, Shannon, reside in Marin County, California. *Risky Business in Rising China* is his first book.

Risky Business in Rising China

冒险生意

For inquiries on book purchases or speaking engagements, email
the author at markriskybusiness@gmail.com

$14.95
ISBN 979-8-9891025-0-1
51495>

9 798989 102501